DICE ON REGARDLESS

DICE ON REGARDLESS
The Story of an RAF Sunderland Pilot

Ken Robinson

R J Leach & Co – London

© K R Robinson 1993

First published 1993
by R J Leach & Co
Military Publishers
73 Priory Grove
Ditton
Aylesford
Kent ME20 6BB

All rights reserved. No part of this book may be reproduced, stored in a retrieval system, or transmitted, in any form or by any means, electronic, mechanical, photocopying, recording or otherwise, without written permission from the author.

British Library Cataloguing in Publication Data

Robinson, Ken
Dice on Regardless: Story of an RAF
Sunderland Pilot
I. Title II. Evans, Ann
940.54

ISBN 1-873050-11-9

Laser typeset by Daisywheel, Wallasey
Printed in Great Britain by Biddles Ltd, Guildford and King's Lynn

This book is dedicated to all who were associated with Sunderland flying boats: to those who designed and built them, to the aircrew who flew them and to the ground staff, maintenance teams and marine crews who worked so devotedly to support their worldwide operations.

Acknowledgements

Although my log book and pilot's notes have provided the main stimulus for recalling my RAF service in the mid-1940s, I have had to rely heavily on the invaluable assistance of many people who have been able both to fill gaps in my recollections and to correct inaccuracies. It would be quite impossible to mention all who have directly or indirectly helped me with my account, but the contributions of those unnamed are no less valued for that.

In the course of research I have been greatly assisted by the staffs of the Imperial War Museum at Lambeth Road and Duxford, the RAF Museum at Hendon and the Public Record Office at Kew, whose substantial cooperation in giving me free access to photographs, technical data and squadron records respectively is much appreciated. I am also grateful to the Ministry of Defence for permission to reproduce diagrams and technical information from Air Publication 1566E (Volume 1 Section 3 and pilot's notes). I should like to thank all those who gave me permission to use photographs, as acknowledged in the List of Illustrations. Every effort has been made to trace the origins of photographs in my personal collection, but some remain unknown.

The data given in Appendix A was collected with difficulty, as most of the manufacturer's records for the Sunderland were no longer available. Many sources were consulted, including the publications listed at the end of the book. I should like to thank Short Brothers plc, in particular Tom Goyer, and Norman Harry, who worked on the design of the Sunderland over 50 years ago, for checking and supplementing the information as far as records and memories permitted.

Several ex-service groups, including the British Pensacola Veterans Association, the Indian Ocean Flying Boat Association and the Aircrew Association, have been helpful in pointing me in the direction of sources of information.

Many RAF friends and colleagues were able to jog my memory about our joint experiences during and after the war, in particular Graham Moffitt, Peter Young, Mick Crowther, Terry Martin, Benny Burton, John Haigh, David Brien and Ray Morgan, all members of my crew. I have discussed the book with many others in recent years, including Dave Banton, Charlie Watkinson, Charlie Todd, Reg Newbon, Denis Stone, Peter Dismore, Les Marshall, Ken Critchlow, Colin Buckmaster, Maxie Beaumont, Sydney Lane, Lew Day and Peter Moffatt, all of whom were able to make useful contributions to the Sunderland narrative.

First-hand information from the 355 squadron Liberator crew's viewpoint (chapter 23) was given by Tom Blackburn and Gord Shawcross, who were tracked down with the help of Philip Robertson and Tom Henthorne (355/356 Squadrons Reunions Association). Two Army officers, my brother-in-law Murray Simon and a former industrial work colleague Dudley Morgan, were able to supply further details of events which took place when our paths crossed in the Far East.

My thanks are also due to the following: my son-in-law John Bashford, for working miracles with some of my amateur wartime photographs; my daughter Ann and her husband Ian (Rockwell Design Consultancy) for the jacket design, maps, layout of photographs, etc.; Cambridge City Library staff and others for making available various books and articles which helped to put my experiences in perspective; John Evans of Pembroke Dock for providing invaluable information; John Woods, Bill Curtin, Ron Pain and Peter Gill, who painstakingly read the book and gave me their most helpful comments, which led to improvements; and, of course, my wife Mary and daughter Kate for their help and understanding over a long period when the book tended to dominate our lives.

A major factor of survival in military flying boats was learning to cope with mechanical problems and the vagaries of the weather. That I did survive such difficulties was in no small way due to the first class flying and technical training received from my US Navy and RAF instructors. I am greatly indebted to them.

Finally, I am grateful to all those in the Royal Air Force, the United States Navy, the Royal Navy, the Royal Canadian Air Force, the Royal Australian Air Force, and others too numerous to mention, who contributed to my experience and without whom the story could not have been written.

Contents

Preface	Introduction. Author's reasons for writing the book	Page 1
Chapter 1	Why he volunteers for the RAF. Enlistment and initial training at ACRC and ITW	Page 4
Chapter 2	America for flying training. First flight at Grosse Île, Michigan. Month in hospital	Page 11
Chapter 3	Going solo. Pensacola, Florida. Setback in pressure chamber	Page 17
Chapter 4	Second spell in hospital. Primary flying training. Aerobatics. Instrument flying. Check procedures. Discipline	Page 23
Chapter 5	Weekly parade. Advanced flying training. Introduction to flying boats. Graduation	Page 27
Chapter 6	General Reconnaissance course at Prince Edward Island, Canada. Disappointment when recommended for boats. Return to UK. Awaits squadron posting at Harrogate	Page 32
Chapter 7	Pembroke Dock. First sight of a Sunderland. Joins 204 Squadron crew as second pilot. Guided tour of aircraft	Page 38
Chapter 8	Exploring the aircraft. Preparations for overseas tour	Page 44
Chapter 9	Handling the flying boat on flight to the Gambia via Gibraltar. First impressions of West Africa	Page 49
Chapter 10	The U-boat war and the Sunderland's role in it. Strategy and tactics	Page 55

Contents (contd)

Chapter 11	Author's first operational flight, escorting small convoy. Initial excitement giving way to frustration. Dead reckoning navigation	Page 61
Chapter 12	Use of detachment bases. Living aboard. Escort of large convoys. Problems of finding and attacking U-boats, assessing damage and identifying survivors. Alarms about engine reliability. Valuable instruction in flying aircraft in all conditions	Page 67
Chapter 13	Unexplained accidents. Engine trouble three hundred miles out to sea. Blockade runners. A U-boat escapes. Close call with barracuda	Page 75
Chapter 14	Plague of locusts. Escorting oil tankers. Tragedies on the squadron. Night take-offs and landings. Appalling weather conditions. More mechanical problems. Suspected malaria after mess party	Page 80
Chapter 15	Engine failure on take-off. The trauma of having to jettison fuel. Bouncing the boat at Dakar. Near misses with the French and with petrol spillage aboard. Another U-boat escapes	Page 85
Chapter 16	Trusting the instruments. Trouble with George. Author commissioned – undignified entry into Officers' Mess. American report from Morocco leads to concentrated week-long U-boat hunt. Increasing number of mechanical failures on squadron. One boat ditches in sea. Pressure for more reliable engines. Dodging lightning on night anti-sub patrol. Difficult flat calm take-off	Page 90
Chapter 17	Germans' problems with U-boat design. Their new Electro-boat. Author returns to UK on naval sloop. Leave in Scotland. Captain's course in Northern Ireland	Page 96

Contents (contd)

Chapter 18	Author trains as skipper with his first crew. Hazardous landing in gale	Page 102
Chapter 19	New U-boat attack technique. The Mk V Sunderland. Prepares new boat for delivery to 209 squadron at Mombasa. Gibraltar	Page 107
Chapter 20	To Kisumu via Sicily, Egypt and Khartoum. Flying blind in cloud over Kenyan hills. Return to UK by BOAC. Marries in Glasgow	Page 112
Chapter 21	Flies another new aircraft (destined for Far East) from Oban to Bahrein, via Gibraltar, Sicily, Egypt and Iraq. Fire on board off North African coast	Page 117
Chapter 22	To Ceylon via Karachi. Joins 240 squadron at Madras. Converting Catalina pilots to Sunderlands. Has engine failure on a meteorological flight. Far East war ends. Crew acquires D240 for rest of tour. Detachment in Burma	Page 122
Chapter 23	Rescue of crew of crashed Liberator of 355 squadron in Burma	Page 127
Chapter 24	Recce of Japanese-held Andaman & Nicobar Islands. ASR cover for fighter aircraft. Early recall from sorties require jettison of hundreds of gallons of fuel. Passenger and freight carrying across Indian Ocean. D240 converted to carry VIPs	Page 135
Chapter 25	Prepares flying boat facilities in Port Blair (Andaman Is.) for visit of Lord Wavell in another Sunderland. D240 springs a leak. Life in Ceylon. Tricky take-off and mooring conditions on lake. Disbandment of 240 squadron. Transfer to 209 squadron (Hong Kong) with same aircraft but new crew	Page 141

Contents (contd)

Chapter 26	Flies Lord Louis Mountbatten from Singapore to Sarawak for discussions with retiring White Rajah. Transports Anglo-Polish Ballet from Hong Kong to Singapore. Author returns to UK by sea	Page 147
Chapter 27	Reflections on five years' RAF service	Page 152

MAPS

Map 1	Area of operation - West Africa tour (204 Squadron) 1943/44 and locations of stopover bases on transit flights to Mombasa and Karachi	Page 158
Map 2	Area of operations in author's Far East tour (240 and 209 Squadrons) 1945/46	Page 160

APPENDICES

Appendix A1	The Sunderland - comparative technical data for Marks I, II, III & V	Page 162
Appendix A2	Explanatory notes on above	Page 165
Appendix B	Drawings of the aircraft (Mk V)	Page 167
Appendix C1	Cutaway drawing of the aircraft	Page 168
Appendix C2	Key to equipment, etc at crew stations (Mk V)	Page 169
Appendix D	Glossary of 300 terms and abbreviations used in the text	Page 170
Appendix E	Bibliography	Page 181
	Index	Page 183

Illustrations

Plate No	Caption/Description	Code
1	No 1 ACRC, London	A *
2	US Navy primary trainer (N3N-3)	B *
3	North American Harvard advanced trainer (SNJ-3)	B *
4	Vultee Valiant advanced trainer (SNV-1)	B *
5	Consolidated flying boat (P2Y)	B *
6	Consolidated Catalina flying boat (PBY-5B)	C *
7	Sunderland Mk III at moorings	C *
8	Sunderland Mk III in flight	C *
9	Sunderland Mk II on the step	C *
10	Sunderland Mk III on the slip	D *
11	Sunderland Mk I at moorings	C *
12	View inside bow compartment	C *
13	The galley	C *
14	Pilots' cabin	C *
15	Navigator's position	C *
16	Wireless operator's position	C *
17	Flight engineer's station	C *
18	Interior view from tail	C *

Illustrations (contd)

19	Mid-upper or dorsal turret	C *
20	The rear turret	C *
21	View from rear bunk area towards tail	C *
22	Mooring a Sunderland	C *
23	Interior of Catalina	B *
24	The Sunderland flight deck	C *
25	Sunderland attack on U-boat	C *
26	204 squadron photograph	A *
27	Sunderland Mk I on convoy escort duty	C *
28	Sunderland Mk II beached on Scottish coast	C *
29	Engineers on maintenance platform	E *
30	Crew of Sunderland A204, February 1944	F *
31	The weekly swimming treat near Freetown	F *
32	Negotiating a flat calm	C *
33	Sunderland Mk V over convoy	C *
34	The author's first crew at 131(c) OTU, Killadeas	A *
35	Sunderland Mk V in flight	C *
36	Sunderland Mk III with centimetric radar	A *
37	The camp at Fanara (Kasfareit)	F *
38	The jetty at Penang	F *
39	Author's crew at start of Far East tour	F *
40	Syriam, Burma	A *

Illustrations (contd)

41	The trots at Koggala, Ceylon	F *
42	Beached Sunderland at Koggala	F *
43	Crashed Liberator, Burma	A *
44	Dropping a Bircham Barrel	A *
45	The author and engineer awaiting Liberator survivors	A *
46	Dinghy carrying rescue party with Liberator survivors	A *
47	240 Squadron photograph, March 1946	A *

Maps

1	First overseas tour, etc	G *
2	Second overseas tour	G *

Drawings

Appx B	Sunderland Mark V	A *
Appx C	Sunderland Mark V	A *

* The above illustrations are reproduced by kind permission of:

    A – Controller of HMSO – © Crown copyright 1992/MOD
    B – United States Navy
    C – Trustees of the Imperial War Museum
    D – Group Captain A M Carey (ex CO, Pembroke Dock)
    E – Reg Newbon (ex 204 squadron)

Those photographs marked F were in the Author's Collection. The maps under reference G were produced by Rockwell Design Consultancy.

Author's Preface

While the experiences of RAF fighter pilots and bomber crews during World War II have received justified coverage in books, films, videos and television programmes, those of flying boat crews appear almost to have gone unnoticed. In recent years, however, we have seen a growing curiosity about their activities as more information has come to light acknowledging the contribution that they made to the war effort.

The activities of Sunderlands were, in many ways, unique, not only because of the unusual nature of their operations, but also by reason of the fact that special facilities had to be provided to enable them to function at all. The crews had much in common with those of other long-range aircraft operating for hours over the ocean, but there was an added dimension. Flying in boats demanded a *sympathy* with the sea not normally required of other aircrew. Skills of seamanship were needed in addition to flying abilities. It was not surprising that crewmen conversed with each other in nautical language and to this day have referred to themselves as web-footers.

Certain operations were indeed peculiar to flying boats. Suitable stretches of water had to be selected and conditions assessed for taking off from, or landing on, them. These manoeuvres had to be carried out in greatly varying conditions. When waterborne, the boat was taxied between alighting area and buoy and crews needed to acquire the skills of mooring and unmooring the aircraft. Any of these operations could prove tricky in some circumstances. The widely differing moods of the sea, and even of relatively sheltered inland areas of water, created unusual hazards.

In addition, the crews were dependent on the ready services of a marine section to ferry them aboard the aircraft and get them ashore again. These indispensable people were available as required to provide refuelling facilities afloat, to sweep the alighting area for debris before a take-off or landing and to assist in beaching the aircraft for maintenance purposes. They also laid flarepaths when needed for night operations.

It might be thought that the maintenance of a flying boat would be no different from that of any other kind of aircraft. This would be a fair assumption from the purely technical standpoint, but it would not take account of the almost impossible conditions under which the tasks frequently had to be carried out. Few people would relish the thought of being suspended on a narrow platform beneath an engine in order to service it when the boat was tossing about in an unrelenting swell, or when there was no way of sheltering from driving rain or intense heat. The flying crews owed a good deal to these stalwarts who provided an impeccable service and seldom let them down.

For much of their time, flying boat aircrew led a very different life from that of their landplane counterparts. It was not uncommon for them to live on board their aircraft when operating from remote detachment bases in different parts of the world. This not only called for teamwork but resourcefulness of the highest order.

For three of my five years' service with the RAF, my life was dominated by flying boats. Like many young men of my age group, I had volunteered for aircrew hoping to be accepted to fly fighters. This was not to be. With some reservations, I was posted to a Sunderland flying boat squadron after my training. There followed two tours of operations, one as a second pilot in West Africa and another as captain of my own aircraft and crew in the Far East.

During over 1500 flying hours on the type, I grew to appreciate just how fortunate I was to have been selected to fly such a superb aircraft. It was so widely respected and valued that at the time of its eventual retirement it was the longest serving military aircraft in the RAF. Developed alongside the pre-war Empire civil flying boat, the Sunderland incorporated standards of comfort not found in other military types. In addition to being thus pampered, crews were able to enjoy the excitement and fascination of using a stretch of water as a runway. As Lettice Curtis in her book *The Forgotten Pilots* so aptly put it "How can a take-off from acres of concrete be compared with the spray, the swishing water and the power boat thrill of speed before the flying boat got airborne?"

The aircraft was not without its problems. Engine failure was not unusual in the earlier versions and this could be both disconcerting and dangerous, particularly when it occurred several hundred miles out to sea. Unfortunately the Mark V, which was to be free of most of the mechanical problems suffered by its predecessors, came too late to demonstrate its superior performance in the war against Germany, although it gave commendable service in many other ways until finally retired by the RAF in 1959.

The most important role of Sunderlands during the European conflict was to deter enemy U-boats from attacking convoys and unaccompanied ships which provided the Allies' lifeline on the high seas. There were some successes too in destroying, or in badly damaging, a number of these submarines.

At the outbreak of the war, the Germans felt that by strangling our merchant shipping they would be able to bring about our early defeat and so make an invasion of the British Isles unnecessary. Only the determination of the Royal Navy escort ships and RAF aircraft, supported later by their American counterparts, prevented the U-boats from achieving their objective.

Because of its long range, the Sunderland was invaluable as a means of keeping our naval forces informed of the presence and movements of enemy ships. For the same reason, it was able to provide detailed meteorological information from over a wide area. Its air-sea rescue role was well known and many people in peril on the seas, and sometimes elsewhere, owed their lives to the timely arrival of a Sunderland flying boat.

It was also used extensively for transporting VIPs and other passengers over long distances in various parts of the world. With the development of high speed jet aircraft capable of carrying much greater loads over vast distances, it gradually became redundant and all but one of the few surviving Sunderlands are now museum pieces.

The objective of this book is in no way to give a comprehensive account of Sunderland activities during the war, or for that matter to provide histories of the squadrons on which I served. It is intended to be a record of the experiences and feelings of one individual who was grateful that after over 1800 flying hours he survived to be able to tell his story. No two Sunderland pilots will give the same account of their experiences. Although there will clearly be many common factors, their personal characteristics, emotions, attitudes, training, even the crew members who worked with them, will make their specific experience unique. We did, of course, learn much from each other and I have attempted to show how the experiences of others influenced my own philosophy and actions.

I have tried to record the realities of flying and living with these magnificent aircraft, the security and the danger, the successes and the failures, the satisfactions and the frustrations, the camaraderie of the crews. My feelings about these experiences, both in the aircraft and ashore, whether in my favour or not, are set down here. They are the feelings of a young man passing through his most impressionable years from 18 to 23, whose maturity was greatly accelerated by the responsibilities thrust upon him.

Much of the narrative has been compiled from my own memory of what took place and from the recollections of my RAF colleagues. After a time interval of nearly fifty years, it is inevitable that some inaccuracies will have crept into this account. Every effort has been made to verify it by reference to the official records of the period and other sources and I apologize to the reader for any errors which might still remain.

I hope that, for those who shared my good fortune in being associated with Sunderland flying boats, this story will revive happy memories. For those who didn't, perhaps an insight into what really went on in these splendid machines will be of some interest.

Ken Robinson - 1993

Chapter 1

I could never honestly claim that flying an aircraft came naturally to me. As a boy I was certainly fascinated with the idea and spent long periods of my leisure time making scale models of contemporary aircraft. During the Battle of Britain in 1940, I followed the exploits of RAF fighter pilots with awe and admiration, not to say a certain amount of envy.

It was inconceivable, however, that I could become a flier myself. Greatly lacking in self-confidence at the tender age of 17, I reckoned that a flying career was for people who had qualities which I simply didn't possess. What those qualities were I wasn't exactly sure, but such was the irrationality of my thinking as an adolescent in those days.

In the last war, some took to flying as a duck takes to water. They were never happier than when sitting in the pilot's seat in command of several thousand pounds worth of flying metal. It wasn't quite like that with me, yet I can't deny that some aspects of flying gave me much pleasure and satisfaction.

I suppose that my attitude was to some extent conditioned by my having to work very hard at everything I did to achieve success. Nothing came easily, but happily I seemed to get there in the end. Perhaps the skills acquired through dogged persistence ensured my own survival and that of my crew and we should be truly grateful for that. One thing is certain; my five years in the RAF developed me as a person in a way that no other experience could have done.

Why then, with such a low level of self-assurance, did I choose to volunteer to train as a pilot? There were plenty of other things that I could have done which would have involved far less effort and caused me considerably less trauma. The decision was eventually to be made for me in dramatic if unhappy circumstances.

Approaching my eighteenth birthday in June 1941, I faced the prospect of being conscripted into whatever arm of the forces the powers that be decreed. If I took the initiative and volunteered for a specific service, there would be a better chance of training for the job of my own choice. I decided to volunteer for the RAF, much to my parents' disapproval, and then had to make up my mind exactly what I should try to do.

Not knowing what was on offer, I was in a quandary until the news reached me of the tragic death of one of my school friends, Dave Trevor. He was a trainee at the torpedo works in Weymouth. During an air raid alert he took to the company's underground shelter with the rest of his workmates. I was told that when some time had elapsed and there was no sign of any activity, he looked out of the shelter to see what, if anything, was going on. At that moment a low-flying Dornier 17 passed overhead, strafing the ground with machine gun fire. Dave was hit in the stomach and died on the way to hospital.

The impact of this tragedy was incredible, suddenly bringing out aggressive feelings in me which were uncharacteristic. I was incensed at the loss of a close friend at the hands of the Germans. Until then, whenever I'd heard of people dying in the war, the information had made no impact. It was as if they were fictitious characters in a novel. Now for the very first time the victim was someone I knew and the news brought me up with a round turn.

I could not stand idly by and do nothing about it. I was thirsting for revenge. About that time, I learned that two other former grammar school friends of mine had been accepted by the RAF for aircrew. If they could do it, why couldn't I? It seemed the most appropriate thing to do in the circumstances. I naïvely pictured myself sitting in the cockpit of a Spitfire with my thumb on the gun button, giving that Dornier all I'd got.

In practice, it wasn't an easy choice. I persistently got cold feet and was all for changing my mind many times. It needed a good deal of courage for me even to step across the threshold of the recruiting centre in Salisbury. Only the nagging vision of Dave pushed me through the door.

"What do you want, lad?"

"Er...I want to fly..."

The sergeant looked at me with an expression which I interpreted as sheer cynicism. I felt thoroughly demoralized. To my surprise, and possibly his, I passed all the tests and went forward to an aircrew medical two weeks later at Weston-super-Mare. Once again, as I climbed the steps of the multi-storied house requisitioned by the RAF, I very nearly turned back, but pressed on with the thought that I did not want to be labelled a coward so early in the game. I was also nurturing a relationship at the time with Mary, the girlfriend I met when we were both sixteen and vowed to marry. I could not bear to think what she would say if she knew of my vacillation.

I astonished both the medicos and myself with my prowess in some of the medical tests. When I had to hold up a column of mercury with my breath for a whole minute, I was still hanging on after two and was told to pack it in before I burst my boiler. The chest expansion test gave equally unlikely results when I managed five inches, not knowing that three and a half were sufficient to get me through. The unbelieving MO asked me how I did it and I explained that I spent much of my free time swimming in the sea. I enjoyed diving and could cover a considerable distance under water. No doubt this helped to develop my lungs.

All this was a boost to my ego and I made my way home to await my call-up with a feeling of smug satisfaction. Put on what was known as deferred service, I had to wait three months before reporting for duty. This was frustrating in the extreme. Having summoned up all the courage I could muster to go ahead with my plan, I was now destined to hang around for three months before I could get on with the job. I was soon to learn that life in the RAF was full of such frustrations. The excitement came in short, sharp bursts and then one sat around for days or even weeks waiting for something to happen.

My first experience of being a member of the Royal Air Force was at No 1 Aircrew Reception Centre (ACRC) in north-west London in October, 1941 (*see plate* 1). Here we were privileged to live in large blocks of luxury flats, but unfortunately they turned out to be very sparsely furnished and the luxury had to be imagined. There were no lifts, so every time we wanted to get to our quarters, we had to climb many flights of stairs. Our meals were served in the Regent's Park Zoo Cafeteria, where we were first introduced to tea laced with bromide to dampen our ardour should we decide to savour the delights of the big city.

The unit was officially based at Lord's Cricket Ground, the hallowed Long Room being used for documentation and FFI inspections. Pay parades took literally hours and we sat in one of the stands gazing at a vacant pitch as we waited for our names to be called. Physical training sessions usually took place in the Park and swimming was arranged in the Mansion House there or Seymour Baths, Marylebone, while lectures were held at Lord's, Seymour Hall or farther afield. We probably entered the Cricket Ground more times during our brief stay at ACRC than most cricket supporters do in a lifetime.

My fellow AC2s and I had our first taste of marching with a steaming NCO breathing down our necks and exhorting us to greater effort. At first, we thought we must look a stupid bunch marching through Regent's Park and St John's Wood in civvies, but once equipped with uniforms and all the trappings we felt more the part and began to take a pride in being aircrew cadets. The white flash in the front of our caps distinguished us from the other erks on the station, but there was no justification for feeling superior. We had a lot to learn. I also reflected with no small concern that we were now official targets in the eyes of the enemy.

One of the humiliations of those first few weeks was getting our jabs. We filed through the sick bay at Abbey Lodge and gritted our teeth as we bared our arms for inoculations and vaccinations. Watching the reactions of some of the victims to this minor discomfort, one wondered how the Air Force was going to turn them into fighting men. When we formed up in the street outside to march back to our quarters, the colour drained from the faces of several of our number and one of them keeled over in a faint, hitting his head on the kerb.

After two weeks at ACRC, we moved to No 9 Initial Training Wing (ITW) at Stratford-upon-Avon. We were part of a large intake of two hundred U/T (under training) aircrew who were allocated to four squadrons. The Officer Commanding the unit was Wing Commander J C M Hay. We didn't envy him his job, to convert a motley collection of sprogs, or raw recruits, into a smart and disciplined body of men fit to be trained for flying duties. We were very soon to find out how he did it.

The town, which was to be our home for the next five weeks, was a source of fascination to me. Having spent the greater part of my life within the boundaries of my native Dorset, I had never had the pleasure of seeing such a rich concentration of Tudor buildings. It was not difficult to be carried back in time to the days when the Bard himself trod these streets, which then would have been little more than mud tracks.

Although many of the larger half-timbered hotels had been requisitioned by the RAF, we were upset to discover that we were to be accommodated in a neglected building which reputedly had been unoccupied for twelve years. Clearly it had been a house of quality in the past, but now it was cold and damp and parts of its structure were considered unsafe. The bannisters, which would have graced the large winding staircase in better times, had been removed by vagrants, presumably for firewood. The whole prospect was stark and uninviting.

The regime that had been mapped out for us at ITW was a strict one and, as the sergeant in the recruiting office had warned me, was "not all beer and skittles." The drill and marching in London was kid's stuff when compared with what was expected of us here. Wherever we went, we were required to march smartly at 120 to 140 paces per minute, swinging our arms to shoulder height and achieving a precision which we thought only possible with automatons. After a few weeks, however, we were marvelling at our polished performances and were forced to conclude that we were the exception to the old saying that you "can't make a silk purse out of a sow's ear."

Not only did we have to spend hours drilling to instructions from a regular NCO, but we were also required to take it in turns to put the flight through the various manoeuvres ourselves. Our barrack-square bellowings resounded around the streets of the otherwise peaceful township of Shakespeare's birth.

A marching column of aircrew cadets was a formidable thing indeed, particularly when one could not remember what instruction came next. In the absence of a suitable command, the flight pressed on relentlessly, oblivious of the obstacles, as I found to my cost. I only just managed to remember the necessary command in time to stop my charges from marching into the River Avon like a family of lemmings. When I'd finished my stint and given the order to "get fell out" they set about me with a vengeance.

Fitness was undoubtedly the god that everyone was expected to worship at Stratford. Regular exercises in singlets and shorts were the order of most days, followed by games and cross-country runs. Frequently, for those of us who were discovered to be practised swimmers, a swim across the Avon was a feature of the latter, the only excuse for non-participation being that the river was frozen over. Weather conditions were seldom allowed to prevent us from taking part in these alfresco activities. Only those who had reported to the sick bay with genuine complaints were exempt.

The sick bay did a roaring trade. Exposure to the winter elements and Spartan living conditions combined to test even some of the most rugged constitutions. Heavy colds and 'flu circulated continuously around our flight. On a bleak, wet day when all the occupants of my room were suffering from these complaints and finding it difficult to keep warm, we discovered that our bedclothes were damp.

There was no hope of drying them out unless the weather improved or we could have a fire. The latter was forbidden because of the shaky state of the building, but I felt that the circumstances justified a bending of the rules. Finding some coal in the basement, I lit a fire in our small bedroom grate.

It was inevitable that I should be found out and before the objective of the exercise could be achieved, an NCO nabbed me and put me on a charge. As luck would have it, one of my roommates, Ted Say, who'd been a Metropolitan policeman, agreed to represent me when the charge was heard, although he'd warned me about sticking my neck out in the first place. Nevertheless, with consummate skill he presented my case in tear-jerking terms and managed to get me off the hook. This wasn't to be the only time that I was to fall foul of the establishment during my RAF service.

Not being a very sporty type, I did not look forward to the games sessions. I was neither physically nor psychologically suited to such activities. On the football field, my well-intentioned but feeble efforts seemed to be completely out of phase with those of the rest of my team. While dashing about frenetically all over the pitch, I seemed to achieve precious little. I must have given the impression of having invented an entirely new set of rules for the game.

Because of my height and weight and singular lack of expertise, I was placed in a fullback position where it was believed I could do the least harm. Nobody had allowed for my incompetence. In one match between the RAF and a local team, I was deeply conscious that the reputation of the service was at stake and that I should therefore put up a good show and not let the side down. In valiantly trying to defend my goal, however, I succeeded in heading the ball straight into it. Thanks to me, the local team won 2-1. The impression I made on my team-mates was far from favourable. Since they were not quite sure whose side I was on, they decided not to ask me to play again, to my intense relief.

It was probably because of my lack of prowess on the sports field that I developed an aversion to competition of any kind. I justified my limited interest in any game apart from cricket, which I found more technically absorbing than other sports, by declaring that I was simply not a competitive animal. Unlike many of my friends, I was not stimulated, but rather demoralized, by competition. Far from bringing out the best in me, it highlighted a decidedly weak side of my character. Had I gone to a public school, where gallantry on the sports field seemed a prerequisite for success, I would have led a life of sheer misery.

When I strove to do well in anything, it was to meet the personal standards I set myself, not in any sense to show that I was better than anyone else. So when I attended lectures which laid the foundation of the theoretical knowledge of aircrew cadets, I didn't concern myself with who came out on top in the tests. It was more important to me to be able to reach a satisfactory all-round standard of performance as a pilot, to play a successful part in the war and indeed survive it.

An event which was to have a dramatic impact on the conduct of the war took place when we were at Stratford. It was Sunday, 7 December 1941. While sitting down to supper in the mess, we overheard snatches of a news report coming from a radio in the kitchen. It became clear that the Japanese Air Force had made a surprise attack on the American naval base at Pearl Harbor in Hawaii, destroying practically the entire US Pacific Fleet at a stroke. A stunned silence fell upon the group of cadets at my table. I was the first to speak, surprising myself with my unusual forthrightness.

"You know what that means. The Nips will be able to sweep through the Pacific islands like a dose of salts. What then? The blighters will stop at nothing. They'll have a go at our possessions in the Far East and we won't have the resources to fight them off. The Allies have got their hands full with the bloody European war..." Hitherto the major part of the war had been waged in the northern hemisphere. Now I could see it developing rapidly worldwide. A cold shiver ran down my spine. I hadn't counted on having to fight the Japanese.

They soon set about overrunning the Pacific islands and Allied possessions throughout much of South East Asia. The Americans made token moves to reinforce the defence of the area, but they had lost just about everything but their aircraft carriers at Hawaii, so they were not in a very strong position to provide the necessary resources.

Hitler clearly appreciated this. Four days after the air attack, he made a serious tactical error in declaring war on the United States. Encouraged by the Americans' embarrassment at the hands of the Japanese, he was counting on the US forces being too preoccupied with their commitments on the other side of the world to involve themselves in the European conflict. He was greatly mistaken.

In spite of the rigours of the routine that my fellow cadets and I were subjected to at ITW, we were generally agreed that we'd never felt fitter. When the day came for us to be leaving Stratford, it was with some regret that we packed our kit and took our last look around the town. True, we were three months nearer to getting into the cockpit of an aeroplane, but although the last few weeks had been pretty tough, we felt so much better for the experience and had strengthened our friendships with each other.

I concluded that my sojourn in Stratford was one of the best things that had happened to me so far. Notwithstanding my lack of skill on the sportsfield, I felt that I'd been accepted as one of the boys, no longer the outsider that I'd felt on joining up, and I was fast gaining confidence. It was a considerable step towards maturity.

Chapter 2

In the early days of World War II, the facilities available in the UK for the training of pilots and aircrew were limited and were not geared to the greatly increasing demands of the war effort. Training aircraft were liable to be a hazard to our own operational aircraft and were also themselves at risk, whether in the air or on the ground, from marauding enemy planes. John Terraine records in his book *The Right of the Line* that as many as 46 trainer aircraft were destroyed by the enemy at Brize Norton in August 1940.

To counter these problems and to step up aircrew output substantially and with some urgency, the number of flying training schools was increased to 333, fewer than half of which were in this country. The remainder were mainly in the larger British possessions, well away from what were at the time the main theatres of war. Canada provided 92 of these schools, second only in number to the UK's 153.

Before the United States entered the war, they were already supplying considerable quantities of war material to Britain under a Lend-Lease Agreement. In 1941, the US Army and Navy Air Forces increased their aircrew training resources in order to be able to accommodate British and other non-US cadets. Over a half, upwards of 150,000, of our flying personnel were trained on the other side of the Atlantic, at least 14,000 of them in the five US schools.

After leaving Stratford-upon-Avon, my colleagues and I spent a week at a Personnel Distribution Centre in Manchester, where we learned that we were shortly to embark for Canada for our flying training. The SS Highland Brigade (14,134 tons) had been converted for troop-carrying and we went on board her at Avonmouth Docks on 2 March.

The voyage to Halifax, Nova Scotia, took us twelve days and, although it was the first time I had left British shores, I did not find the trip particularly memorable. We were accommodated in very cramped, smelly and stuffy conditions below decks and had the new experience of sleeping in hammocks (the most economical way of using the space available). Compared with what the founding fathers of the New World had to put up with this was no doubt luxurious, but most of us had the quaint idea that we were worthy of better conditions.

One thing I did learn with gratitude on this trip was that I was not prone to seasickness. Three days out from port the weather deteriorated rapidly and very soon the ship was rolling and tossing in heavy seas. Many of the cadets turned green at breakfast time, rushing up to the main deck to lean miserably over the rails. I quickly scooped up and devoured the boiled eggs that they'd left behind on the tables, firmly believing that the only antidote to seasickness was a full stomach. This theory certainly worked for me and I suffered little discomfort from the turbulent conditions, much to my companions' annoyance.

The most unpleasant aspect of the crossing was the continual griping of some of my fellow passengers. They'd never been confined in such restricting conditions before and boredom undoubtedly contributed to their irritability. When I chastised one of them for holding forth tirelessly about everything and everyone in sight, he pleaded that there was "nothing else to do but bind."

This was a foretaste of what was to come. I felt at this moment that I was just unlucky having been put down in the midst of a group of moaners who simply had to be kicking against the establishment. Little did I know that this was par for the course and an occupational hazard in the RAF. When airmen weren't fully occupied in fighting the enemy, they were sounding off about the service and all its perceived shortcomings. In some ways it was understandable. They'd all been taken away from their families, from the shelter, security and comfort of their own homes, to be thrown together in what was for them a totally unknown and unnatural environment. Not everyone was equipped to handle the shock of this dramatic change.

A journey of about 150 miles by train from Halifax brought us to Moncton, New Brunswick. Here we were to wait over six weeks for our postings to flying stations. Someone reading from a local guidebook observed that the place had been known as *The Bend* before it was renamed Moncton in 1855. The cynics who had made such a nuisance of themselves on the crossing insisted that the expression 'being driven round the bend' must have originated here.

When postings began to come through, we discovered that our group was about to be split up. Some were to go to Canadian (RCAF) units such as Calgary, others were destined for the United States. I found myself in the latter category. The journey to Detroit was broken by short stops in Montreal and Toronto. Here the well-stocked shopping centres were a novelty after the austerity of over two years of war at home. Brilliantly illuminated at night, they provided a welcome, almost bewildering, change from the blackout to which we'd all become accustomed. Nonetheless, I didn't take much in at the time, being too preoccupied with the imminent prospect of at last starting my flying training. Like my pals, I was impatient to get on with it, but unlike them I saw no future in making a fuss about things over which I could have no control.

The US Naval Reserve Aviation Base was on Grosse Île, an island in the Detroit river, just south of the city. About eight miles long and one and a half miles wide, the island was gained by a road bridge near Wyandotte, approximately eight miles from the centre of Detroit. As our coach arrived at the station gates, everyone else was craning his neck to get the best view of the aircraft drawn up on the tarmac. I had my head tilted back, trying in vain to stem the flow from a bleeding nose. This activity occupied me to such an extent that I was denied the pleasure of seeing anything of my new surroundings. It was, appropriately enough, 1 April 1942.

The local population made us most welcome. The Battle of Britain was still fresh in their minds and anyone in RAF uniform was seen as something of a hero. I was befriended by a delightful Irish/American family called Owens. Nothing was too much trouble for them. They frequently collected me from the camp and took me to their home in Wyandotte, where I was sometimes accommodated overnight. Wined and dined in a manner to which I had not previously been accustomed, I was quite prepared to bask, albeit guiltily, in the reflected glory of 'the few'.

We were in the air for the first time two days after arrival on the base. In a hangar the day's flying schedules were displayed on a board, telling us which instructors would be taking us up and which aircraft we'd be using. The primary training, which took place over three or four weeks, consisted of twelve to fifteen flights of up to an hour with an instructor, followed by a solo flight of fifteen to twenty minutes. The latter simply involved a take-off, a circuit of the field and a landing.

We scanned the board, looking eagerly for our names. Five minutes before the stated time, I collected my parachute and signed the necessary documents in the office. Donning flying helmet and goggles and feeling embarrassingly like a latter-day Biggles, I strode off in the direction of my aircraft. It was standing on the apron, a mechanic sitting in the forward seat running up the engine. When he saw me, he climbed out on to the lower wing and invited me to take my place in the rear seat.

Realizing that I was a new boy to all this, he showed me how to strap myself in and I plied him with questions about the aircraft. It was an N3N-3 naval biplane (*see plate* 2), a solid-looking dual-control primary trainer, resplendent in bright yellow livery. Powered by a Pratt and Whitney J5 Whirlwind radial engine, it looked more substantial than the British Tiger Moth, in which many pilots learned to fly at home. Although affectionately known as the Yellow Peril, it had proved itself to be a very safe and reliable aircraft.

Soon my instructor appeared, carrying a parachute over one shoulder and swinging his helmet in the other hand. Reaching the aircraft, he strapped the 'chute on properly and pulled his helmet loosely over his head. I checked the name on the leather patch on the left side of his flying jacket. He smiled briefly, climbed on to the lower wing and called out against the noise of the engine, "Robinson?"

"Yes, sir."

"Name's Clabaugh. Glad to know you. Ever flown before?"

"Never, sir."

"Right... Looking forward to it?" I nodded. "I'll give you a run-down on the controls and then we'll take her up."

As he settled himself into the cockpit, I took stock of the aircraft. The nose was pointing up towards the sky like a long-range field gun, restricting my forward vision. The propeller, or fan as it was more commonly known by those who sought slang expressions for just about everything, rotated throughout a wide arc ahead. Inside the cockpit, just below the transparent windshield, there was a vaguely familiar cluster of instruments which had yet to be explained to me in practical detail.

Near the floor were the rudder pedals which moved backwards and forwards and parallel to it. The control column or joystick, which could be tilted fore and aft and from side to side, came up from the floor between my legs. It was all very basic. Indeed, the cables and chains connecting the operating controls to the control surfaces seemed so flimsy that I found it difficult to believe they were strong enough for the job expected of them.

Clabaugh explained that the intercom system, or Gosport, was not very sophisticated. He had to shout at me through a rubber tube and I couldn't answer back. I simply had to use sign language. After I'd coupled it up and he'd checked that it worked, he demonstrated the effect of moving the various controls, telling me to look out along the wings or back towards the tail to see the aileron, elevator and rudder movements.

He outlined the procedure for checking engine performance, signalled to the mechanic to remove the chocks from the wheels and then taxied the aircraft around the perimeter of the field before turning it into the wind for take-off. Carrying out his final cockpit check with obvious care, he described each step, telling me to memorize it. The throttle was then opened and the engine revs increased until the noise was deafening. Despite the presence of the windshield, the slipstream rushing past the cockpit caused a colossal draught and the aircraft began to roll sluggishly forward. I watched the blades of grass being flattened by the rush of air over them and then became aware that the wings and their supporting struts and wires were flapping as though about to disintegrate.

Fortunately, we'd been warned about this in the classroom and assured that if the wings weren't flexible they'd very likely fall off. It was alarming to see it for the first time and I wondered whether the amount of flapping I was witnessing was within safe limits. As we gathered speed across the bumpy field, the tail began to lift and I could now look out over the nose and see exactly where we were going. Suddenly, the bumping ceased and the ground receded. We were airborne.

The pilot throttled back and we were able to continue climbing with less power. I felt discomfort in my ears due to the changing pressure as we gained height. We'd been told that the air pressure decreased as you climbed and you needed to swallow to equalize the pressure on both sides of the eardrums. Coming down, as pressure increased, it was more effective to yawn, which was something I had great difficulty in doing to order.

As the airfield disappeared behind us, the port wing dropped and we began to turn to make a circuit of the base. Feeling insecure as we banked, I clung on to the side of the cockpit for fear of falling out. In spite of being safely strapped in, I found myself worrying about what would happen if the seat belt failed and I was pitched out before we'd gained enough height for me to use my parachute.

These thoughts were interrupted by Clabaugh who looked very relaxed and certainly didn't share my alarm. "I'm going to climb up to 2000 feet and then you can take the controls." He obviously thought that with that amount of height in hand he would have time to take the necessary action should I do anything stupid. Completing this manoeuvre, he said, "OK, Robinson. We're flying at 2000 feet and we're on a heading of 250 degrees. Look at the nose of the airplane and see where it comes in relation to the horizon. That's where it always needs to be when you're flying straight and level, right? Now take over the controls and see if you can maintain height, airspeed and course. You've got it."

I made a determined effort to do what Clabaugh had said. The nose went up and the airspeed started to fall off. Stick forward, push the nose down...whoops, too far... The airspeed picked up again as the nose dropped. Each time I took corrective action I found I overshot and had to reverse the procedure. It occurred to me that my path in the air must have resembled that of a roller coaster at the fair.

After a while I began to get the feel of the controls and my corrections became more subtle. I found that I was having greater success in maintaining the required altitude. While concentrating on that, I'd forgotten our heading. I glanced at the gyro compass...230 degrees and spinning. Bank to the right, rudder and aileron...oh no! 254 degrees... straighten out... that's better. What's our height? 1980 feet. Oh hell!

Clabaugh, seeing my obvious discomfort, came to the rescue. "OK, I've got it. Don't worry about it, you're doing just fine. It takes time to get used to the controls. Now try a 180 degree turn. Turn to starboard on to 070, maintaining your height and airspeed. OK?" I took the controls again. Applying right rudder and stick, I went into the turn, at the same time losing height rapidly. I broke out into a cold sweat. This won't bloody well do, I admonished myself. Nose up...

The correcting manoeuvre was so positive that I could feel the pull of gravity as the aircraft changed suddenly from a nose-down to a nose-up attitude. By the time I'd recovered my height, I'd greatly overshot the course I was to steer and the gyro was showing 085 degrees. With difficulty I made the necessary adjustments and then the instructor called out that he was taking over again. "I've got it. We're due back at base now. I'll do one circuit of the field and then put her down." I was glad to be relieved of the controls. I didn't think much of my first attempt at flying an aeroplane.

As we approached the airfield, Clabaugh cut the throttle right back to lose height to about 1000 feet. My ears felt blocked. Sounds became muffled. I managed a yawn and the discomfort cleared. The engine plopped intermittently and I thought there might be something wrong with it. When the throttle was opened again to level out, however, the motor responded normally.

At the end of the downwind leg of the circuit, Clabaugh throttled back again, turning to port and losing height for the final approach. The ground came up fast to meet us and I hoped that we'd flatten out in time. When we were within 200-250 feet of the grass, our rate of descent lessened and we were between 50 and 60 feet above the perimeter of the field when we crossed it. A few feet from the ground the aircraft assumed a nose-up attitude and I braced myself for the touchdown.

It was a perfect three point landing. The ride became bumpy again as the wheels ran along the turf. The blades of grass were being whipped by the slipstream and everything seemed to be flapping in the breeze once more as we sped across the field. The N3N gradually lost momentum until it almost stopped and then Clabaugh turned it towards the concrete apron in front of the hangar and taxied in slowly. As he ran the biplane on to the chocks, he cut the engine and climbed out of the cockpit onto the wing. Removing helmet and 'chute, he waited for me to get down rather uncertainly from the aircraft.

"Well? What did you think of your first flight?"

"I enjoyed it," I answered, tongue in cheek, "but I made a bit of a pig's ear of it, didn't I?"

"Not at all. You didn't do any worse than anyone else at first attempt."

He disappeared into the instructors' room, leaving me to contemplate what I regarded as a pretty poor show. I always set myself high standards, getting very depressed when I did not appear to be achieving them.

Chapter 3

After my next flight at Grosse Île, I had a disappointing setback which prevented me from flying with Clabaugh again. The nose-bleed referred to earlier turned out to be the precursor of a month of discomfort in hospital with a bout of sinusitis. Having grown up with this problem, I had learned to live with it. At my RAF medical, the staff had shown no interest in it at all. Since I had never had any treatment for the complaint, they presumably did not consider it important. This surprised me, as I'd always been led to believe that aircrew needed to be the fittest. Now I found myself lying on my back, regularly taking sulpha drugs and having inhalants.

The latter involved a comic performance. I was given a jug of boiling water in which some menthol crystals had been dissolved. A sheet was draped over me and I inhaled the vapours under the tent for ten or fifteen minutes. Once during this tedious procedure I fell asleep and tipped the jug over, spilling the boiling contents onto myself and scalding my elbow and crutch.

The nurse who came running to my assistance when I let out a penetrating yelp of pain asked me where I was hurt. I showed her my elbow, which she treated with a yellow antiseptic called acriflavine. Modesty forbade me from disclosing the location of the other injury. My bashfulness resulted in my suffering over a week of unnecessary discomfort while the blister in my crutch cleared up without treatment.

This ignominious start to my flying career delayed my training for a whole month. All my friends moved on ahead of me and so I found myself having to make new ones on a later course. One of my former companions had visited me regularly in the sick bay, updating me on his new experiences which, of course, filled me with envy. I was itching to get out and start flying again, but the medical staff insisted that my treatment should take its inexorable course. It was tantalizing to lie in bed listening to the revving up of aircraft engines. When I finally emerged from my detention, it was really like starting all over again.

One of my new colleagues relayed a report to me which I would have preferred not to have heard. When I was telling him how keen I was to get into the air again, he asked me why I was in so much of a hurry. Flying was full of hazards, so why was I so anxious to expose myself to them? I was suspicious, because he didn't seem the type to worry too much about normal flying risks. In fact, he was much more likely to take the line that it couldn't possibly happen to him. When I pressed him for an explanation, he told me that one of the cadets on an earlier course had baled out of his primary trainer and his parachute had failed to open. Naïvely, I asked what had happened to him.

"He made a bloody big hole in the ground, didn't he?"

To cheer me up further, the narrator claimed that when the other 'chutes on the base were checked, it was doubted whether some of those would have opened in an emergency, because they'd been packed incorrectly. I didn't know whether to believe him or not, but I wasn't very amused.

Over the next three weeks, I got into the routine of making short flights with Anderson, another agreeable instructor with whom I made satisfactory progress. It was impressed on me that flying an aircraft required precision in all things. The constant cry was "needle, ball and airspeed" which, being interpreted, meant precision in flying a course using a compass or gyro, precision in putting on just the right amount of bank when making a turn and precision in adjusting the aircraft's power and attitude to maintain the necessary airspeed.

The ball was a bubble in a tube not unlike a spirit level. The tube was slightly curved and the ball had to be kept in the middle when in a normal flying attitude. If when executing a turn the wrong amount of aileron or rudder was applied, the ball would swing over to one side, indicating that the aircraft was slipping (or skidding) instead of banking correctly.

The instruction in the cockpit included taxiing, normal take-offs and landings, climbs, turns, spirals, slips and emergency landings. I found my introduction to spins a bit unnerving, since I hadn't known quite what to expect. Anderson explained what was going to happen, but I was still unprepared for it when the time came. Throttling back the engine, he held the stick back in his stomach until the aircraft, losing speed, eventually stalled and the nose dropped like a stone. He then kicked the rudder pedal and the aircraft flipped over into a spin. The ground rotated like a merry-go-round and was rapidly getting nearer. I was forced back into the cockpit by gravity, so was not in any danger of falling out. My anxieties turned instead to what I'd have to do if the instructor blacked out or had a heart attack.

When the altimeter was showing about 700 feet, I felt violent movements of rudder and stick and the aircraft came out of the spin in a deep gliding attitude. Gradually it resumed level flight at about 500 feet. My fingers released their vice-like grip on the sides of the cockpit and I heard the instructor saying, "You're not permitted to do spins on your own, understand? If you inadvertently get into one, you now know how to deal with it."

Did I? I'd been too mesmerized to hear Anderson's commentary on the recovery procedure.

A good deal of satisfaction was derived from doing side slips. These manoeuvres enabled you to lose height rapidly when making an emergency landing without power and in a confined space. A slip to port required a port-wing-down attitude while applying opposite (starboard) rudder and vice versa for a starboard slip. A few feet off the ground a normal gliding attitude was resumed before raising the nose for touchdown. I'd often wondered how to handle a forced landing in a restricted space in the event of an engine failure. It was encouraging to learn a procedure which could get me out of trouble in such circumstances, always providing that a suitable space presented itself in the first place.

The flying programme was punctuated by classes in a variety of subjects related to all aspects of military flying. We also had to take regular (organized) exercise, however tired we might feel, and participate in the inevitable parades and drill. All these activities were an anti-climax to the excitement of flying, which was what I had joined the RAF to do. As the programme progressed, however, I realized that there was no way in which I could fly on operations without having a thorough theoretical grounding. It would also be asking for trouble to do so if I were not perfectly fit.

The time came for my first solo flight. In the few hours of tuition with my regular instructor, I had learned all the tricks I needed to enable me to take off, do a circuit of the field and land again. The training had been sound and I was confident. I was looking forward to it. After collecting my 'chute, I paused at the flight board and checked the number of my aircraft. A self-satisfied smile crossed my face briefly as I read, "First pilot – Robinson, K." Drawing myself up to my full height, I marched briskly out onto the apron.

It was not unheard of for pilots to try to take off with the clamps still on the control surfaces. I wanted to make sure that I didn't follow their example, so I walked around the aircraft once to check that everything was in order. The precaution probably wasn't justified, since it was part of the normal cockpit drill to see that the surfaces responded to the appropriate movements of the stick and rudder bar. However, I was cautious enough to think that there was always the risk of something like a tin of dope or a spanner being left on the aircraft and causing a hazard.

I strapped myself in and took great care over checking the operation of the controls and running up the engine, reminding myself, as I did on every flight that I made as first pilot, that there was no room for human error in flying. Everything had to be checked and double-checked and if you were not satisfied, you yelled for somebody and had something done about it.

I was satisfied, gave the mechanic the thumbs up for the chocks to be removed and taxied off around the edge of the field until I was in a suitable position downwind. Turning into the ten knot breeze, I carried out a scrupulously precise cockpit check. Having assured myself that nothing else was airborne in the vicinity, I opened the throttle. The roar of the engine was music in my ears as I concentrated on steering a straight course and on keeping my wings level. The aircraft gathered speed and gradually became more responsive. The tail lifted with a little help as I eased the joystick forward and within seconds the N3N was airborne. As I climbed out of the field and started my circuit to port, I found myself working out how I would deal with an emergency. I knew the drill, but would I do what was required instinctively? There'd be no time to look up the handbook, even if I'd had one. I stopped worrying as I reached cruising altitude and started on the downwind leg. Extremely elated, I was unable to resist shouting at the top of my voice.

Then I sobered up again as I realized that the most tricky manoeuvre, that of putting the biplane down safely, was yet to come. I wanted to opt out of that part of the exercise, but a little voice inside me reminded me that what goes up must come down, so there was no choice. I talked myself down. Now, what's the drill? Start turn to port, throttle back, watch airspeed, check height above the perimeter... help! too low...put on power, watch rate of descent, throttle back again, check altitude and airspeed, wings level, keep the damned thing straight, stick back, wait for it... touchdown...bumpy ride...keep it *straight*... The trainer gradually rolled to a halt. I had done it. I'd soloed.

As I jumped down from the N3N after parking it against the chocks, I looked at my watch. The whole operation had only taken eighteen minutes, but it was one of the most exhilarating experiences of my life. This was my last flight from Grosse Île and I couldn't wait to move on to the next stage of my training, which was to be at the US Naval Air Station at Pensacola, Florida.

Back in the barracks, I was met at the door by the chap who'd given me the parachute horror story. I'd never seen him looking so agitated. "God, man, am I glad to see *you*!"

"Why? Didn't you think you'd come back from your solo?"

"Not *me*, you jerk, *you*... Didn't you know that the bloody flagpole went right between your wheels on that approach?"

The Naval Air Station at Pensacola was a most imposing place. A number of airfields were spread over a wide area of the flat terrain of northern Florida and there was also a flying boat station on the adjacent shore of the Gulf of Mexico. The central establishment was equipped with smart buildings, generously spaced in regimented rows with well-kept areas of grass between and around them.

Some of the buildings were faced with architectural features in the Palladian style, making them look like Greek temples. They were in immaculate condition and my first reaction was that it all looked very formal and in a way threatening. I reckoned that we might be in for a tough time here.

There was no doubt that things were run on strictly military lines at the 'Annapolis of the Air'. Some of the large impressive buildings housed dormitories equipped with bunk beds. I settled for a top one, reasoning that if I was first in bed I was less likely to be disturbed by someone getting into the bottom bunk.

The biggest shock that awaited the new members of the British Flight Battalion was to learn that reveille would be at 5 am. We were rudely awakened each morning by an enlisted man walking briskly through the block shouting "*Rev*-alee, *rev*-alee...hit the deck!" and banging on the bunks of those of us showing reluctance to do so. The names of cadets intending to report for sick call were taken and ten minutes later the rest of us were forming up on the grass outside building 624, suitably clad in singlets, shorts and plimsolls, for our daily dose of callisthenics in the gloom before the dawn.

After this "degrading ritual", as one of our number put it, we returned exhausted to our quarters to carry out the morning's ablutions before we went to breakfast in the smart dining hall at 6 am. Work began at 6.35 and consisted of a full and active programme of classes and flying lessons.

The recreational activities matched the military ones. There were excellent provisions for indoor and outdoor games and sports, a luxurious air-conditioned (this was new to most of us) theatre, which showed the latest movies and attracted leading performers like Louis Armstrong and Glenn Miller, and a shop called the Post Exchange (or PX) which sold just about everything. A suitably equipped naval hospital was available on the station and there was also a well-attended chapel.

The flying programme consisted of four main stages. The first was a continuation of the primary training started at Grosse Île, the second involved instrument flying in advanced trainers, the third formation flying and the fourth flying boat training.

I embarked on stage one, in the now familiar Yellow Peril, with enthusiasm. In the early flights I covered much the same ground as before but with another instructor, Lt Deneen, who also introduced me to a variety of new aerial manoeuvres. I was just beginning to enjoy doing one or two aerobatics when I had another unfortunate experience which set my flying programme back by a further month.

As part of the process of assessing student pilots' suitability for operational flying duties, it was necessary for them to undergo tests in a pressure chamber. This was a 'tank' in which the pressure and the oxygen content of the atmosphere could be controlled. It was thus possible for conditions at various altitudes to be simulated, so that the effects on aircrew of pressure variations and lack of oxygen could be measured. The students were seated at tables and given simple arithmetical tests at different 'altitudes' with and without oxygen. The possible effects on their performance when actually flying at those altitudes could then be predicted.

Before being allowed into the chamber we were asked if anyone was suffering from colds or similar complaints. Those who were had to come back at some other time. I had my customary sniffles but did not associate them with a cold, so I marched boldly in with the others. As the pressure was gradually reduced to simulate climbing to about 30,000 feet, I was feeling fine and managed to clear my ears satisfactorily. When the pressure was increased for the 'descent', however, I suffered excruciating pain in the ears and had to ask the NCO in charge to stop the process. So as to cause me minimum discomfort, he then increased the pressure in easy stages.

When we eventually reached sea-level conditions again, I found that I was deaf. The sensation was like swimming under water, where the sounds are muffled and almost unintelligible. As I was leaving the chamber, the NCO asked me how I felt. "Uh?" I queried, not having the least idea what he was saying.

He shouted "I said, if you don't feel better tomorrow, be sure to attend sick call and get the doc to look at you." I nodded and wandered disconsolately back to the barracks in a silent world of my own.

Chapter 4

The following morning brought no improvement in my condition and I joined the queue of patients at sick call. After a thorough examination, I was admitted to the naval hospital for a course of treatment which once again prevented me from getting on with the job. The treatment followed much the same pattern initially as in Detroit, but when it failed to bring the desired results, other means, such as draining my sinuses, were tried.

For much of the time I was not bedridden and therefore had to make my own way to sick call. On one such occasion, a doctor who had a reputation for seeing the removal of tonsils as the cure for all maladies, examined me. After gazing expectantly down my throat, he threw the spatula into the bin with obvious disgust.

"What's the trouble, doc? Disappointed?"

"What d'you mean, disappointed?"

"No tonsils. I had them out when I was five."

I was promptly ordered to get out and left the room with "goddamn limeys" ringing in my ears.

Once again, my companions had moved on ahead of me in the training programme. Fortunately for me, however, we were still in the same quarters, so my close friendship with them was not broken at this stage. In a sense there were advantages, because they were able to keep me informed of what I could expect in the next stage of my training. As I was the kind of person who needed time to absorb information and prepare myself for what lay ahead, I was very grateful for the opportunity to be forewarned in this way.

Back in the cockpit of an N3N-3, I found myself going over the programme covered at Grosse Île and refining my skills in handling the aircraft in normal manoeuvres. I was gratified to find that much emphasis was placed on precision and emergency landings and I had to practise these at length when I was flying solo again.

Having to put the aircraft down in a marked circle in the middle of a field after the instructor had closed the throttle unexpectedly was a challenge I enjoyed. I made a determined effort to master this technique, knowing that one day I might have to face an emergency where competence in such skills would be paramount. It was of even greater importance to our Fleet Air Arm colleagues, who would have to land their aircraft in a small space on an aircraft carrier deck as a matter of routine.

The next stage in my primary training was not without its problems. I was introduced to aerobatics which included loops, rolls and other unnatural manoeuvres. While most of them came reasonably easily to me when under instruction, in some instances I had difficulty in summoning up the courage to carry them out when I was flying alone. Maybe I still lacked confidence in being able to get myself out of trouble if the need arose.

One such daunting manoeuvre for me was the Immelmann turn, which comprised a half-roll off the top of a loop. When I'd completed the first half of the loop and had to right the aircraft from an upside down position, I temporarily lost my nerve and completed the loop instead. This happened on a number of solo flights, until I realized just how irrational I was being...I could do loops and I could do rolls perfectly well, so why not a roll off a loop? The next time I took to the air on my own I gave myself an ultimatum: "Do an Immelmann turn properly or resign and remuster as an air-gunner... That's the last thing I want! Here goes..."

Progressing from one stage of training to another required the passing of flying checks with instructors other than your own. An up check qualified you for transfer to the next stage. A down check usually had to be followed by two up checks with independent instructors. Two down checks in a row could mean one of two things. If the regular instructor's recommendation was strong enough and the student's track record supported it, some extra instruction time might be allowed, after which the check procedure would be followed again. Without such a recommendation, the cadet would have failed the course and would find himself on the way back to Canada to remuster in another trade.

At one stage in my primary training I found myself facing a critical situation. I'd collected two down checks followed by extra time and one up check in which I'd scraped through by the skin of my teeth. I was about to try for the second up check and was understandably very nervous about it. My worries were compounded when I consulted the flight board and found that I was scheduled to fly with an instructor who had a reputation for being 'anti-limey'. I felt like packing my bags and leaving on the next train. Instead, I picked up my 'chute and climbed into the aircraft praying for a miracle. After checking things over, I started the engine and then waited... and waited...and waited...

I watched the other aircraft taxiing out and taking off until at last I found myself sitting on the tarmac in blissful isolation. "What the hell's happened to him?" Getting more and more agitated as every minute passed, I was hoping now that the instructor wouldn't show up at all, but eventually a lone figure emerged from the hangar and sauntered in my direction, showing no sign of urgency. I cursed my luck that I was not going to be reprieved after all. Resigned to my fate, I braced myself for the ordeal ahead.

The dreaded instructor clambered on to the wing, leaned across the cockpit and asked "Are you Robinson?"

"Y-es, sir."

"British?" My nod brought a grunt from him as he climbed into his seat.

I decided it would be foolhardy to throw in the towel now, although the temptation was great. Everything depended on this flight, so I willed myself to put all I'd got into it. Unfortunately, it was one of the perversities of my nature that the harder I tried, the worse my performance became. Paranoiac about the smallest errors which might reasonably have been overlooked, I found myself making far bigger ones which just couldn't be ignored.

I didn't enjoy criticism and tended to concentrate my attention more on what was actually said about my performance than on what effort I needed to put in to improve it. The instructor's displeasure was incurred at a very early stage when, believing that enough time had already been lost, I set off around the perimeter track with abnormal urgency.

"Robinson, you're supposed to be *taxiing* this goddamn airplane, not *flying* it!"

I slowed down. Take it easy, for God's sake...this is your last chance. You've got plenty of time... Reaching a suitable position for take-off, I turned the aircraft into the wind, reminding myself that I had to make sure everything was covered in my cockpit check. This was one of the things which upset instructors if we didn't get it right.

I was still mentally working through my checklist when I felt the controls wrested from me and we were suddenly airborne. Impatient with waiting, the instructor had taken the kite off himself without so much as a word. My nerves got the better of me. I became hot and bothered, no longer aware of what was happening. The commands I was given were carried out as if by a robot and I was unable to absorb the criticisms which seemed to be coming thick and fast. I was far too obsessed with the prospect of failure.

Providence then took a hand. The sky became black with cumulonimbus thunderclouds and the aircraft began tossing about in the turbulence like a small craft in a raging sea. Flashes of lightning pierced the gloom and got nearer with every minute. I became aware of the instructor's voice screaming down the tube, "Let's get the hell out of it. Back to base, Robinson, d'ya hear?" Proper to the end, I tried to execute a perfect 180 degree turn with a shallow bank, but found the instructor taking over again and completing a steep manoeuvre in a fraction of the time.

What exactly happened after that I can't remember. My only recollection was sitting in the aircraft on the tarmac in torrential rain as the instructor jumped down from the cockpit and shouted, "Guess that'll have to be an incomplete..." He then propelled himself towards the hangar through the teeming rain.

For several minutes I sat in the open cockpit with the rain pouring down my face before the penny dropped. An incomplete! I'd been reprieved after all! The check was null and void. It had to be done all over again...but with whom? I gazed at the leaden sky and said "Thanks... but please don't let it be the same guy next time." It wasn't. Next time it was a more understanding instructor who in consequence was treated to a much more acceptable performance. I passed and went on to the next stage.

Failing to make the grade as a pilot wasn't the only reason that a cadet could find himself remustering in Canada. Offending too often against the establishment could have the same effect. There was a system of merits and demerits — credits and debits — awarded for good and bad behaviour respectively. Accrual of too many demerits could result in relegation, irrespective of flying performance. In cases where pilot ability was borderline, a few merits or demerits could tip the scales either way.

I wasn't impressed with the discipline on the camp. At times I thought it bordered on the childish. On one occasion, I went on parade in the hangar holding a pair of plimsolls in my left hand. The officer in charge decided that I couldn't stand to attention properly so accoutred and he ordered me to fall out. Taking me into the middle of the hangar, he threw a piece of wood onto the ground and said, "Now stand there and salute that until I get back." After recovering from the initial humiliation, I saw the funny side of it. He'd got it all wrong. In the RAF we'd always been led to believe that 'if it moves, you salute it; if it doesn't, you paint it'.

The time came for me to move on to the first stage of flying in advanced trainers. This was in Harvard and Yale aircraft, which looked much the same except that the former had an undercarriage which was retractable while the latter's was fixed. The Harvard (*see plate* 3) was equipped with a Pratt and Whitney R1340 (600hp) engine and the Yale a Wright 985 (450hp).

This stage of training involved blind flying or flying entirely on instruments. Sitting in the cockpit staring at the instrument panel and not having any opportunity to check my position by means of outside landmarks was not my idea of flying. It was very easy to become thoroughly bored.

One of my instructors recognized this and, in an effort to relieve the monotony, showed me what low flying was like in an advanced trainer. As we skimmed over dense trees in a large area of Florida swampland, he told me that this was the home of alligators, although I never actually saw any. Nevertheless, I kept my fingers crossed that the need wouldn't arise for us to make a forced landing.

In spite of my reservations about blind flying, I soon learned the importance of trusting the instruments. I found that when flying in the dark or in conditions of poor visibility, my sense of balance and equilibrium tended to play tricks. I experimented with trying to fly a straight and level course through cloud by the seat of my pants, that is ignoring the instruments, only to discover when I emerged from the cloud that I was in a steep turn and losing height rapidly.

At other times, when religiously following what the instrument panel was telling me, the sensation I felt did not always agree with that information. It was unsettling until I finally came to terms with it and put my faith in technology.

Chapter 5

One of the activities that the British Flight Battalion considered a bind was the weekly parade. Just about everybody on the camp was expected to turn out for this military display. First the column of officers, then the NCOs and enlisted men and finally the BFB, which included the Fleet Air Arm cadets, all marched through the camp demonstrating their own particular standards of smartness.

The CO of the station took the salute. Some of the British students, accustomed to the RAF practice of swinging their arms fore and aft to shoulder height while holding their heads and bodies erect, were amused at the American style in which the arms appeared to swing loosely across the body.

One day at breakfast, we schemed to liven up the proceedings by taking the mickey out of our hosts. Playing our parts as if rehearsed, we copied the American technique as accurately as we could with possibly a little exaggeration. The CO and his officers were livid and demanded immediate disciplinary action. All the villains were confined to camp for the whole of the following weekend.

This enforced incarceration gave me an excuse for spending more time writing to Mary. My dedication to this activity greatly amused my companions. Their loved ones were lucky to hear from them once every week or two. I wrote something on most days and Mary looked forward to the postie's call before she set off for work in the centre of Glasgow. She responded in like vein and I could not complain about lack of regular news from home. Her encouragement spurred me on to greater effort whenever the going was rough. We always numbered our letters to each other and were agreeably surprised to find that none of our mail failed to arrive safely, in spite of heavy Allied shipping losses about this time.

The next stage in the flying programme proved most stimulating. It involved familiarization with another advanced trainer, the Vultee Valiant (*see plate* 4). This was a trim aircraft with fixed undercarriage, powered by the same engine as the Yale. The standard manoeuvres learnt on the Yellow Peril were practised both with an instructor and solo. I enjoyed formation flying immensely. Holding one's aircraft in position in a V or echelon formation required skilful handling of all the controls and success in carrying out such manoeuvres gave tremendous satisfaction.

It was not always easy to judge exactly how much gun, or throttle, was needed to keep one's position relative to the other aircraft. Changing station in the formation, for example executing crossovers or crossunders, was also quite a tricky operation. There was a tendency to overshoot and there weren't any brakes that you could apply.

Perhaps the most exhilarating aspect of formation flying was the breakaway. This entailed the three aircraft leaving the formation separately and landing on the airstrip in sequence. It was usual for trainee pilots to carry out this manoeuvre from a right echelon formation. The signal, which caused much amusement, consisted of number one blowing a kiss to number two, who passed it on to number three.

When number one was satisfied that the message had been received by the others, he patted his head to signify that he was about to break away and number two responded similarly, his message being duly received by number three. Number one then banked steeply to port, at the same time falling into a glide towards the airfield. This procedure was then repeated by numbers two and three, the latter following the former into the landing circuit. The breakaway was a source of pleasure to most of us.

Because of the risk of collision when in a vulnerable position near the ground, a pilot would normally keep as far away as possible from other aircraft when taking off or landing. Deliberately carrying out these manoeuvres in formation could therefore be a little unnerving. To take off in V-formation, the two wingmen had to be airborne *before* the leader so that they flew slightly above him. This was potentially dangerous, considering the difficulties that a wingman might face if he had to make an emergency landing with another aircraft only a few feet below him. Fortunately I never had to handle this situation.

The hazards when flying in formation could, of course, be compounded if something went wrong in any one of the aircraft. For instance, I learned that there had been a tragic accident in primary trainers at Grosse Île. It was customary, when a cadet was flying without an instructor, for a sack of sand to be strapped into the rear cockpit as ballast. On this occasion, the sack in one of the aircraft broke loose, fouling the joystick and causing a violent manoeuvre which resulted in the aircraft crashing into its neighbour, which in turn flew into the third aircraft in the formation. All three British student pilots were killed.

I embarked on the final stage of my flying training with mixed feelings. While fascinated with the idea of having to take off from and land on water, I had not really joined the Air Force to fly in boats. I hoped I would not have to do so eventually on operations, although the prospect of avoiding this now seemed to be bleak.

When I sat at the controls of a Consolidated P2Y flying boat (*see plate 5*), it was another totally new experience. An ungainly looking biplane, of which only 46 were built, it was affectionately (or denigratingly, depending on your viewpoint) known as the 'flying bedstead'. The hull sat low in the water and the high upper wing, connected to the lower one by struts and wires and carrying two Wright 1820/90 (700hp) radial engines, towered above and aft of the closed-in cockpit. There was a raised tailplane with twin fins and rudders mounted on it.

The boat was partially beached in shallow water facing out to sea, held in this position by a cable between the rear of the hull and a winch ashore. A mobile wooden catwalk was provided to enable the crew to board the aircraft. It transpired that she had been up the slipway for minor repairs and we were about to take her out for the first flight following the work. Normally she would have been moored to a buoy in the Gulf.

I was astonished at the size of the flying boat. Entering by a waist hatch about halfway along her hull, I had to walk forward at least twenty feet in a doubled-up attitude to reach the cabin. Hitherto I'd flown in aircraft in which the two seats had been in tandem. In the flying boat the two pilots sat side by side with space between them. The first pilot sat in the port seat, the second in the starboard. A crew of at least two other airmen was necessary to carry out various duties including mooring and unmooring. The engine instruments and controls were, of course, duplicated.

Sitting in this odd-looking contraption for the first time with the prospect of getting airborne in it was a strange experience. Ensign W B Ansbro, my first flying boat instructor, appreciated my confusion and gave me a meticulous briefing before we set off on our first flight. It had not occurred to me that handling a flying boat both on and off the water could be so different from anything I'd done before. I had to come to terms with the idea of being a seaman as well as an aviator. This meant taking account of a new dimension, the condition of the sea as well as that of the air. Often the two would be in conflict and one had to use one's judgement to decide how the effects could be reconciled.

Ansbro started the engines and the aircraft literally vibrated into life. The signal was given to let go the cable and the boat made for the open waters of the Gulf. It tossed and rolled in the swell and I felt sorry for the lads who'd been such poor sailors on the Atlantic crossing. They would have a miserable time of it if they ended up on boats, at risk from both seasickness and airsickness.

While the boat was sailing across wind, the engine on the windward side had to be run at higher revs to prevent her weathercocking into the breeze. As the engines reached normal operating temperature, Ansbro ran them up and checked the magnetos, switching off each in turn to ensure that the other was working satisfactorily. On reaching the take-off area, he throttled back and allowed the aircraft to swing into wind of her own accord. He then did his cockpit check, explaining every move.

A new feature of the procedure for me was that the pilot had to confirm with the crew that, among other things, they had closed all the hatches and were ready for take-off. From now on I realized that I'd no longer have just myself to consider, but would be taking on a responsibility for a number of other crew members, each of whom had an important role to play.

The pilot opened the throttles and the big flying boat lumbered forward. The tearing sound of the water on the bottom of her hull was alarming. As she gathered speed, she developed a bow wave and the spray could be seen whipping past the cabin in the slipstream on either side. The stabilizing floats suspended from the lower wing were well clear of the water. Initially the aircraft's nose was thrusting upwards proudly, but as the boat approached flying speed, the hull rode up onto its planing surface and levelled out briefly before finally leaving the water.

The tearing sound suddenly stopped, but the engines were very noisy and, since they were not synchronized, there was a marked throbbing sound. It occurred to me that the pulsating drone which seemed to be characteristic of multi-engined German aircraft was possibly due their pilots not bothering to synchronize the engines.

Once the boat was airborne, Ansbro put her into a climbing attitude, adjusting the throttles and airscrew pitch controls for the appropriate climbing speed. When we reached cruising altitude, he throttled back again and set the controls for level flight. It was then that he took time to eliminate the throbbing sound by adjusting the pitch on one of the airscrews. The ride became more comfortable.

Before long I was asked to take over the controls. The feel of the flying boat was not at all like that of a single-engined landplane. The controls were heavier, predictably, and the reactions of the aircraft to movements of wheel and rudder were therefore much slower. Nonetheless, there was something very stately about the way she responded and I concluded that this could be regarded as luxury travel compared with being cooped up in the restricted cockpit of a fighter.

My initiation into twin-engined luxury was to be brief and the instructor shortly took over again and explained what he was doing as he came in to land. As the hull touched down on the water, it sounded as though the bottom was being ripped out. It was a good landing and I wondered what a bad one would be like. What I didn't know then was just how much this noise and this sensation were to mean to me in the years to come. As the boat came off the step, the nose reared up, there was a rush of water past the bow and the hull settled comfortably in a level attitude again. Ansbro gave the starboard engine a boost to turn the aircraft out of the wind and the boat made for her moorings.

After passing the appropriate tests on the P2Y, we moved on to the Consolidated PBY-5B, better known as the Catalina (*see plate* 6). This was a more sophisticated military flying boat which was extensively used on operational duties, being a slow, economical and reliable aircraft ideally suited to long-range patrol work. It was a high-winged monoplane with a shallow hull and a single fin and rudder. The twin Pratt and Whitney 1830/92 engines each developed 1200 hp. In order to reduce drag, the floats near the ends of the mainplane folded up in flight to form the wingtips.

Familiarization flights in the Catalina were followed by a programme involving instrument flying, navigation flights, bombing and gunnery practice and night flying. While working through this schedule, I learned with some disappointment that we would not be joining an operational unit immediately after getting our wings. We were to go to Prince Edward Island in the St Lawrence River estuary for what was ominously called a General Reconnaissance course.

I asked the adjutant, "It's a foregone conclusion that I'll end up in boats after all, then?"

"Not necessarily," he replied cryptically. "The decision as to what type of operational unit you'll be posted to depends partly on your showing on the GR course. The staff at PEI will make their recommendations to Air Ministry based on that." I still had a faint glimmer of hope. My fate was not yet sealed.

Graduation came on Christmas Day 1942 without any flourish of trumpets. Not surprisingly, people were otherwise occupied, so the award of pilot's wings was a mere formality. I thought there was a touch of irony about my entering the United States on All Fools' Day and passing out with my wings on Christmas Day. It was a bit of a comedown to find that the BFB had run out of RAF pilots' brevets to sew on our uniforms. Having been given permission to wear US Navy wings instead to signify that we had qualified, we bought these from the PX.

As soon as I received my sergeant's stripes, I got out my 'housewife, airmen for the use of', and stitched them on to my tunic. Settling down to write a long letter to Mary telling her of this new milestone in my career, I had to break the bad news that I would not be coming straight home. I imagined her enjoying the Christmas festivities with her parents, who were both expert cooks, and wondered what I might be missing. Then the reality hit me that there was a dire shortage of food in the UK, so they'd hardly be living it up. When I made my way to the dining hall for my own Christmas blowout, a sense of guilt came over me.

Chapter 6

In the middle of January 1943, after another two weeks at Moncton, I completed my journey to Charlottetown, Prince Edward Island, in an icebreaker. The St Lawrence River was frozen over and everything was clothed in a thick blanket of snow. The ship ploughed her resolute way through the floes, making horrendous cracking noises as she broke up the ice and swept it aside.

We learned that we would be operating in landplanes, which was just as well since flying boats would have been useless in these conditions. I wondered what the countryside would look like after the thaw. One thing was certain. It was extremely cold and the immediate outlook was dismal. The prospect of flying around here was not very inviting, particularly after the near tropical climate of Florida.

The object of the nine-week course at PEI was to polish up the skills of the newly-qualified pilots in navigation and supporting subjects. To this end, we had no further experience in the driving seat, but flew as navigators in Avro Ansons. It was excessively chilly work and we were equipped with wool-lined flying suits and boots, a far cry from the lightweight drill uniforms used in the deep south. Even so, I found that my hands became stiff with the cold as I pored over my charts, measured drifts and worked out courses, heights and speeds for my pilot to fly. Not even the process of manually winding the undercarriage in and out, requiring no less than 150 turns of the handle, did anything for my circulation.

Notwithstanding these discomforts, I found navigation right up my street and proved successful at it. At the end of the course, the examination results were posted on the notice board. If you were at the top of the list you were awarded the 'strawberry'; if at the bottom, you got the 'raspberry'. Thenceforth I became known as Strawb by a select few of my contemporaries!

This success undoubtedly sealed my fate so far as flying boats were concerned. Towards the end of the course, one of our classroom instructors told us that the Air Ministry wanted to have some indication of the type of aircraft we'd like to fly on operations. He said that there was no guarantee that our choice would be accepted, but it would be one of the factors taken into account when the powers that be made their decisions.

We were asked to list various types of aircraft in order of preference. I found no difficulty with this, having made up my mind long ago. At the top I put all the glamour jobs – single-engine day fighters, twin-engine low-level day fighters, night fighters... Relegated to the very bottom were long-range bombers and flying boats. As I was putting the finishing touches to my list, I was aware of the instructor looking over my shoulder and I turned to see him shaking his head.

"No chance. We'll be recommending you for boats."

I was shattered. "Why? I don't see any future for me in boats."

He told me that with my showing on the course, particularly in navigation, he had no option. He was sorry if I didn't like it. Anyway, if it was action I was looking for, there was no shortage of that on boat squadrons, especially over the Bay of Biscay.

With that he gave me a broad grin and moved on to the next man in the row. I was very angry and not convinced by the arguments, but what could I do about it? If his recommendation was a foregone conclusion, why bother to ask me for my choice?

It was customary for groups to arrange end-of-course dinner parties to which they invited the staff as their guests. My companions and I arrived at the Queen Hotel some time before the staff were expected and we lost no time in getting the party under way. By the time the instructor appeared in the foyer, I was well oiled and thirsting for the officer's blood. "I'll teach him to recommend me for bloody boats," I promised. One of my companionions, Don Cross, tried to restrain me, saying "Take it easy, Strawb, he's only doing his job. He won't be taking the final decision."

"No, but the adj. at Pensacola implied that the Air Ministry'll take a hell of a lot of notice of what he says," I slurred. "There's the sod now!"

Lunging across the floor of the foyer, I started to flail my arms inaccurately at the bewildered officer. Exactly what happened next, no one seems to be able to recall. Subsequently, I learned that I was conveniently removed from the party for the next two and a half hours. Don and Cliff Short apologized to the instructor for their friend's appalling behaviour, explaining that it was nothing personal but he felt the decision about flying boats very keenly.

I was settled in an armchair in a small lounge which was otherwise unoccupied and I remained there incommunicado until the party was over. After my friends had revived me with difficulty, I was ready to join the celebrations, only to be told that they were all over and my taxi awaited me outside.

The following day was the day of reckoning. I awoke with the realization that I'd made a downright fool of myself and my RAF career was likely to be in ruins before it had really begun. A court martial was the least that I could expect for assaulting an officer. The poor chap was only trying to do his job. Why should I have taken it out on him? I suppose he's got the charge sheet made out already. Oh hell!

Suddenly deciding what action I should take, I smartened myself up and made for his office. He looked up from his desk as I saluted. "Good morning, sergeant."

"Morning, sir. I've come to apologize for last night. I was carried away by my disappointment at being recommended for boats. There was no excuse for my behaviour...I should not have attacked you...I'm extremely sorry..." My apology petered out. I didn't know what else I could say.

I stood petrified, awaiting his judgement. He had been impassive throughout. Then in his good time he spoke, the gist of his message being that I'd acted unwisely last night. Had he been drinking as much as I obviously had, we might have ended up brawling, with very serious consequences for us both. As it happened, he didn't drink and so had the advantage over me from the outset.

He fully understood my concern about the decision. Now he suggested that I forgot all about last night and made the best of my opportunities. He wanted to tell me that I should be proud of the fact that I'd been recommended so strongly for boats. It was a highly responsible job calling for special qualities, so I should think on that. He wished me good day and I simply stood there rooted to the spot.

Reprieved yet again? I just couldn't believe it. My relief at this unexpected outcome was clearly evident. I stammered something about his being most understanding, then saluted smartly and turned towards the door. He briefly wished me luck and from that moment I was looking forward to becoming a flying boat captain.

Back at my quarters, Don was just surfacing. "Well, you don't look as though you've been fired, so what are you grinning about? Did he drop dead or something?" he asked with his customary jocularity, his pink face wreathed in smiles.

Uncharacteristically, I ignored the humour this time, admonishing him with "Don't you insult that instructor, mate. He's a bloody brick."

In mid-April, we boarded RMS Queen Elizabeth for the return voyage to the UK. The famous ocean-going liner and her sister ship RMS Queen Mary had been converted for use as troopships for the duration of the war and frequently made the Atlantic crossing with thousands of servicemen. Because of their superior speed and manoeuvrability, they did not travel in convoys, but were deemed to be able to avoid submarines more readily on their own. The living quarters were very much better than those experienced on the outward voyage and there was an added advantage that the crossing only took four and a half days against the other troopship's twelve.

Although most of us didn't know what was going on for much of the voyage, there were U-boat alerts from time to time and the big ship weaved a tortuous course at high speed, denying the threatening enemy an easy target.

The first landfall was made at night, so we were unaware that we were just off the northern coast of Ireland. By daybreak it was possible to see the Mull of Kintyre through the mist and we realized that we were making for the Clyde. We eventually disembarked at Greenock and I bemoaned the fact that I was so close to Mary but unable to get in touch with her. Instead, I had to join the train destined for Harrogate.

Number 7 PRC at Harrogate was another of those holding units which my fellow sufferers and I had grown to hate. We did not appreciate the problems of those who had to move servicemen about the world in the best interests of the war effort. As far as we were concerned, we were just kicking our heels in these noncombatant units for weeks on end while the war was going on somewhere else and probably needed us.

It became clear that the friendships that we'd made during training were being broken up, because over the next few weeks we were freely distributed among a number of units at home and overseas. In some instances, instead of being posted to operational squadrons, as expected and strongly desired, aircrew found themselves doing commando courses at Whitley Bay. Understandably, since I was not the athletic type, I felt that these activities were a waste of time and an underuse of resources. I hoped that I would not be selected for one of them. Among other things, I did not want to do myself a mischief and be invalided out of the service having got this far.

One of the diversions breaking the monotony of life at Harrogate was the Link Trainer, a flight simulator which provided instrument flying practice without the use of an expensive aircraft. I had two sessions in this infernal machine and became very frustrated with it, because on the one hand it was claustrophobic and on the other it didn't appear to simulate accurately any aircraft that I'd flown so far. I concluded that British aircraft must have behaved differently from American ones. Knowing that the alternative to the Link Trainer activity would probably be something less acceptable, I became philosophical about it and convinced myself that any experience was better than none.

I learned that I was to have two weeks leave before my fate was finally sealed. After a week with my parents in Dorset, I hastened to Glasgow to see Mary for the first time since we'd met three and a half years earlier. I was also to have my first meeting with her parents. This turned out to be anything but the ordeal I'd anticipated. Her mother was a delightful, warm, friendly person who made me immediately welcome. Her father had been a seafaring man who now had a senior desk job in shipping. His conversation was full of interesting anecdotes about his many years at sea. They readily accepted me as an honorary member of the family, which was very gratifying and added to the pleasures of my first leave with them.

On one of our evening strolls in Jordanhill, Mary asked me where I was likely to be posted. I had to admit that quite honestly I had no idea. I suspected that the Harrogate people didn't even know themselves yet. Even if they did, they'd keep the information quiet until the last minute, for fear of it getting into the wrong hands. Not that the Germans would be overly worried about where *I* was, but troop movements generally were considered to be top secret.

Our predecessors at Harrogate had been scattered to the four winds, so my own destination could be anywhere. I wasn't even certain what kind of aircraft I'd be flying. I related the arguments that went on in Canada about that last topic, but was careful not to give Mary the unsavoury details of the happenings in Prince Edward Island, of which I was not very proud.

We talked about my having come to terms with the prospect of driving flying boats. My preoccupation with becoming a fighter pilot had faded fast. What sort of fighter pilot would I have made, anyway? Would my reactions have been quick enough? If not, I couldn't have expected to last long. And what about the trouble I'd had with my ears in the pressure chamber at Pensacola? Could I have flown at the heights required in fighters? Boats spent most of their time not more than a few thousand feet above the water. Maybe that's why they wanted me to fly boats; I wouldn't have to fly too high, so I wouldn't have any ear problems. Perhaps they had more sense than I gave them credit for, but why didn't they tell me the real reasons?

On my return to Harrogate, I was detailed to take charge of the RAF contingent which was to participate in an all-services pageant at one of the local theatres. In addition to the one from the RAF, there were to be groups from the Army, Navy, Nursing services, Civil Defence services and so on. A rehearsal was to take place in a couple of days. When the time came, I got my contingent formed up in the road and marched them off smartly to the venue.

A few isolated people were scattered about in various parts of the theatre, but mine was the only complete contingent present so far. I was unable to find anybody in authority, so characteristically we sat around impatiently waiting for something to happen. Half-an-hour went by and the agreed deadline passed without significant developments. In their customary way, the RAF boys were moaning like mad and complaining about the organization. I was livid. I'd kept to my side of the bargain, but nobody else had, so to hell with it.

"Come on, lads, outside."

"What's to do, sarge?"

"You'll see. Get fell in." They formed up again in the road. "Atten-*tion*! To the right, dis-*miss*!" The RAF contingent broke up, and with satisfied smirks on their faces, dispersed.

The following day, I stopped at the blackboard outside the Station Warrant Officer's office. There in bold characters was written the instruction SGT ROBINSON – REPORT TO SWO – URGENT.

"My God!" I exclaimed under my breath, "I'm on a fizzer after the fiasco yesterday. How am I going to flannel my way out of this one?" I opened the door behind which the SWO was sitting at a desk working through a pile of papers.

"Sergeant Robinson reporting..."

The SWO interrupted me with "Your posting's come through, sergeant. Here are your papers," he snapped. "Go straight down to stores and draw out some tropical kit."

"Where am I going, then, sir?"

"Pembroke Dock."

"Pembroke Dock? What do I need tropical kit there for?"

"You'll find out when you get there."

The Station Warrant Officer returned to his papers, signifying that he'd given me all the information I was getting. There was, of course, no mention of the pageant.

Good grief! They certainly believe in springing surprises on you, I muttered to myself, as I paused outside the office to reflect on this brief but highly significant interview.

Walking over to the blackboard, I picked up a piece of chalk and wrote across the instruction against my name, POSTED.

Chapter 7

The train journey to Pembroke Dock in May 1943 was not a very enjoyable one. Apart from the feeling of isolation having been parted from my friends, I was troubled by the uncertainty of what my fate was to be. There was little doubt now that I was to join a flying boat squadron, since PD was a well-known flying boat base. But why the tropical kit?

Approaching the RAF station, I saw a huge fin and rudder looming above the perimeter wall (*see appendix* B). I'd never set eyes on a Sunderland before, but this diagnostic feature was unmistakable from the aircraft recognition lectures attended at PEI. Contrary to my earlier reservations about flying boats, I was unable to suppress a certain feeling of excitement at seeing these handsome machines for the first time and in the knowledge that I would soon be flying them. Several of the aircraft were scattered around the station, some on the concrete aprons or part-way up the slipways (*see plate* 10), others moored at buoys on the water. I was overawed.

At the Orderly Room I found a message telling me to seek out Pilot Officer K F Dickson on arrival. A corporal directed me to my quarters, where I had a quick wash and unpacked my large holdall, or goon bag as I called it, before going off in search of the officer. He was busy in his room writing a letter and got up as I introduced myself. Greeting me warmly in an unmistakably Australian accent, he added that I was very welcome on his crew. I looked at him inquiringly.

"Thanks. I'm afraid I've not been told anything about my posting. The SWO at Harrogate was very cagey when I asked him why I had to bring tropical kit. I hope you'll be able to put me out of my misery."

His face broke into a grin as he appeared to express satisfaction that his crew's movements were being kept confidential. "You're here to join my crew as second pilot." He seemed to delight in keeping me in suspense, but eventually decided to break the news that I'd been waiting for. "I'm skipper of Sunderland D for Dog of 204 squadron. We're actually based at Bathurst in the Gambia. The reason we're here is that the boat's having a major overhaul. The job's nearly finished, so we'll soon be on our way back."

So that was it. The suspense had been killing me and now that I knew what was in store, I wasn't sure whether to be pleased or disappointed. New horizons were opening up for me, but somehow West Africa didn't really appeal. I suddenly realized how self-centred I was in thinking that way. The war was being waged worldwide and one's personal preferences as to location were irrelevant. At least I'd be flying again. It was probably the only way to keep cool in West Africa, anyway, so the promise of this would help to soften the blow.

I explained to Dickson rather sheepishly that I hadn't even had sight of a Sunderland before, let alone flown one. I couldn't imagine that I'd be much use to him to start with, since I'd never handled four engines. He reassured me that if I'd flown Cats I'd be half-way there...at least.

"You can get some practice on the way out to the Coast."

"What happened to your other second dicky?"

"He's just gone off on his skipper's course."

"Oh." There was relief in my voice. At least it was a good reason for him to be leaving the crew. There could have been other reasons which would not have been so agreeable. "When do you think we'll be going?"

"Within a few days, if things go to plan. The engines have been thoroughly checked on the slip. They seem to be OK, but we now need to air test the aircraft and do a loop swing. We must make sure that we're quite satisfied with her before we set off. But we'll soon be on our way to the sun again."

Dickson's enthusiasm for getting back to the white man's grave came as a surprise to me. Maybe it wasn't such a bad place after all. I shouldn't prejudge these things. Take them as they come.

I went on to bombard him with questions about the aircraft, the crew, the squadron, West Africa and everything else I wanted to know. He gave me some technical information about the boat and personal details of the crew. 'D for Dog' was a Mark III Sunderland (*see plates* 7 and 8 and *appendix* A) fitted with four Bristol Pegasus XVIII engines developing 1050hp each. It was seen to be an improvement over the Mark I (*see plate* 27) which was equipped with BP XXIIs developing 1010hp each and the Mark II (also having BP XVIIIs), but it still suffered from the embarrassing drawback that the airscrews could not be fully feathered.

In the event of an engine failure, the propeller would just go on windmilling. If you lost all the oil, the engine would seize up. In the worst case, the airscrew could spin off and there was no way of knowing in which direction it was going to fly. Dickson cheered me up further with the thought that when you were sitting in either of the pilots' seats, the inner prop on your side was uncomfortably close.

I was staggered to learn that the crew normally comprised ten members, as many as thirteen if you were operating over European waters where the risk of enemy fighter attack was greatest. For this trip there would only be eight of us. Until the skipper explained the duties of crew members, I found it difficult to believe that there were so many jobs to be done on board. This was a far cry from the four or five people flying around the Gulf of Mexico on training trips.

For an aircraft with a range of something like sixteen hours, there had to be reliefs for every job. My mind boggled at the captain's responsibilities on operational sorties – £100,000 worth (1940s prices!) of flying hardware and at least nine lives in addition to his own. I was now beginning to understand what the instructor meant by his parting remarks to me at PEI.

The following day the boat was to be air tested and I was to experience my first flight in a four-engined aircraft. She had been launched from the slipway and, after the beaching gear had been removed, towed out to a buoy to which she was finally moored. All this had been going on while I'd been at breakfast and I was sorry to have missed it. Anyway, I knew that there would be plenty of other opportunities to see these rituals in the future.

When the crew were ready we were all driven out to the aircraft in a motorized dinghy (*see plate* 11), a craft with which I was to become very familiar over the next three years. As we approached the flying boat, I was once again astounded at the size of it. The huge plump hull loomed out of the water to a height of between twelve and fifteen feet, excluding the fin. The wing area seemed enormous and I was later told that it was 1487 square feet; the wing span was more than 112 feet, the hull over 85 feet long and the overall height from keel to top of fin was in excess of 30 feet. A sizeable aircraft as warplanes went in the early 1940s.

Dickson offered to show me round before we took off. The dinghy drew alongside the boat on the port side and the crew entered through the forward hatch. Once the skipper and I had boarded, we stood aside in the bow compartment to allow the rest of the crew to get aboard and go about their various duties. We had to bend down to avoid banging our heads on the top of the nose section, but I was soon to discover that this was the only compartment except the rear turret area where this precaution was necessary for anyone of medium height. Luxury indeed.

The front turret had been withdrawn into the bow compartment to enable the crewmen to moor and unmoor the boat. There was a bollard, hinged at the bottom, which was normally horizontal when the aircraft was in flight but was now fixed in an upright position adjacent to the bomb-aimer's hatch. Strapped to the hull on the port side were a mooring ladder and an anchor (*see plate* 12) for use when there were no suitable fixed mooring facilities.

On the starboard side, there was a J-type inflatable dinghy and alongside a companionway leading to the flight deck was the toilet compartment, complete with lavatory and wash basin, both small but unexpectedly comfortable. Just aft of the forward hatch through which we'd boarded the aircraft was the entrance to the wardroom and a through route to the tail.

The skipper referred to the men in the bows as riggers. I was unfamiliar with the term as applied to aircrew and he explained that they were Straight Air Gunners who, in addition to looking after the guns, ammunition and bomb equipment, were also responsible for the airframe. Their varied tasks included mooring and unmooring, carrying out galley duties and deploying the drogues for slowing the boat down in the water when approaching the buoy. It was not unusual, however, for other crew members to assist with these jobs.

Moving towards the rear of the aircraft, we passed through the wardroom which contained two bunks doubling as seats on either side of a table with hinged flaps. Further aft was the galley where food and drinks were prepared (*see plate* 13). The equipment included two primus stoves separated by a small oven. Another companionway ascended to the rear end of the flight deck and on either side of the galley was a square hatch used, among other things, for deployment of the drogues, which were stowed in semi-circular receptacles just below the hatches.

Beyond the galley was the bomb bay in which eight 250lb torpex-filled depth charges were normally suspended from racks. These racks would be run out along the underside of the wings when the DCs were made ready for an attack. Under the port bomb door was a removable wedge-shaped panel which enabled a spare engine or other sizeable cargo to be loaded.

The next compartment had two more bunks in it and then there was a very spacious area leading up to the tail of the aircraft and the rear turret (*see plate* 21). The equipment in this space included a fitter's bench and there was a rear hatch on the starboard side providing an exit at a higher level above the water line than the forward hatch.

Attached to one of the bulkheads was the IFF (Identification Friend or Foe) transmitter, provided to enable our own forces to identify us as friendly. It could be switched to a distress frequency in an emergency. The control box in the pilot's cabin included a detonating device so that the equipment could be destroyed should there be any risk of it falling into enemy hands.

The forward companionway came up between the two pilots' seats on the flight deck (*see plate* 14). Immediately aft of the starboard seat was a small darkened cubby-hole housing the ASV (Air to Surface Vessel) radar equipment. The display was on a six inch diameter cathode ray tube with linear vertical scales offering four ranges. A very rough indication of the direction of the target could be obtained by observing the width of the blip and its disposition on either side of the scale. Adjacent to the radar position was the navigator's chart table, equipped with instruments used for dead-reckoning navigation (*see plate* 15).

On the port side there was a wireless operator's position (*see plate* 16), dominated by its R1155 receiver and T1154 transmitter. The latter was conspicuous by its enormous brilliantly coloured control knobs. The main spar, the strongest part of the aircraft, crossed the fuselage from wing to wing behind this and the navigator's table. Beyond it on the starboard side the flight engineer had his station (*see plate* 17). There was one other compartment on the flight deck, where the mid-upper, or dorsal, turret was normally located (*see plate* 19). This turret replaced the two waist hatches in the Mark I (*see plate* 18). A second J-type dinghy was stowed here.

I was suitably impressed. Although I had yet to get airborne in the flying boat, I certainly appreciated how much more comfortable it must be than fighters or bombers, or even Catalinas, where space was so restricted (*see plate* 23). I was slightly over six feet in height, yet I was able to stand erect in most of the compartments. It was much like being on a ship. I decided that it wasn't going to be so bad flying in these things after all.

I settled myself into the starboard seat alongside the skipper. From his position on the port side he explained all the controls to me and I had to admit that at first I found it a little difficult coming to terms with four of everything. The riggers were busy in the bows uncoupling the mooring pendants which held the boat to the buoy and putting a short slip, or rope, through the spreader so that it could be unhitched readily from the bollard as soon as the pilot gave the order (*see plate* 22). The intercom was checked and each crew member was asked to report in.

The skipper called up the control tower on the R/T (radio telephone) to establish contact so that he would be able to get clearance for take-off eventually. The hatch above the navigator's position was open and the flight mechanic climbed out onto the starboard wing to start the auxiliary power unit (APU) which would ensure that there was sufficient electrical power to start the engines. Access to the APU was gained by unhinging part of the leading edge of the wing between the hull and the starboard inner engine.

The APU motor was turned over with a starter rope in the manner of an outboard engine and it fired first time, which I later learned was a fairly rare occurrence. The flight engineer checked the panel of instruments in front of him and gave the skipper the OK to start the engines. The Australian adjusted the throttle, mixture and pitch controls and performed several other checks before starting the outer engines, first port and then starboard. When satisfied that they were both running smoothly, he signalled to the men in the bows to cast off. One of the riggers unhitched the short slip from the bollard, the spreader fell away and the buoy disappeared along the port side of the boat.

It wasn't until the aircraft was free of the trots, or rows of mooring buoys, that the inner engines were started. The flight mechanic stopped the APU, replaced and secured the leading edge hatch, returned to the flight deck and closed the engineer's hatch. All four engines were then allowed to warm up to operating temperature as the aircraft made her way slowly out towards the take-off area. While the engineer carefully watched his dials, the skipper ran up the engines in pairs and checked the magnetos.

After that, he carried out his cockpit check, making sure that the crew reported that they were at their stations, that the bow turret was closed and that all hatches were secure. Adjusting the trim on the control surfaces, he checked that the latter were operating correctly, ran the flaps out to one third and obtained clearance from the tower for take-off. Throughout this procedure he gave me a running commentary.

The flying boat was by now facing into wind with a substantial stretch of water ahead of her. Pulling the control column fully back, the pilot opened the throttles of the two outer engines. The boat began to move forward sluggishly and the bow reared up with apparent reluctance, plunging ahead laboriously like a vessel not really designed for the job. Then as the inner engines were opened up, the aircraft assumed a more determined attitude, surging forward and sending up bow waves on either side of her hull.

The engine noise was ear-splitting and yet, even though on the flight deck, I could still hear the water tearing at her planing surfaces. As she gathered speed, the skipper moved the control column slowly forward, easing the hull onto the step, so that the boat was soon planing along the surface of the water on her keel. A few more seconds in a level position and the bow wave suddenly disappeared. The tearing noise on the bottom of the hull ceased as the water began to recede. The huge aircraft was airborne and Dickson clasped all four throttles, drawing them back together to a suitable boost setting for climbing. Over the intercom he asked me to reduce the revs by adjusting the airscrew pitch controls. The flaps were then retracted and the trim adjusted.

We climbed to the required cruising altitude and I began to reassess my feelings about flying boats. This was comfortable flying and I felt at home in this spacious machine. The skipper suggested I had a look around to see what I thought of her. Unplugging my intercom, I stepped down between the pilots' seats and moved the sliding hatch to reveal the companionway to the lower deck. Descending to the bow compartment, I retraced the route taken when shown over the boat earlier. In the wardroom, two wireless operators were leaning on a bulkhead chatting. One had his headset plugged in, in case either was summoned by the skipper.

Asked what I thought of the "old crate" I gave her an unqualified seal of approval. When I suggested that they didn't have too hard a time by the look of it, one of them went on the defensive immediately and explained that life wasn't always so easy. Since this was only an air test there wasn't much for them to do, but when on ops they spent hours either in the gun turrets or listening in to the radio communications set. From the way this was said and the reaction evoked from his companion, I deduced that neither of them was too enamoured of his regular operational duties.

As one of the men eventually put it, "...you get a bit cheesed off sitting in a turret looking at what seems like an empty sea for hours on end. It's not so bad if you actually come across something, but often we don't see a damn thing from start to finish of a trip. Several hours of that sort of concentration is more than enough."

I moved on into the galley. Both hatches were open and the sound from the engines and slipstream was much in evidence. It was also extremely draughty. One of the crew was looking out of the starboard hatch admiring the scenery. Due to the noise he was unaware of my presence so I carried on with my inspection, moving towards the tail. When I reached it after what seemed a very long walk along a compartment which tapered into a narrow tunnel (*see plate* 21 and *appendix* C), I couldn't work out how to get the turret open. Collecting the rigger from the galley, I asked him to introduce me to the mysteries of the rear gun position.

Chapter 8

Once settled in the rear gun position, I felt utterly detached from the outside world. The rotatable turret was like a small round greenhouse and, even though its guns and ammunition were not installed, the space was so restricted that I wondered how I would get out once shut up inside. There was an escape hatch for the rear gunner in the hull just forward of the turret, but he wouldn't be able to use that in an emergency until he'd extricated himself from the turret itself. As I sat there surveying the wide panorama of land, sea and sky, I somehow did not feel part of the scene. Behind me were solid metal doors which when closed gave little clue as to what lay beyond. The sensation was as if I were suspended in midair in a ski lift, yet without any visible means of support.

There was little evidence of movement at first, but the feeling of helpless isolation was later made worse by the pilot's sudden action in putting the flying boat into a steep turn. I felt that my greenhouse was going out of control and there was nothing I could do about it. I looked around me as if to make sure that the rest of the aircraft and the crew were still there. It was then that I discovered how to operate the turret by using the control handle in front of me. Hoping it was not connected in some way to a device for jettisoning the whole thing, I moved it gingerly and found myself rotating to port. The tailplane reassuringly came into view and I was relieved to find that I was not alone in space.

Returning the turret to its central position, I pondered on how fortunate I was that I had not had to remuster as an air gunner. I felt that rear gunners deserved the highest admiration for the job they did. In spite of the four-barrelled weaponry over which they normally had control (*see plate* 20), they must have felt that they were sitting targets out there. Furthermore, if the intercom failed to operate and they were unable to keep in touch with what was going on, they could quite easily imagine that they'd been deserted by the rest of the crew. I unlatched the doors behind me and climbed out into the fuselage again. Glad to have escaped from this claustrophobic prison, I hurriedly made my way back to the galley.

As I was climbing the companionway from the galley to the engineer's position the rigger called out, "OK?" I nodded and thanked him timidly, not wanting to explain how I really felt. On opening the hinged hatch at the top of the steps, I nearly knocked the flight engineer off balance. He had just been leaving his position to call to the flight mechanic to take over from him when the hatch had flown up and given him a resounding slap on the buttocks. "Oh, sorry, old man. I had no idea you were there."

"That's all right, mate. You'll learn... Give my relief a shout, will you?" I complied and the two changed places.

The navigator was standing by his table leaning on the main spar (*see plate* 24). He also had little to do on this local trip, but he didn't trust the skipper not to go too far from base and get us all lost. Every few minutes he looked out of the cabin window to make sure that we weren't.

"Like to have a look at the equipment?" He gave me a briefing on the radar, D/F radio, astro-compass and drift recorder. He also showed me the Dalton Computer, a device already familiar from my training at PEI, which enabled you to work out the wind direction and speed and the course that the aircraft had to fly to get from A to B.

One of the wireless operators was now listening intently to the radio, from time to time changing channels to check its performance and to find out who was on the air. He took his headset off, handed it to me and I held it to my ear. All I heard was a sequence of Morse signals being transmitted at too fast a speed for me to decipher them. Although I'd learned how to use the Morse code, the specialist operators not surprisingly left me standing. I returned the headset, then made my way back to the pilots' cabin.

When I'd plugged into the intercom, Dickson asked me what I thought about the aircraft, now that I'd flown in her. The expression on my face said it all. My mind flashed back to the fuss I'd made about being nominated for boats. I had those guilt feelings again, but fortunately I wasn't allowed to dwell on them.

"You can take over now," the skipper told me and I grabbed the starboard wheel as he took his hands off the port one. Since the flying controls were duplicated, it was possible to fly the aircraft from either seat.

I was agreeably surprised at how responsive the Sunderland was. While I couldn't say that it was light on the controls, it seemed to cooperate with what I was asking it to do. In fact, it cooperated just a bit too well and I was reminded of my first attempt to fly the Yellow Peril, when I kept overshooting and the biplane was careering all over the sky. This time, however, the overshoots were not too serious, for which no doubt the other members of the crew were truly thankful.

I asked the skipper why it was that when I took over the aircraft from him, it immediately lost both height and airspeed. It didn't make sense to me, since we were nowhere near stalling speed. He explained it away by saying that it was just a matter of fine adjustment, but this seemed to be begging the question. It was some time before I found out the true reason by trial and error.

Dickson took over the controls again and announced to the crew that he was ready to do the loop swing. Luckily I knew what this meant, otherwise I might have thought that he was going to try to loop the aircraft, which would have been a rather ambitious manoeuvre. The loop was in fact a directional aerial situated on the top of the fuselage and was used for taking radio bearings. Distortions in its readings, known as quadrantal error, arose due to signals being reflected from various parts of the airframe and arriving at the aerial with time delays. Television viewers who have experienced ghosting on their sets, due to reflections from large obstructions such as gas holders, will be familiar with this effect. The loop swing procedure enabled the errors to be computed so that the necessary corrections could be applied when taking bearings. A similar procedure was needed to compute errors in magnetic compass readings.

When the loop swing was completed, the engineer appeared between the seats in the pilots' cabin and leaned on the back of one of them, looking intently at the instruments. Dickson asked him whether he thought the engines were in good shape and was told that everything was performing satisfactorily. He then announced that we could set off for Africa within the week. The engineer looked put out and protested that he'd made some personal arrangements for the following Tuesday. The Australian eyed him with a mischievous expression and told him that he'd have to transfer his arrangements to Gibraltar, because that's where we were likely to be.

He added that after a trip across the Bay we would have earned a celebration. I laughed at the joke and then considered the implications. The Bay was alive with Junkers 88s thirsting for the blood of people like us. This was a real danger to me, but the others appeared to think nothing of it.

The skipper sounded the buzzer signifying to the crew that he was going down. They reported back to him that all the hatches were closed and that they were ready. He called up the tower for clearance to land and then set about making his circuit of the alighting area. As he began his letdown from 1000 feet he asked me to put the airscrews into fine pitch and run out two thirds flap. He then throttled back, first on the two inner engines and then on the outers, resetting the outer engines and adjusting the rate of descent by the use of the inners to ensure maximum control. When he judged that he could make the desired touchdown by means of a glide without power, he throttled right back and began to flatten out.

The hull skimmed along just above the water for some distance and then the keel made contact with it and the bottom tearing sound returned, getting louder as the engine noise diminished and the hull gradually settled its weight into the water. As the boat came off the step, the bow reared up and the pilot opened the outer engines momentarily, moving the control column progressively further back to prevent the spray from hitting the propellers as the bow eased itself into the water again. The aircraft slowed to taxiing speed and the pilot turned her towards the trots.

In the next ten minutes, I learned a good deal about seamanship in flying boats as Dickson made his approach to the buoy. It was important to do this as slowly as possible to give the riggers a fighting chance to pick up the floating spreader with a boathook and secure it over the bollard. Since the aircraft tended to weathercock if left to her own devices, it was sensible to approach into the wind, provided it was of significant strength and the tide did not conflict with it. In light wind conditions, the inner engines would normally be cut and full flap used to create as much drag as possible.

If the boat was still travelling too fast, one or both of the drogues could be thrown out of the galley hatches. The drogues were large canvas truncated cones like bottomless buckets and, since they created considerable drag, they had to be used skilfully. Once deployed, it was extremely difficult to spill the water from them to bring them inboard again when the aircraft was under way or if there was a strong tide.

On this occasion we were able to make a perfect approach into a ten knot wind using the outer engines only. As the tide was on the turn, it was not a significant factor and we did not need the drogues. The riggers secured the spreader with swift movements and the outer engines were then cut. By means of the engine starter buttons the propellers were repositioned so that all four were in the same configuration. The riggers set about mooring the aircraft properly, which required that they picked up two strops or pendants which were suspended from the buoy.

One of these was shackled to a fixed bridle on the keel via an extension bridle which took the strain of the boat at her moorings. The other was fixed to the end of an anchor chain which hung loosely over the bollard and was secured to a winch in the centre of the bow compartment. This was a precaution in case the keel bridles failed for any reason. The spreader was then removed from the bollard and allowed to float freely in the water. When the operation was complete, I told the skipper that I hadn't realized that such a performance was involved.

"Well, remember that the unladen weight is about fifteen tons and with a full payload it's nearer twenty-five tons. In rough conditions, that would put a hell of a strain on those hawsers. A thin bit of rope wouldn't hold her for long." The Australian grinned, then told me that we'd better call a dinghy, otherwise we'd be out there all night. He picked up an Aldis lamp and started flashing the shore with the letter D for dinghy, *dah-dit-dit*. A dinghy driver responded with the letter R for Roger, *dit-dah-dit*, to indicate that the message was received and understood. Within seconds he had started his engine and was making for the Sunderland. Five minutes later the crew was ashore.

During the next few days we carried out several more brief air tests to make final checks that everything was in order. On our return to shore on Monday, 31 May the skipper and I called at the Operations Room to confirm the arrangements for tomorrow. Weather conditions were perfect. We'd be in a high pressure area for most of the trip to Gibraltar, the cloud would be five tenths and the wind light and variable.

I was puzzled that there weren't any armaments aboard and asked Dickson when we'd be loading them. "We haven't any," he said nonchalantly. "We left them behind in Bathurst. No point in carrying guns and ammo about on transit trips like this. It's only extra weight."

"So we won't have anything to fight back with if we're attacked by Ju88s?"

"That's right. But we're not counting on anything like that."

I was incredulous. "Then I suppose we'll go over the Bay at night?"

"No, I like to be able to see where I'm going. We'll take off at first light."

Nonplussed, I just couldn't think of anything else to say. I was not at all encouraged by some of the stories I'd heard from crews operating regularly out of Pembroke Dock. It was not unusual for them to be shot up by German aircraft or by U-boats in the Bay. Under attack, a flying boat was, of course, subject to much the same risks as a landplane. However, there was an added danger of getting her hull peppered with holes, making a landing on water particularly hazardous if not disastrous. In some circumstances, it was possible to rip the bottom out on touchdown.

Only two days earlier a Mk II boat with a large hole in her hull, sustained in heavy seas when involved in an air-sea rescue mission, made a successful landing on the grass alongside the runway at Angle aerodrome, not far from PD. The knowledge that the crew survived the experience offered some comfort. It was reassuring to know that one could get away with landing a Sunderland with reasonable safety on land. I never envied anyone having to bring a landplane down in the sea.

Chapter 9

In the early hours of 1 June 1943, I received my call and roused myself to prepare for the day's experience. I had very mixed feelings about this trip. While accepting that there were challenges which many people would have jumped at, I lacked any enchantment with Africa and was plagued with thoughts of the extra distance that the move would put between Mary and myself. The UK leave that I'd had on my return from Canada had helped to forge a strong bond between us and it had been a wrench having to be parted so soon from the girl I loved.

Added to this, the fear of running the gauntlet of a fighter-infested Bay of Biscay without any means of defending myself bore in on me periodically and I considered that all in all this was no great deal. I had to remind myself again that there was a war to be fought and won and personal factors were of secondary consideration.

After the inevitable RAF breakfast of bacon and eggs, I joined the skipper, navigator and a wireless operator in the Operations Room. The briefing was a mere formality, because the trip was a straightforward one and conditions had not changed much since the previous day. The flight plan provided us with a route skirting the Bay of Biscay well to the west, but I wasn't convinced that we'd be outside the range of Ju88 fighters operating from the French airfields.

Following the air test yesterday, a refuelling barge had moored alongside the aircraft and over two thousand gallons of 100 octane fuel had been put into the ten tanks in the wings. Most of this would be used up on the flight, since an average consumption of nearly one hundred and fifty gallons an hour was allowed for and the trip was expected to last at least twelve hours.

Once on board, the crew busied themselves with their individual duties. The captain took particular care over his preparations because, he told me, there was no margin for error when you were taking off with a full load of petrol. The engines would have to do a considerable amount of work "to get that lot into the air". Allowance would have to be made for a much longer take-off run than for a local trip when we weren't carrying a fraction of the weight. In fact, when it came to the point, I estimated that we took at least twice as long to come unstuck as we had done the previous day.

Airborne, we circled the tower and waggled our wings in a pilot's gesture of farewell. The skipper set course manually for the Scilly Isles, climbing to 5000 feet. Visibility was excellent and the islands soon came into view. Dickson asked the navigator for a course from the Bishop Rock lighthouse and it was not very long before we were out over the Atlantic and all trace of our homeland disappeared behind us. I wondered when I was likely to see it again.

The skipper showed me how to put George the automatic pilot into operation and how to make the minor adjustments necessary from time to time to ensure that the aircraft maintained straight and level flight on the right course. He also demonstrated the method used to synchronize the propellers. Seen from the cockpit the two props on either side of the fuselage were conveniently in line with each other. The stroboscopic effect could therefore be used when adjusting the pitch to equalize the revs. The pulsating throb then disappeared and the regular noise of the engines became less noticeable.

For the first time I experienced what it was like to be floating in the air over a vast area of sea with nothing else in view. The sensation was extraordinary and in some ways alarming. Could there possibly be anyone else out here in this enormous expanse? The open space seemed unlimited and I speculated on how long it might be before anybody found us if we had to make a forced landing miles from anywhere. How much we had to rely on radio contact with the outside world! Although the surface of the sea was broken only by small wavelets as the wind was light, it was possible to detect a substantial swell moving eerily in the direction of the Continent. The energy contained in that undulating movement must have been tremendous.

I scanned the skies anxiously for enemy aircraft, while the rest of the crew seemed totally relaxed. They were quite used to this sort of thing and I couldn't understand how they could be so unfearing. That lesson had yet to be learnt. In the meantime, I occupied myself with thoughts of what would happen if enemy aircraft did take an interest in the lumbering flying boat which would not be able to use speed to make an escape.

Given enough warning we would have to fly as low as we could over the sea to protect our vulnerable under-belly. What a beautiful target we'd make from above! Taken by surprise, there'd be only one course of action open to us. If we got into a very tight turn, the much faster fighters would find it difficult, if not impossible, to draw a bead on us. I still thought it was a dodgy business without so much as a peashooter to fire back at them.

My thoughts were mercifully interrupted by the skipper. "Would you like to swap places now?" He slipped into the second pilot's seat after I'd vacated it and I settled myself in the first pilot's position and checked our speed, altitude and course. No adjustments seemed necessary, so I sat back thinking I was in for an easy time of it, letting George do all the work. Not so. Dickson said, "Just so that you can get a bit of practice, take George out and climb to 6000 feet, making sure you stay on course."

I responded, but found that as I tried to handle a fist full of throttles to adjust the engine speeds with my right hand, my left hand failed to produce the appropriate corrections to the boat's attitude as first one wing and then the other dropped. Having put this right, I then discovered to my annoyance that I'd drifted several degrees off our intended heading.

I imagined the navigator back there biting his finger nails and wondering how the devil he was going to keep us on our computed track when the pilot couldn't steer a straight course. "OK, I'll keep her going straight," offered the skipper, "you concentrate on adjusting the engines for the right climbing speed."

On reaching 6000 feet, I levelled out and throttled back to settle the aircraft down at the correct cruising speed. I found myself making all the mistakes I'd made in the primary trainer in the early stages of my training and it embarrassed me to think that I was wearing wings signifying that I was a qualified pilot.

Unfortunately, although a highly skilled and competent pilot himself, my skipper didn't really know how to handle someone like me. Nevertheless, he showed infinite patience, which is something I would have been short of had I been put in his position.

In the event, I overcame these difficulties in time and discovered for myself why I lost height and airspeed every time I took over the controls. My conclusion was that the Sunderland flew naturally in a slightly nose-down attitude. After setting boost and revs for the correct cruising attitude, any attempt to fly the boat with the nose higher than it should be resulted in the loss of both height and airspeed.

When we reached a point west of northern Portugal, we flew parallel with the coast about thirty miles out from it. I realized, much to my relief, that we'd negotiated the Bay without seeing a thing. Maybe the skipper's decision not to carry all the extra weight of armaments was right after all. Even so, it had seemed to me to be a bit of a gamble and in any event we were still not home and dry yet.

As it turned out, the trip proved uneventful and we finally reached the gateway to the Mediterranean in the early evening. From the southern end of the isthmus known as La Linea, the huge Rock of Gibraltar thrust itself proudly into the sky. The ships in the harbour seemed to be cradled in its arms. My knowledge of the Rock to date did not extend beyond the Barbary Apes and I imagined them sitting there watching us suspiciously as we circled, waiting for permission to land.

The wind was blowing from the west, which meant an approach from behind the Rock, across the isthmus and towards the town of Algeciras. As the aircraft skirted the east side and turned across the narrow neck of land, she began to shake erratically from the turbulence caused by air currents rising up the west face of the Rock, but she settled down again as we made our final approach across the harbour. The touchdown was between two naval escort vessels at anchor and we could see their crews enjoying a ringside seat for the landing.

The next day, the second of June, was my twentieth birthday. We spent it in a leisurely way checking the aircraft and refuelling her ready for the next leg of the flight to Bathurst, today known as Banjul. It was now quite hot and it was a pleasure to change into lightweight khaki shirts and shorts. As I stood on the wing watching the refuelling operation, I could feel the warmth from the metal skin of the aircraft through the soles of my shoes. Although the breeze had freshened a little, the petrol vapour could be seen rising in the heat haze above the large expanse of wing.

On the trip from the UK we'd used about eighteen hundred gallons of fuel and this thought put the cost of running the war into perspective for me. I could now understand how important it was for the Allies to have continuing and uninterrupted access to vast quantities of oil if they were to win this conflict.

We took off again at first light the following morning. It was cool and pleasant and there was a slight sea mist. The estimated duration of the flight was about twelve and a half hours, which seemed to me a lifetime. We had no specific operational duties to occupy us, although we were expected to keep our eyes open for any enemy U-boats, surface vessels or aircraft which might happen to be along our track. Had we seen any, we'd have been unable to engage them, being completely bereft of armaments, so we'd have had to report them to someone who could.

We set course immediately for a point a few miles off the Moroccan coast and the temperature gradually increased as we moved south. It was comfortable in the air, but I began to imagine what we had to look forward to when we eventually set foot on the Coast.

I alternated watches with the skipper in the first pilot's seat and gradually became more competent in my flying skill with the Sunderland. When Dickson was beside me, I flew the aircraft manually, to get more practice under instruction. At other times, such as when he was below in the wardroom having a meal or resting (trusting soul!), I let George do the work. I just hoped that if anything went wrong, the skipper would have time to cover the distance from the wardroom to the flight deck before I ditched everybody in the sea. I was not yet skilled in the art of making emergency landings in this type of boat.

It was while I was contemplating these possibilities that I suddenly became aware of the fact that we were not carrying parachutes. Curiously, I had not noticed this before, either at Pembroke Dock or on the way out to Gib. We all had Mae West life jackets, of course, in case we came down in the drink. In the wing there was also an inflatable dinghy, in which we would be able to paddle around in that vast expanse of ocean until someone found out we were there and decided to come and pick us up, if we were so lucky.

But what if the aircraft went out of control and we couldn't make an emergency landing? When the skipper appeared again, I put the point to him. "Oh, no, we don't carry parachutes. We wouldn't have much opportunity to use them, would we? We normally fly lower than this on ops, say 1000 to 2000 feet, so if anything really went wrong there wouldn't be time for anyone to get to a hatch and bale out. That's one of the hazards of flying in boats."

As we continued southwards roughly parallel to the coast, the navigator periodically pointed out landmarks of interest on his Mercator chart. At one point he indicated that we were due west of Port Étienne, now known as Nouadhibou, although we were too far away from it to be able to distinguish anything. I was told that it was a small settlement on the edge of the Sahara and hardly an area of scenic beauty, anyway.

"We've got a detachment base there. It's often more convenient to drop in to PE after a long sortie north of the Gambia than to go back to base. We can knock off several hours' flying time if we have to operate this far north. It's about four hours away from Bathurst." This flexibility impressed me and I hoped that the squadron was always as well organized.

I was beginning to get tired. We'd been in the air for twelve and a half hours and we hadn't turned coastwards yet. "How much longer?" I asked the navigator.

"Oh, about forty minutes now. The wind's backed round to the south and slowed us up a bit... Bathurst is nothing to get excited about, you know. You're better off up here. It'll be hot and sticky and smelly and..."

"OK, spare me the details. I know we're not going to some tropical paradise."

We were soon waterborne after arriving at the capital of the Gambia, which was located near the mouth of the big river of that name. As we disembarked from the dinghy alongside a long wooden jetty, I witnessed a scene which was to have a lasting impression on me. Three of the barefooted local lads were having their evening meal at the end of the jetty. Sitting cross-legged around a rusty old iron drum, they were plunging their hands into it, bringing out a mixture which looked like pigswill and stuffing it hungrily into their mouths. My education to date had painted a different picture of life in our African colonial possessions and I found the reality somewhat disturbing.

After debriefing in the Ops Room, we made our way to our quarters. The crews were accommodated in long single-storied huts on the sandy beach, the water lapping the shore only a few yards away. A low sea wall and makeshift ovens constructed from loose bricks and bits of corrugated iron were the only features breaking up the open area of fine white sand.

Dancing on his haunches ape-like around one of these ovens was a very tanned individual, aged about twenty-five, dressed only in a pair of tattered shorts. He was making unintelligible sounds as he waved his long arms about in an aimless fashion. I eyed him questioningly and someone, detecting my mystification, said "Oh, that's only Harry. He's Coasty."

"What do you mean by that?"

"He's been out here too damned long. That's what the Coast does to perfectly normal people. Don't worry about him. He's not always like that. He likes to put on a show for newcomers. He's a bit of a wag, really."

"I'm not so sure. Where there's smoke there's fire!"

The NCO, or non-commissioned officer, members of the crew had their own hut, which was very convenient. It meant that we could keep together and didn't have to be disturbed by other crews who might be called out at different times, for example when making early morning take-offs. My bed was more or less in the centre of our hut. It was a standard issue iron bed with three biscuit mattresses and the ubiquitous RAF drab grey blankets. Hanging over the centre of the bed was a mosquito net tied up in a large knot.

We had to get used to the idea of giving mosquitoes a wide berth here. At home they didn't worry me much. Here, one bite was enough to put you in the sick bay with malaria, a complaint which could plague you for the rest of your life. We were advised to take quinine tablets regularly as a safeguard against catching malaria, or at least as a means of minimizing its effects.

I soon learned that one of the worst features of serving my country in West Africa was the food. The cook's speciality in the sergeants' mess was the soya link. I had been warned that this secret weapon was on offer with monotonous regularity at breakfast every morning. Since most of them were left on the plates with equal regularity, it was assumed that they were the same ones being recycled.

I awaited my first breakfast in fear and trepidation. When the plate was thrust into my hand, there they were sure enough. Two of the dreaded soya links were huddled together on one side of the plate as though they were not on speaking terms with the baked beans. To be more complimentary to them than they deserved, they were a kind of sausage with a distinctive form arising from their having been crammed together uncomfortably in a can before being served. The pressures that had flattened their ends had forced them into a shape not unlike that of a dog's bone, wider at the ends than in the middle.

They certainly looked as though they'd seen the light of day before this occasion. I tried a piece tentatively and resolved never to try them again. They had a taste and texture that beggared description. I disposed of the beans and then decided to have some bread and jam. Picking up a slice of bread, I noticed that it had a mottled appearance. "What are these little black specks?"

"That's your protein ration. They're weevils. Pretty harmless, really... They don't eat much... They're dead, you know... We pick 'em out before we eat the bread if we've got the time."

Chapter 10

Number 204 Squadron was formed in 1918 from number 4 Squadron Royal Naval Air Service, which had been operating in France during the First World War. It was disbanded in 1919, but reformed in 1929 at Mount Batten, Plymouth, as part of Coastal Command. Equipped with Sunderland flying boats in 1939, it moved to West Africa two years later to counter the U-boat threat along the shipping lanes of the South Atlantic.

When I joined 204 in the middle of 1943, it was commanded by Wing Commander C E W Evison and the Flight Commander was Flight Lieutenant J C Paré. The squadron crest showed a cormorant drying its wings and the motto was 'Praedam mari quaero − I seek my prey in the sea'.

During the European war from 1939 to 1945, Britain was by no means self-sufficient as a nation. Most of her food supplies and raw materials had to be transported from all over the world by her substantial merchant fleet. Large numbers of service personnel and considerable quantities of war materials also had to be moved safely from one part of the globe to another. It was imperative to keep the sea lanes open for this vital traffic.

The merchant vessels required protection against enemy U-boats and surface raiders which found them easy prey, particularly when unaccompanied. Although often armed, their guns were no match for the armaments of German vessels intent on preventing them from reaching their destinations. The U-boats lay in wait for them and picked them off with disturbing success.

The British response to this serious hazard was to use a First World War ploy, forming the merchant ships into convoys accompanied by Royal Navy escort vessels, usually sloops, corvettes and destroyers. The detection equipment used by the escorts was mainly ASDIC and radio D/F, while their most important anti-submarine weapon was the depth charge.

The ships with the most valuable cargoes were positioned in the centre of the convoy, affording them maximum protection. Predictably, the fastest were at the front and the slowest, including those most likely to fall behind, eg due to engine trouble, at the rear. Many convoys progressed at no more than eight knots and since the escorts were capable of at least twice that speed, they were able to manoeuvre as necessary around the outside of the convoy, providing a shield against marauding U-boats.

One of the difficulties was that if there were several enemy submarines, one or more could draw off the escort ships while the others attacked the ships which had become exposed. Furthermore, if an escort vessel at the rear of the convoy went to the aid of a straggler in trouble, this would also remove cover from some of the other ships. The protection was greatly improved with the deployment of aircraft of Coastal Command. These could seek out the enemy and give our ships considerably more warning of the threat of a torpedo attack. They were also able to offer a strike facility which did not require the diversion of the escort vessels from the convoy.

Since the Atlantic convoys made such slow progress and it could be several hours before an aircraft reached them from its coastal base, it was important that any air support should be carried out by long range aircraft. The Sunderland could stay airborne for as much as sixteen hours, so that in theory it could remain with a convoy for up to twelve hours, during which time the ships would have steamed less than one hundred nautical miles. Extravagant as this support may have seemed, it was sufficiently successful in getting vital supplies through to their destinations to have amply justified the commitment of resources. Once out of range of West African squadrons, the UK-bound convoys were covered for the even more hazardous passage through the North Atlantic and the Western Approaches by aircraft operating from North Africa, Gibraltar and the British Isles.

Our major role in West Africa was therefore to liaise with the Royal Navy in protecting our shipping and its valuable cargoes from the U-boat menace in the South Atlantic (*see plate* 27). It was also necessary to vigorously pursue the submarines and, where possible, destroy them (*see plate* 25). There were, of course, other enemy marauders on the lookout for easy targets. These were heavily armed surface raiders which were quite happy to take on something weaker than themselves and even in some instances their equals in fire power. The range of our aircraft, and the bird's eye view they provided, made them ideal as spotters and so they were able to locate enemy shipping and transmit its position to the Royal Navy for suitable action. We had to be constantly on our guard against German ships masquerading as neutrals and we could but report them to base and get someone else to check them out.

The cat and mouse activities of the U-boats and their pursuers involved a battle of wits throughout the period of the European war. The pendulum swung from one side to the other as each gained the advantage and counter measures had to be devised to combat the new situation. Germany had started the war with fifty-six U-boats, which their Commander-in-Chief, Grossadmiral Karl Dönitz, had considered wholly inadequate to enable him to blockade the UK and to deal a decisive blow against the Royal Navy. Only about a third of these submarines were operational at any one time. He therefore had to concentrate his efforts in areas of high shipping density, that is, in the vicinity of harbours rather than on the high seas.

He achieved considerable early success. Many of our merchantmen were then armed in an effort to give them some sort of protection. All but the fastest travelled in convoys, a strategy which had saved Britain from being starved out in the First World War. We were, however, embarrassingly short of both escort ships and aircraft, so that as the U-boats began to penetrate ever deeper into the mid-Atlantic our convoys were forced to try to avoid them altogether by careful diversionary routing. This was reasonably effective due to there being only a small number of enemy submarines in a vast area of ocean.

The German response was to begin hunting the convoys in packs in the most likely areas of contact, but the shortage of U-boats made this policy impracticable at that time and it was temporarily abandoned. There were also problems with torpedo failures which proved perplexing to U-boat commanders when their carefully laid plans to sink their prey were thus thwarted. As these difficulties were overcome, their successes against our merchant fleet increased.

At about the same time, France was being overrun by the Germans and Britain faced the threat of invasion. Valuable escort vessels had to be taken off convoy work to be deployed around the shores of the UK. The result was an alarming increase in sinkings of our ships and the position became so serious in terms of vital supplies failing to get through that the anti-invasion forces had to part with the escort vessels again in order to give better support to the convoys, in particular those coming from America.

With the fall of France in mid-1940, the U-boats were soon able to operate from the west coast ports of that country. At Brest, Lorient, St Nazaire, La Pallice (near La Rochelle) and Bordeaux, impregnable pens were built to accommodate the submarines when they were being repaired, refuelled, etc.

This meant that they no longer had to travel across the North Sea and around the north of the British Isles in order to take up stations in their Atlantic hunting grounds. The pendulum had swung in their favour again. They now had a profitable period of several months towards the end of 1940 and were particularly successful at night when the merchant ships were at their most vulnerable.

A desperate plea to the Americans resulted in more destroyers becoming available but it was not until the invasion threat had receded that the convoys really reaped the benefit. The Germans returned to hunting in packs and the deterioration in the situation led to the setting up in Liverpool of a new Western Approaches Command. Cooperation between the RAF and the Royal Navy had not always been of the highest order in the inter-war years. The naval top brass felt that operational flying to protect our shipping was the responsibility of the Navy. The RAF on the other hand regarded themselves as the guardians of the airspace wherever aerial operations had to be carried out.

The argument continued for some years until the compromise solution was reached that the Navy should control the Fleet Air Arm and the RAF should be responsible for Coastal Command. The move of 15 Group Coastal Command from Mount Batten to Liverpool in February 1941 proved of considerable value in establishing closer collaboration between the two services. Further measures to improve efficiency in the battle against the U-boat menace were the stepping up of anti-submarine training and of the production of ASV equipment for installation in convoy escort vessels.

The enemy were now having difficulty in maintaining their operational U-boat strength at even the 1939 level, since the number of losses was not being replaced due mainly to lack of production priority. The difficulties they experienced in tracking down convoys resulted in their employing long-range aircraft such as the Focke-Wolf Condor to do the spotting for them. Gradually American destroyers and long-range Liberator aircraft became available for escort work and in the early months of 1941 things began to improve for Britain.

Several of the U-boat aces, such as the redoubtable Kapitänleutnant Gunther Prien (U47) who sank HMS Royal Oak in Scapa Flow in 1939, were sent to the bottom with their crews. Others were forced to abandon their damaged boats and were captured. Both landplane and flying boat support for our convoys increased with marked results, U-boats being driven out of the areas where they would have been able to do the most damage.

A dramatic attack on U110 in May 1941 led to the capture of a German Enigma coding machine complete with instructions in its use. In the months to come this proved invaluable in ascertaining U-boat Command's strategy and future intentions. The improvement in our intelligence resulted in a decline in enemy successes and an increase in their losses for a limited period. It came as an unwelcome surprise to the Germans to learn that two of their U-boat supply ships operating in mid-Atlantic had been located by their adversaries and sunk. The outcome was that for a time they diverted their attention to the West African convoys.

Early in 1942, U-boat activity switched to the Western Atlantic, Hitler having declared war on the United States following the Japanese attack on Pearl Harbor. The offensive, which the Americans were unprepared for, had startling success. When they recovered from the shock, they concentrated their efforts on stepping up production of destroyers and aircraft to patrol their Atlantic coastline. It was going to take months before these would become operational and the U-boats were now being refuelled and rearmed by the new Milch Cow U-boats, which were functioning uncomfortably close to the United States' eastern seaboard.

Gradually, the new anti-submarine vessels and aircraft became available and merchant ship losses began to decline. Nevertheless, Allied losses generally still exceeded production and a determined effort had to be made on both sides of the Atlantic to produce more ships. By the end of the year, new production had at last overtaken the losses.

At the time, U-boats had to spend several hours in every twenty-four on the surface in order to recharge their batteries and renew their air supplies. They chose to do this at night because there was less risk of their being detected and attacked. In the middle of 1942, some of Britain's long-range aircraft were fitted with searchlights known as Leigh Lights which, with the assistance of ASV, enabled them to surprise and attack U-boats on the surface.

The enemy then switched from night- to day-time surfacing. This was not very successful for them, because they were more easily located by patrolling aircraft in daylight. A brief period of success followed for the aircraft, until the U-boats were equipped with their new Metox receiver which was capable of detecting the signals from the airborne metric ASV equipment. Its range was more than double that of the ASV itself and its rotatable aerial provided a means of indicating the direction from which the aircraft was approaching. Thus the U-boat had early warning of its hunter's presence and was able to alter course, making it more difficult for the aircraft to get into a suitable position for an attack. The unexpected introduction of this equipment was to cause my colleagues and me considerable frustration some months later.

When we arrived in West Africa in June 1943, the battles between large U-boat packs and large well-defended convoys in the North Atlantic area had swung in the Allies' favour. The Germans had more U-boats there than at any time previously, but their successes fell markedly and their own losses were heavy. Air cover was proving a substantial contributory factor to Allied success, with a new ASV MkIII centimetric radar playing a key role. Unfortunately, it was not available to us during my stay on the Coast.

The submarine packs were now congregating in mid-Atlantic and there was a very good chance that they'd turn their attention to our West African convoys again. Or so we thought. What we didn't know was that U-boat Command was having the greatest difficulty carrying out its commitments. Leutnant Heinz Schaeffer, commanding one of the boats operating out of St Nazaire, recorded the following in his book, *U-boat 977*:

"Our original plan was to operate off Freetown with eight boats. But two had gone down when we first sailed in company; three were missing, probably sunk; the sixth had to return to base heavily damaged by bombs and the seventh through lack of fuel. So of all the eight boats assigned to the task only we were fit for action. We did make some tentative attacks, but they were futile, for we were dealing with ships too fast for us to catch. They picked us up with their instruments, showed us their stern and vanished, and soon afterwards the planes came out to hunt us. We were no longer the cat, we were the mouse... This wasn't war but a sheer struggle for existence." (Schaeffer's was the last U-boat to reach port after Dönitz sent his signal on 4 May 1945 instructing all his boats to cease hostilities.)

By this time, the German U-boat Command felt that it had lost the initiative and would not be able to meet its objective unless its submarine design was radically improved. The boats needed greater speed and the ability to remain submerged for longer periods. While waiting for the new designs to become available, the enemy equipped existing boats with flak batteries which would enable them to defend themselves if caught on the surface by prowling aircraft. These anti-aircraft installations were on 'bandstands' aft of the conning tower, which gave them a blind spot forward. Allied aircraft exploited this by making depth charge attacks at a fine angle across the bows, thus preventing the Germans from deploying their guns until it was too late. Many such battles took place in the Bay of Biscay, the aircraft generally having the advantage.

In his excellent book *U333 - The Story of a U-Boat Ace*, Peter Cremer recorded that in the period from the end of April to the beginning of August 1943, the British "...sank 26 U-boats in the Bay and damaged 17, which were forced to turn back. The German Navy had tried to counter these attacks with U-boats heavily armed as 'flak-traps', but had abandoned the scheme. After all, it was not the task of U-boats to shoot down aircraft, but to avoid them."

I was in the air for my first convoy escort trip a week after arrival on the Coast. At the early morning briefing, we learned that the small convoy consisted of four merchant vessels (MVs) with a generous escort of four naval ships. The cargoes must have been very important indeed. We were only briefed on the convoy's position at a given time and the latest information on its speed and direction. We were never told what the ships we escorted were carrying.

The weather report promised us fair conditions for the sortie. It was the dry season and the only hazard we were likely to encounter was dust and sand being carried from the Sahara on the north-east trade winds. We collected our charts and the information about the convoy and were told what other aircraft or ships were expected to be in the area. While there were no reports about the possible presence of submarines, we were nevertheless warned to be on full alert. It was not unknown for them to break through the net undetected. Another aircraft was to take over from us after about ten hours, so we knew roughly how long we could stay with the convoy. We were then given the letter of the day and the necessary code books for the coding and decoding of radio messages.

We were airborne at first light. The navigator had calculated our estimated time of arrival, or ETA, in the vicinity of the convoy. He then had to compute its actual position at that time. Aiming for a point a few miles ahead of the convoy, he worked out a course for us to fly. Dickson set the grid on the compass beside him and turned on to the appropriate heading.

Chapter 11

The navigation used by flying boats was 'dead reckoning'. It depended on reasonable visibility so that it was possible to measure the aircraft's drift, the angle between the course being steered and the actual track of the aircraft over the ground or water. The wind direction and its speed accounted for any difference between course and track.

The first course steered on a sortie would be calculated using the wind direction and speed given by the meteorological forecast. It was then necessary to take early drift readings in the air to confirm this information. If the drift was different from expected, a manoeuvre was necessary to determine the true direction and speed of the wind, so that a new course could be computed.

The most common method was to turn 60 degrees to port for a given time, then 120 degrees to starboard for the same period, resuming the original heading by turning 60 degrees to port again. On each of the three legs a drift would be taken. The information would be drawn on the Dalton Computer, corrections being made for the differences in time between the readings, and the wind direction and speed calculated. This information would then be used to work out a new course and determine the aircraft's position.

Drifts could be taken in several ways, all fairly primitive but none the less effective. The drift recorder in the navigator's position gave a view of a section of the surface immediately below the aircraft. A calibrated ring with a grid of parallel lines was rotated until features on the ground or water appeared to move along these lines. The drift could then be read off directly from the scale. The rear turret was calibrated for the purpose of reporting bearings of targets or landmarks, but it could also be used for drift readings. An object on the ground or water could be followed with the guns and the reading taken from the scale. This method was particularly useful when flying over a calm sea, when the drift recorder was unusable. It was then necessary to throw out a smoke puff or flare on which the guns could be trained when it was floating in the water. The aircraft's bomb sight, located in the bows, could be used in a similar way to the drift recorder.

There was, of course, nothing to compare with fixes on known landmarks for establishing an aircraft's position. Unfortunately, most of its time was spent out of sight of land, but this facility was particularly useful when making a landfall. If transmissions from fixed radio stations were within range, bearings could be obtained from the D/F loop. Two different stations some distance apart could provide a fix. The problem for us was that the number and range of radio stations in the South Atlantic was very limited.

Provided weather conditions were favourable and heavenly bodies could be seen, star shots at night or sun shots by day were taken using a sextant. After making corrections and calculations, a position line for each shot was drawn on the chart. Two of these from different stars, preferably three to improve the accuracy, produced a fix.

Inclement weather conditions created severe problems for flying boats in every way. On the water, a heavy swell or high winds could put the aircraft at considerable risk (*see plate* 28). Taking off or landing in such conditions was hazardous and demanded additional skills, bearing in mind that the 'runway' might be moving about unpredictably! The limited navigational aids available meant that it was also very difficult to carry out an accurate flight plan in poor weather. The enemy marauders were therefore given greater respite from possible attack and were in a stronger position to carry out their own objectives.

ASV was of some use in these conditions, but even if it successfully homed an aircraft on to its target, an attack might not be practicable or very effective if the visibility was inadequate. On the other hand, there were times when it was possible to make surprise attacks under cover of heavy cloud when the visibility was just good enough over the target. Flying low over the sea to avoid cloud and fool the German detection devices had its own problems. The inaccuracy of barometric altimeters meant that it was unsafe to fly blind just above the surface of the water.

I was glad to find that for this and subsequent long-range sorties we were suitably protected with armaments. The Germans were impressed with the Sunderland's arsenal and referred to the boat as the 'flying porcupine'. Normally equipped with two .303 Browning machine guns in each of the front and dorsal turrets and four in the rear turret, the so-called sting in the tail, it was capable of giving a very good account of itself when attacked by enemy fighters. It could also cause U-boat crews some discomfort if they were caught on the surface. In the bomb bay the eight 250 lb depth charges were strung up on electrically operated carriers which could quickly be run out under the wings when preparing for an attack.

The risk of meeting enemy fighters in the West African theatre was minimal and our dorsal turrets were therefore removed in order to reduce drag and so increase our speed and range. I still felt that we were adequately equipped to cope with any U-boat action against us and I found myself worrying more about the prospect of mechanical failures when we were several hundred miles out to sea. I consoled myself with the thought that there was a fighting chance of our being able to make a reasonably safe landing on the water and for aid to be available within hours, thanks to cooperation between our RAF and Royal Navy colleagues.

My feelings as we headed out into the Atlantic to make our rendezvous with the convoy were, however, mainly of satisfaction and excited anticipation. After a year and a half of training, I was at last on operations.

Being 'on ops' was the ambition of everyone who chose aircrew for his RAF war service and those of us who went through the aircrew production machine were frustrated at the time it took to reach this stage, even without the medical setbacks which had dogged my own training. The few who joined the service very early in the war, or even before it, did not seem to be subjected to anything like the same discouraging delays. The mass production of aircrews in the US and in various parts of the British Empire had not yet begun, so they were more fortunate in being able to get on with their operational flying within a very short time. Whether or not their being thrown in at the deep end in this way was to their ultimate advantage is debatable. Would their losses have been fewer had they received more thorough training?

Suddenly for me all the delays and setbacks experienced during my own training were just memories and I could now get down to the job. Although it wasn't the job I'd volunteered for in the first place, I had now come to terms with my earlier disappointments and was determined to make the best of my forthcoming flying experience in boats.

One of our WOPs was stationed in the radar position, assiduously scanning the ASV screen for blips which would indicate shipping in the area. His target was the convoy itself, but he had to be equally aware of the possibility of other ships, in particular U-boats. Eventually he reported that something was coming up on the screen. It was a fairly healthy response at about twenty miles, but at this range it was impossible to say whether it was from one target or several. A number of ships could produce blips which merged together on the screen, making them appear as one.

We couldn't guarantee that this response was from our convoy, so the skipper alerted the crew to the possibilities and told them to keep a sharp lookout and report anything they saw immediately. He asked the navigator how the position of the contact tied up with his own calculations. He'd expected the convoy to be five miles closer to us, but on the same bearing. The pilot decided to stay on course until more information was available.

The visibility was hazy and we had to strain our eyes to scan the horizon. When the radar op reported that the blip had broken up into several and that they were now about twelve miles away, I picked up something ahead through the binoculars. The skipper confirmed that there was certainly a ship ahead but he couldn't make any accurate identification yet. He continued to explore the horizon and then announced that he could now see more than one vessel. The nearest one appeared to be a British sloop.

He told me to get the Very cartridges ready and asked the navigator for a course to a point about ten miles ahead of the convoy, so that we would avoid approaching it up sun. Since enemy aircraft had a habit of attacking out of the sun, we did not want to be mistaken for one. Before long, we were able to see all eight ships which met the descriptions given at our briefing that morning.

When making the first contact with a convoy, it was vitally necessary to get our identification right, otherwise we could be giving ourselves a good deal of trouble. We had to be certain we'd identified our vessels correctly before having any direct communication with them. We then approached them cautiously, firing Very cartridges of the appropriate colour of the day.

It was forbidden to break radio silence in the vicinity of a convoy except for emergencies. The reasons for this were clear. The air needed to be kept open for us to receive any reports concerning the disposition of enemy forces and of course we had to deny them the opportunity of determining our own or the convoy's position. An additional precaution was that our radio messages were cyphered to make them unintelligible to the enemy. The fewer chances they had of cracking the cypher the better. We were careful, therefore, to communicate with convoys using visual methods, mainly the Aldis signalling lamp, unless they themselves indicated that we could use the R/T.

In reaching the agreed point ahead of our convoy, we had skirted it to the east and north and could now approach it up sun. This enabled the escort ships to have a clear view of us and of our signals. I fired the Very pistol out of the second pilot's window and received my only permanent scar of the war, apart from the scalds suffered in the US Naval Hospital. The recoil from the pistol caused a neat half-inch cut in my forefinger!

There was an exchange of brief coded messages by Aldis lamp, until the Navy was quite satisfied as to our identity. Then followed messages of greeting, after which we agreed the area for our first patrol, this time in plain language. We also gave an indication of approximately how long it would be before we rejoined the convoy. On this sortie, I flew as third pilot and when not in one of the pilot's seats I helped with the navigation. The second pilot was P/O A G (Tony) Staffiere, an officer with whom I struck up a close friendship, to be cut short in tragic fashion just over a year later. I flew with Tony on a number of occasions during my West African tour.

The ships, steaming slowly but purposefully northwards at about ten knots, were spaced at least 400 yards apart. Their wakes added the only bright relief to a blue-green expanse of ocean punctuated by small grey shapes. From our viewpoint, the wakes were a giveaway, visible from some miles distant. From sea level they would be less evident and the ships' camouflage more effective. This was a small convoy by any standards, but it was my first experience of escort work and I felt that at long last I was doing something useful. I had not really known what this work entailed and in the months to come I was to be astounded at the size of some of the convoys we escorted and also the apparent inconsistency of the escort/MV ratio.

Sitting above these eight ships with ocean spreading to infinity all around them, it was difficult to believe that they were in any kind of danger. Indeed, I felt that, but for technology, there'd be little chance of their being detected at all except by purely accidental encounter. The reality was, of course, very different. As long as they were at sea, they were at risk. We were there to protect these vessels, their crews and their cargoes from what were likely to be sudden attacks by an enemy who would do everything to ensure that he gave no warning of his presence. It was clear from the reception we got that the escort ships valued the support that we were giving them. We wanted their confidence in us to be justified.

Flying over the convoy, we checked its course and speed. Measuring the former was straightforward enough, since it was only necessary to fly on the same heading as the convoy and then read off the course from the compass. The speed was slightly less easy to establish, because it involved a certain degree of judgement and a knowledge of the type of ship. The length of her wake gave a rough indication of the speed of the vessel. If it was the same length as the vessel, she was steaming at or near her cruising speed. At full speed, her wake might be twice or maybe three times her own length. We therefore had to know the cruising and full speeds of the type of vessel we were observing. We found it easier to get someone on one of the ships to tell us her speed in this instance. When shadowing an enemy vessel, this might be a little more tricky!

The most commonly used and indeed most effective method of sweeping an area of ocean in search of the enemy, or any other target, was the creeping-line-ahead, or CLA, search. This entailed deciding the boundaries of the square or rectangular area that you wished to search and then covering the whole area with parallel sweeps from one side to the other. Successive sweeps would be spaced at twice the visibility by day or twice the workable ASV range by night.

In other words, if you wished to cover a square proceeding in a northerly direction, you would begin in the centre of the southern boundary of the square, flying first to the south-western tip, then turning north for a distance of twice the visibility, east for the full width of the square, north again for twice the visibility, west again for the full width of the square, and so on. In this way, every part of the area should be seen at least once during the search and no part should be missed. Of course, you could never be sure that, while you were busy sweeping the south-west sector, for example, there wasn't something ominous going on in the north-east sector or elsewhere.

When at the controls, flying a CLA was good practice for me in steering an accurate course for fifty miles or so at a time and in making 90 degree turns on to new headings. Because of our periodic changes in direction it was useful for the navigator, too. He was able to check the drift on different headings fairly regularly and so could be more confident of the accuracy of our calculated position.

As many pairs of eyes as possible were brought to bear on scouring the area. The five main lookout posts in the aircraft were manned for the duration of the search. Occasionally this cover was supplemented by other crew members who were engaged on their normal duties but were also in a position to look out of conveniently placed hatches, such as those in the galley. The ASV was continuously manned and was expected to give us first warning of any ships within its range. Keyed up throughout the search, I anticipated some dramatic development on my very first operation, but much to my disappointment we covered the area thoroughly without seeing anything.

Several hours later we were back with the convoy, reporting on our search and agreeing another sector with the leading escort vessel. The new CLA proved equally unexciting and we returned to the convoy a second time with a negative report. Our relief aircraft was due at any moment and our fuel supply was, according to the engineer, just enough to get us back to base "with a teaspoonful or so to spare." It was time for us to take our leave and the escort thanked us for our help as we set course for base.

On the way, I discussed the trip with the skipper, showing my obvious disappointment. "Don't worry. We may not have seen anything, but if there they'd have kept their heads down. As long as they're prevented from putting their periscopes up, they can't attack anything. The ships will be grateful for that, believe me."

"But periscopes are small things. How can we be sure we didn't miss any out there?"

"We can't be a hundred per cent sure of that, but at least if they *were* there, they didn't attack, did they? We might be able to take some of the credit for that. You're right that a periscope is comparatively small, but it will disturb the water quite a bit when the boat's under way. We'd have seen the telltale feather that it puts up behind it as it cuts through the water. Since the sea wasn't choppy, we'd have been able to see that for miles..."

He did his best to console me, knowing better than I did that I'd have many more such disappointments in the months to come. At the time, I was not at all convinced by his arguments, but many flying hours later I found myself using the same ones to justify my presence on the Coast.

It was not until at least thirty years on, when information from both sides in the U-boat war became freely available, that I was finally persuaded that we had been an effective deterrent to the enemy much of the time and had made a significant contribution to the protection of our vital merchant shipping.

Chapter 12

Not all our escort duties were carried out with convoys. At times we accompanied single ships, such as ocean going liners, most of which hoped that their superior speed would keep them out of trouble. The Île de France was one such vessel steaming northwards in our area and we were detailed to escort her. We carried out our customary anti-submarine patrol (ASP) around her for about four hours but saw nothing. Several days later we were in the air for over twelve hours, this time escorting the liner Orion which was also proceeding northwards. Again there were no alarms, but in the course of our patrol we sighted two other ships, one of which was an armed merchant cruiser.

Obviously, we had to be prepared for encounters with anything which sailed the high seas and it was vital that we could make ready identification. It would be a bit late to consult the recognition books after we'd been shot down. For the same reason, our knowledge of both friendly and enemy aircraft had to be extremely good. While we'd been put through our paces on both counts at PEI, I was constantly seeking to keep myself up to date. There was too much at stake to be complacent about such things.

Our escort of the Orion was to be continued the following day. She had, of course, made much more progress than the eight knot convoys, so we landed at Port Étienne to reduce our non-productive flying time to a minimum.

This was my first experience of operating from a detachment base. Isolated would have been the most accurate way of describing PE. It was a tiny settlement on the western edge of the Sahara, on the border between Rio de Oro, now known as Western Sahara, and Mauritania. The RAF base consisted simply of a few temporary huts. The flying boat facilities, such as they were, were contained within a sheltered stretch of water protected from the Atlantic by a neck of land.

Sand was the most common commodity and there was little else. There was no accommodation for crews ashore, so we had to sleep and eat on board. Our only reasonably civilized sleeping accommodation consisted of the four bunks already referred to, two in the wardroom and two in the compartment aft of the bomb bay. There were twelve of us. In case of emergency, we needed to mount a boat guard of two crew members throughout the night. That meant that additional sleeping facilities had to be found for the other six. They simply stacked out on air beds and blankets wherever they could find enough space on the decks.

The cooking facilities were in almost constant demand, since there were always crew members on duty and requiring tea and sustenance. Basic as the conditions might sound, I always enjoyed this relaxed kind of life away from the relative formality of base. Everyone pulled his weight in getting the chores done (woe betide anyone who didn't!) and the camaraderie had to be seen to be believed.

On returning from one of our flights from PE late one afternoon, we had a leisurely supper prepared by one of the wireless operators and then sat around in the wardroom talking shop in the characteristic manner of RAF aircrews. I learned that on the day that we'd been air testing D204 at Pembroke Dock, J204 captained by F/O T J Hibberd had been making an early morning take-off at Bathurst when it crashed into a 95 squadron Sunderland which was waterborne at the time. J stayed in the air for several hours and eventually landed near the end of the slipway and promptly sank. She was a write-off and the other aircraft was seriously damaged but mercifully no one was hurt. Until then I'd thought that I'd worked out all the possible ways of writing off a flying boat, but I had not allowed for this one.

We were soon airborne once more for over thirteen hours escorting a convoy of thirty-nine MVs, the largest I had seen so far. It was accompanied by only six naval escorts and seemed to stretch into infinity. In reality it was contained within an area of about four or five square miles allowing for the normal spacing between ships in convoy, which was about four cables (eight hundred yards) abeam and half that distance in line ahead.

It was an impressive sight, especially when viewed towards the sun. The calm sea reflected the light as from a mirror and the ships looked like toys carefully placed in ranks on the surface. It was enough to make any U-boat commander's mouth water. Happily, our searches revealed nothing alien in the area and the convoy continued on its slow but determined way without being molested.

The days between flights at PE were usually lazy days. There was nothing much to do apart from the normal chores of keeping our 'houseboat' in order, sunning ourselves on the mainplane, or swimming in the blue waters of the harbour. Sunbathing was not a very comfortable occupation. The wing was far too hot to lie on, even with several thicknesses of blanket under you. We sometimes went ashore, more to stretch our legs than for any other reason, and on one occasion several of us visited a nearby Bedouin camp.

The settlement was very primitive. A number of shabby tents housed the dusky inhabitants, who seemed to be impregnated with the dust of the sandy wastes of the Sahara. Outside one of the tents was a shaky structure which served as a table and on which food was evidently prepared. I was intrigued to know what kind of animal provided the fly-infested joints of meat displayed there. Pointing to these, I asked one of the nomads what they were. While he didn't understand English, he did seem to get the gist of the question and indicated a camel tethered to a stake nearby.

Lunch on board the aircraft frequently consisted of baked beans and Spam. I was becoming bored with the latter, although I had to concede that it was very much more palatable than soya links. In one of my letters home I made the mistake of telling Mary what I thought about it and her reply was less than sympathetic. Spam was a luxury in the UK and people considered themselves fortunate if they were able to get hold of it. I was suitably chastened, but my opinion remained unaltered.

Our transit trips between bases were seldom without some operational content. As these locations were several hundred miles apart, it made sense to fly far enough out into the Atlantic to be able to sweep the tracks of known convoys, even if we did not have time to escort them. This was additional cover which cost little but could be profitable in terms of keeping enemy submarines down. The mere presence of aircraft in the vicinity of a convoy could be sufficient deterrent to all but the most dedicated and/or suicidal U-boat commanders.

Shortly after we returned to Bathurst, we learned that F/O C C (Clem) Mayberry, another Australian captain, was flying G204 from PE on an escort trip when a 750 ton U-boat was sighted on the surface during the evening. It immediately dived and G attacked with her depth charges. Bubbles were seen to rise from the vicinity of the sub, but no wreckage was sighted and no claim of any damage could be made.

This was typical of the frustrations which attended U-boat attacks by our aircraft following ASV and subsequent visual contact. A submarine on the surface usually had warning of its attacker's approach and there was clearly a time delay for the aircraft to reach the target and reduce height to fifty feet. The U-boat became a moving target whose speed changed considerably once it submerged. It might take a certain amount of evasive action under the water which could upset the aircraft's run-in. Depth charges, set to explode at twenty-five feet, took time to reach the water and sink to that depth. There was also the complication that they followed a different trajectory in the water than in the air. Although the DCs might appear to be accurately placed with respect to the target, if it was not at or near twenty-five feet in depth when they exploded it would most likely survive the attack.

There was very little time for the pilot to do all the mental sums and to anticipate what the enemy was going to do. Even if his calculations were right, he could not be sure that he had been successful unless there was positive evidence in the form of considerable wreckage or oil floating on the surface. There may be no evidence at all of minor damage which could nevertheless incapacitate a U-boat sufficiently to prevent it reaching its base.

One of the tricks used by U-boat commanders to shake off their pursuers was a device called Bold, short for Kobold, meaning a deceiving spirit (*see* Cremer – U333). The idea was suggested by Hitler himself in September 1942. The boat ejected a canister from which a chemical was released into the water, causing a dense concentration of hydrogen gas. The resulting bubbles coming to the surface simulated the presence of a U-boat.

To further create the illusion of a kill, odd items of clothing, cleaning cloths, etc were sometimes jettisoned simultaneously. By the time the hunters had searched the area around the disturbance, the submarine had escaped to a safe distance.

Thus there was no foolproof way of determining whether any damage had in fact been done, or the extent of such damage, unless it was spectacular. This uncertainty was exasperating for most aircrews who managed to make attacks on U-boats. Many had to wait for over 30 years before they learned what had happened to their adversaries.

When we arrived in Bathurst our skipper, now a Flying Officer, and several other members of the crew were posted. The remainder flew with the CO, W/Cdr Evison, and F/Lt H V Horner on a night anti-submarine patrol during which we located a large convoy and later sighted a 5000 ton MV. Although once again direct contact with the enemy was not made, the sortie was considered of such value that Air Headquarters, AHQ, saw fit to send congratulations to the squadron, with special instructions to inform the crew. We were never privileged to know why this trip was seen to be so important. It was no different from any other as far as we could see. Even the squadron records were silent on this point. We landed at Jui, Freetown, at dawn and returned to Bathurst in the afternoon.

Three days later P204 took off from PE at first light to carry out a convoy escort mission. It developed engine trouble and had to ditch in the sea. An unsuccessful search was carried out by other aircraft, including a Sunderland of 95 squadron, which also had engine trouble but returned to its base safely. After four anxious days, a signal was received that the crew of P204 had been picked up by a Spanish fishing boat and were safely interned in Rio de Oro.

This was not to be the only alarm about engine reliability during my year on the Coast. It proved my major concern, but I would in no way suggest that this had anything to do with the standard of maintenance on the squadron. I had nothing but the greatest admiration for our 'ground' crews. They carried out their duties with commendable dedication, frequently under the most unpleasant, at times almost impossible, conditions. The intense heat, together with very high humidity, made working on aircraft engines a most uncomfortable activity even in calm weather. When the aircraft was on the water, the mechanics perched on slender platforms slung beneath the engines (*see plate* 29). These were often in constant motion due to choppy seas or a rolling swell. If engine parts or tools were dropped, they were lost for ever at the bottom of the sea. It was an unenviable task, but an absolutely vital one.

The difficulties we had arose mainly from the fact that the engines were being overworked. Weaknesses developed which caused failures not always easy to anticipate, often arising after two or three hours in the air. Oil leaks and loss of oil pressure were common and, as I had learned from crews at Pembroke Dock, such problems could be unnerving if they occurred several hundred miles out to sea.

Had it been possible to feather the propeller and so prevent it from windmilling, it would have been far less serious. Instead, the spinning prop caused considerable drag, demanding much more from the other engines which were not always able to deliver. An additional hazard had been explained to me by Dickson soon after I'd joined him. If all the oil was lost from the faulty engine, it could seize up and the prop could spin off – in any direction.

If we did not get much experience of live attacks on U-boats, we were certainly not deprived of practice bombing and gunnery sessions. We were all deeply conscious of the fact that if we were ever privileged to close with the enemy, the encounter would be over in a matter of seconds and there was unlikely to be the chance of a second attempt. It was essential that we were always on our toes and able to react instinctively when the opportunity arose. This applied equally to the gunners as to the pilot, because if the U-boat was caught on the surface, it was their job to strafe its decks with machine gun fire. The bombing and gunnery flights were designed to sharpen up these skills.

My first bombing practice was with F/Lt Horner in one of the few Mk I Sunderlands (*see appendix* A) on the squadron. The objective was to fly over the target at a height of fifty feet and to straddle it with a stick of depth charges. In other words, half the DCs should fall along one side of the target and half along the other side. If the angle between the aircraft's track and the target's heading was fine, let us say less than 15 degrees, this should bring all the bombs within a lethal distance of the target.

The precise moment of pressing the button was absolutely critical. If you pressed it too early, your bombs fell harmlessly astern of the target; if too late, they would drop too far ahead. The split-second timing required, coupled with the final correction to the aircraft's track over the target, was not at all easy to achieve. I consistently found that my reactions were sluggish and I overshot, but with practice I was able to improve my performance. The gunners had a whale of a time. They had the advantage of being able to spray their target for several seconds, while my DCs had to be released in one operation and dead on target. This was the only time that I envied them their jobs.

With the departure of its Australian skipper, D204 was taken over by a new crew captained by F/O T J Hibberd. Tom Hibberd was an older pilot whose mature advice and support gave me added confidence in my flying ability. After two months on the squadron, I had mastered the problems I'd initially encountered with Sunderlands and it was now a question of consolidation and practice. I was soon to be airborne in D204 with the Flight Commander, F/Lt Paré, for practice in circuits and bumps, ie taking off and landing.

John Paré, a Rhodesian, was well respected on the squadron. A dark, well-built, striking man, he had a suntan which was the envy of everyone.

His flying skills were generally accepted to be of a high order and I greatly valued the instruction that I received at his hands. Among other things, I learned from him that one should anticipate exactly what the aircraft is going to do, rather than wait until something happens and then try to correct it. This was valuable advice indeed. It became second nature to *feel* that the nose or a wing was about to drop and to be applying corrective measures by the time it actually occurred. One became an integral part of the aircraft and one's reactions were instinctive, with satisfying results.

The technique could be seen when George was in operation. The wheel was constantly twitching as the autopilot made small corrections, *preventing* the aircraft from changing its attitude rather than waiting until it did. Only in the roughest of conditions would one see any large, apparently ponderous, adjustments being made. This clearly confirmed John Paré's philosophy.

He also impressed on me the necessity to assess the conditions accurately when making an approach to land. For example, if the air was turbulent, a powered approach was probably going to be safer than the conventional glide because of the added control it gave to the pilot. If it was impossible to make the approach into wind, it was important to recognize that, even if a last minute correction to the aircraft's heading was made on touchdown, there would be a tendency for the boat to pull to one side and for the wing on the lee side to drop. This was no different from landing any aircraft in these conditions, of course, but with flying boats there were the added risks of ripping a float off or digging the nose in and turning the aircraft into a submarine.

Another danger point was when the boat lost speed so that it no longer responded to movements of the control surfaces. A strong and unexpected gust of wind from one side or the other at this stage could be very hazardous. There were times when one had to wrestle violently with the controls to make any impression on the boat's attitude.

In the early afternoon of 12 August 1943, Flight Sergeant C H (Charlie) Watkinson and his crew, over eight hours into a sortie in H204, found two dinghies about 200 miles south-west of Dakar. They were three miles apart, one empty, the other containing seven survivors. The men were believed to be from Liberator D of 200 squadron which had attacked a U-boat the previous day and failed to return to its base at Rufisque near Dakar.

The WOM/AG, F/Sgt Denis Stone, sent a sighting report which resulted in the corvette HMS Clarkia being detached from her convoy escort duty. She immediately set course for the reported position. A heavy swell was running and conditions were considered too rough for H to attempt a rescue landing. Flame floats and emergency packs with a good luck message were dropped. Sgt Reg Newbon (St.AG) collected all the crew's cigarettes, sealed them in coffee jars and attached them to one of the emergency packs. H stayed on station for four hours, eventually landing at Bathurst at 20.00 hours.

Three hours later, John Paré and his crew took off in F204 and just before five o'clock the next morning they located the occupied dinghy and dropped a flare marker and flame floats. Their WOM/AG, F/Sgt Les Marshall, who had been in the J204 crash mentioned earlier in this chapter, recalls homing Clarkia on to the dinghy. The seven occupants were eventually rescued by the Navy at about half past six. They were unexpectedly found to be the sole survivors from the 46-man crew of the attacked U-boat. Those who perished did so either from chlorine gas poisoning or attacks by sharks.

In his autobiography, Peter Cremer of U333 wrote that the boat destroyed in the attack was U468 (a type VIIC submarine of 750 tons displacement, surfaced) commanded by a former colleague, Oberleutnant Klemens Schamong. The Liberator was hit by heavy gunfire and crashed into the sea after straddling the U-boat with its depth charges. Unhappily, the aircraft's entire eight-man crew was lost. Its skipper, F/O Lloyd A Trigg, DFC, RNZAF, was posthumously awarded the VC, largely as a result of the German survivors' eyewitness reports which referred to the crew's coolness and courage.

A sequel to the incident was that Schamong contacted Charlie Watkinson in December 1991 and thanked him and his crew for their efforts. He explained that he and some of his men, who were bitten by fish while struggling in the water, managed to reach the nearer of the dinghies, which had been ejected from the Liberator when it hit the sea. The supplies dropped by H204 had been very welcome, as the survivors had not been looking forward to the prospect of spending another night without food or water.

Such an error of identification was not at all difficult to make, especially if, as in this instance, the dinghies were RAF issue! The occupants of a dinghy might not always have the means, or indeed the stamina, to communicate clearly with aircraft circling above them, particularly in the darkness. They would normally be equipped with flares or Very cartridges with which to draw attention to themselves, but if they did not have a serviceable radio transmitter they would not have the means to carry on a dialogue with their potential rescuers. An aircraft could flash signals to them with an Aldis lamp, but they might not easily be able to respond.

A method which was reasonably effective in daylight was to drop messages in a Bircham Barrel (*see plate* 44). This required a high standard of 'bombing' accuracy if the barrel was to be easily accessible to the survivors. A number of questions could be written down and instructions given as to what hand signals the survivors should use to convey their answers to the aircraft crew. At night, even this method would be impracticable unless some form of illumination could be used for a lengthy period. This would clearly be inadvisable if the attention of unwelcome visitors might be attracted by it.

The Liberator incident gave us some encouragement that there was a useful job to be done in our theatre of operations. We were envious of its success against the U-boat, but not of the crew's unhappy fate. We had been warned that the Germans had now equipped their U-boats with flak batteries and were likely to sit up on the surface and shoot back. This didn't disturb us unduly, as we felt that we were more than a match for them. I still had a niggling concern about other hazards which were not directly attributable to the enemy.

Chapter 13

Not long after the U468 episode, L204 returned from an anti-submarine patrol and, while carrying out its circuit to land, suddenly dived into the sea as it was making a left hand turn. The cause was uncertain, but from eye-witness reports and a subsequent inquiry, it was presumed that the aircraft stalled in the turn. F/O J G Finney and all his crew were lost.

This kind of accident was very worrying. When a pilot is taking off or landing his aircraft, whatever type it might be, he is usually at his most cautious, because he knows that these manoeuvres are the most critical in flying. On the landing approach he watches his height, airspeed and rate of descent with extreme care. The gliding speed is lower than the cruising speed and is therefore closer to stalling, but there is usually a safe enough margin, unless one carries out any unusual manoeuvres such as a very steep turn. We shall never know what really went wrong on Finney's last tragic flight.

Our next operational trip was not without its problems. We were about three hours out on an A/S patrol when we developed engine trouble. The oil pressure on one of the engines began to drop and since we were at least ninety minutes flying time away from base, we had to turn for home as soon as the fault was detected. As it happened, we'd found it extremely difficult to carry out our mission effectively due to very poor weather conditions. There were two good reasons, therefore, for abandoning it. As we set course for base, I fell to thinking about what complications might set in. Since Tony Staffiere was in the second pilot's seat at the time, I was at something of a loose end. The mission had been aborted and our only objective now was to get home safely.

The vacuum in my mind had to be filled with something. In the manner of reporters starved of real news, I filled it with speculation as to what might happen. I talked to the engineer, who was no wiser about the problem than I was. The oil pressure had dropped by about twenty per cent and was fluctuating around a new low level. This didn't really tell him anything in the absence of more symptoms. I imagined I could hear knocking in the faulty engine. He smiled and said he couldn't hear anything. I went below and looked out of the galley hatch at the offending engine to see if there was any sign of an oil leak. There wasn't. The spectre of uncertainty reared its ugly head again.

We didn't know what the problem was or what might be the consequences. What if the engine blew up? We wouldn't stand a chance. Even if the aircraft was still capable of alighting on the sea, the conditions were by no means favourable. Assuming we *were* able to make a safe forced landing and take to the dinghies, how long would it be before we were located out here? That would depend to some extent on whether or not we managed to send out a Mayday distress call before we ditched and whether or not anybody heard it. What if we ended up in the drink without a dinghy? I was a strong swimmer, but had never tried to cover two hundred miles in shark infested waters! These were some of the alarmist thoughts which raced through my mind over the next hour and a half.

Every ten minutes or so I looked for oil leaks and checked the dial readings with the engineer. There was little change in the position, although something was obviously wrong. The pressure continued to oscillate around a considerably lower value than normal, yet it didn't fall any further. Those ninety minutes seemed like ninety hours to me and then, to my intense relief, we crossed the coastline and prepared to land at our base at Half Die, Bathurst. There was something ominous about that name. It no doubt arose because of the high mortality rate among the early white settlers on the Coast. I hoped it had no more recent significance.

I never found out the cause of our mechanical trouble and preferred not to know. If it had simply been a faulty gauge, I would have kicked myself for getting so agitated about it. Had it been something much more serious, I didn't want to think about our possible fate had luck not been on our side.

Crews were always very relieved to reach base after sorties which were in some way eventful, whether by reason of action with the enemy, bad weather conditions or worrying mechanical problems like the one just described. They regarded base as a safe haven, even though it might be vulnerable to attack from the air or bombardment from ships at sea. One thing they could be sure of was that they would not return from a sortie to find that their runway had been bombed and rendered unusable in their absence. To landplanes this was a very real threat. It would, of course, have been possible for enemy aircraft to lay mines in the alighting area, although I don't remember hearing about any instances of this at a flying boat base. In any event, provided the flying boat could be forewarned of the hazard, it could normally be diverted or if short of fuel could hopefully find itself another stretch of water in which to put down.

Throughout the war, it was naturally a key objective of both sides to prevent valuable supplies from reaching the enemy's territory and so try to force him to surrender by putting him under siege. Captains of the faster merchant vessels, proceeding individually, frequently had to run the German blockade, using all the cunning they could muster to escape the attentions of the enemy. Some acquired remarkable expertise in so doing and, although many of their ships were tracked down and sunk, a substantial number managed to elude their pursuers. The skill of these doughty skippers made a valuable contribution towards thwarting the Germans, helping to ensure that their objective, to starve the British nation out, was not achieved.

In the same way, enemy merchantmen had to steer clear of Allied forces on the high seas and our own efforts to locate these blockade runners, which were often disguised as neutrals, met with mixed success. While some were picked up fairly easily, others managed to avoid us altogether, more by luck than judgement, we liked to think. The Atlantic was, of course, a vast place and only a very limited part of it could be searched at any one time.

Convoy escort work and anti-submarine patrols continued throughout my year's tour on the Coast. The convoys varied in size up to sixty merchant ships plus escorts. As previously mentioned, the number of escorts seemed to bear no logical relationship to the number of MVs. It was reasonable to suppose that the major factors affecting this would have been the importance of the cargoes and the actual availability of naval escort ships. Britain clearly did not have an unlimited supply of destroyers, sloops and corvettes, even with the benefit of US aid, and there were considerable demands on them.

Most of the time, A/S patrols were boring, once one had got over the initial euphoria of having contact with the enemy in prospect, but they demanded a high level of concentration from everyone on board. While we relied to a great extent on the ASV giving us the first indication that there was a potential target in the area, we could not for one moment relax our vigil of searching with our own eyes. The radar might not give an adequate response from a periscope, but hopefully the feather this produced when the submarine was under way would be visible to a sharp-eyed member of the crew.

On one occasion we were carrying out a CLA search (*see page* 65) some twenty-five to thirty miles from a convoy when the ASV operator reported a blip on our starboard bow about twenty miles away. In the absence of information about other shipping in the area, we made the reasonable assumption that the response came from an enemy vessel. It was dusk and we concluded that if it was a U-boat he was desperate for air and had therefore surfaced, not expecting any aircraft to be in the vicinity. The skipper sounded the klaxon for action stations and gave instructions to be homed onto the target.

The crew responded with enthusiasm and efficiency. This was it. We were going to get our chance at last. The gunners prepared their armaments in rapt anticipation of the fray. The remaining crew members gazed out of any available hatch, vying with each other to be the first to make the visual contact. One of them clutched the F24 camera as he manned the starboard galley hatch. The atmosphere was electric.

At brief intervals, the ASV operator was calling out the distance and approximate bearing over the intercom and everyone listened attentively and with mounting excitement. Fifteen miles, slightly starboard...twelve, dead ahead...ten... The skipper deployed the depth charges under the wings and all was made ready. He let down to fifty feet in order to be able to get into position to strike without delay. Then a shout came from the radar operator, "It's bloody gone, skipper! Can't see a damned thing now..."

The pilot climbed again to two hundred feet, thinking perhaps that the blip had simply been lost in the 'noise' due to reflections from the surface of the water. "Any better?"

"No, skip, we've lost him..."

We continued on our course, scanning the sea for our target, our eyes now having got used to the failing light. A flare was dropped in the estimated position of our quarry and we circled the area, searching in vain. Whatever had given rise to the response was no longer there. It was obvious that it had been a submarine, otherwise why would it have just disappeared like that after having provided a steady response for a prolonged period? It was equally obvious that, now that it knew we were there, it would not reappear. We had failed again. Why? There could only be one explanation. It was able to detect our radar long before we were close enough to be able to see it, let alone attack it. We couldn't surprise it. Those blighters were all laughing their Teutonic heads off at us down there.

The DCs were returned to the bomb bay and the skipper asked the navigator for a course back to the convoy. When we arrived, we told one of the escort vessels what had happened and it was then time for us to set course for base. A very disappointed crew landed at Bathurst. In the Ops Room our disillusionment was clearly evident.

"Don't fret, chaps," said the operations officer, "you probably achieved more than you think. That sub won't go near our convoy now that it knows we're covering it. Since it was almost dark when he picked you up, he probably thinks you're going to be around all night, so he won't try anything." Somehow, I wasn't consoled and neither were the rest of the crew. We should like to have had the opportunity of having a go at him.

On one of our visits to Port Étienne, sardonically referred to by one crew member as the "Mecca of the West Coast", we arrived there after carrying out a convoy escort task and were to spend several days at the outpost before returning to Bathurst. Swimming was considered a must every day. The water was a Mediterranean blue and very inviting.

Several of us dived from the rear door and made for a small island. Flat and featureless, it was little more than a sandbank. When we went ashore, we had great difficulty in moving about without stepping on a crab, albeit a small one. There were literally thousands of the tiny creatures all over the island and they seemed to move as one with military precision. Concluding that we were trespassing on their preserves, we made a strategic withdrawal.

Back at the boat, we spent another half-hour diving into the water from various parts of the aircraft and swimming around it. At one point, I was clinging on to the port float when I became aware of a movement in the water between me and the bows. It was made by a sizeable creature and whatever it was, it seemed to be taking more than a passing interest in me and was moving in my direction. I didn't wait to make a positive identification. Sensing that it was not too friendly, I yelled a warning to the others and struck out for the stern of the boat as if fired from a torpedo tube.

As I circled the after end of the keel at high speed, a ladder was deployed from the rear hatch and I managed to clamber quickly aboard. I was just in time to miss making the personal acquaintance of a most voracious looking creature with rows of sharp teeth. Having been deprived of a substantial meal, which it would undoubtedly have shared with others, it steamed disconsolately past the rear hatch and out towards the starboard float. It was a barracuda. I had heard that these sea fish were not averse to attacking bathers with somewhat fearsome results and I breathed a sigh of relief that I hadn't stopped to argue with it.

I got no sympathy from the lads when I scrambled aboard and collapsed on one of the rear bunks, exhausted from my exertions. Instead, the episode gave one of them an idea and he immediately made preparations to do some fishing to supplement our rations. This met with general approval and I asked him what he proposed using as bait. "Spam, of course, what else?" I should have known better.

Before very long, the fish were biting and several small ones were transported to the galley and prepared for cooking. When one of them, which looked like a sea bream, was used as bait, something took it with such ferocity that the angler was nearly catapulted out through the rear hatch. I helped him land the monster and it turned out to be a barracuda. As it entered the hatch, it managed to free itself from the improvised hook, which wasn't designed for anything of this size and strength, and it fell down through a gap between deck and hull and into the bilges. Somewhat put out by this development, I called out "Oh, hell, that's done it. We'll never get the ruddy thing out of there. We'll have to wait until it expires."

"Don't talk rot," somebody retorted, "we can take up the deck boards and go down after him."

"You can if you like, but you won't catch me doing it. One encounter with a live barracuda is more than enough for one day."

It took some time for the beast to be recovered, because it kept thrashing about and repositioning itself among the stringers and bulkheads in such a way as to become more inaccessible. At last, after a struggle lasting about fifteen minutes, two of the crew emerged triumphant holding a decapitated barracuda aloft. The next half-hour or so was spent cutting it up into steaks and frying them. They were delicious, making up for the monotonous beans and Spam diet we'd had at lunchtime. I made secret apologies to Mary for using Spam as fish bait.

Chapter 14

On one of the flights made with Charlie Watkinson and his crew, we were returning to PE when we were mystified by a huge reddish shape ahead of us which was rapidly getting bigger. None of us had seen anything quite like it before. It was no ordinary cloud, but appeared to be a seething mass of life, although no one seemed to know exactly what it was.

If we remained airborne any longer, we ran the risk of flying into the unknown, possibly endangering both ourselves and the aircraft. The skipper informed us that he intended to go in immediately, without the customary circuit. There were no other aircraft about and the alighting area was clear, so this did not present a problem. We had just managed to get moored up when the sky suddenly darkened and there was an incredible sound as though we were being bombarded by hailstones.

The aircraft was under fire from vast numbers of seemingly armour plated creatures which the riggers in the bow, who were exposed to them and so bore the full brunt of their attack, identified as "giant grasshoppers". Someone called out that they were locusts and that there were "millions of the blighters". Everything in the area became smothered with them and the noise as they rattled down onto the aircraft's metal skin was alarming. There was no let-up in the onslaught for several minutes and we were not too enthusiastic about braving it to go ashore. This was prudent, as I have since learned that locusts weigh two or three grams and if you get hit in the face by several of them in full flight, you really know it.

I went down into the bow compartment, which had been judiciously vacated by the riggers, and it was full of the insects. They were obviously on their last legs, crawling about lethargically. We concluded that they'd flown a long way and were suffering from exhaustion and starvation. One of the crew, who seemed more knowledgeable about these things than I was, said that they were a migratory species that could have come from Morocco, but judging by their condition had more likely flown over from East Africa on the trade winds. One thing was certain – there was no food for them here, so PE was about to become a locust graveyard. I'd heard that cooked locusts were something of a delicacy to the Bedouins, but they didn't suit the European palate. When I tentatively suggested that we might supplement our own rations, I was firmly shouted down.

The bombardment subsided after about fifteen minutes and when we were able to look around us we found that just about everything was blanketed in locusts. When the dinghy arrived, it was carrying a good complement of them. On finally getting ashore, we found it impossible to put a foot down without crushing several at a time. They had penetrated the huts and were crawling up the walls and over the furniture, but their

Plate 1 No 1 ACRC, London. The author is 6th from left in 3rd row

Plate 2   US Navy primary trainer (N3N-3), nicknamed Yellow Peril

Plate 3   North American Harvard advanced trainer (SNJ-3)

Plate 4   Vultee Valiant advanced trainer (SNV-1)

Plate 5   Consolidated flying boat (P2Y), nicknamed Flying Bedstead

Plate 6 Consolidated Catalina flying boat (PBY-5B). Note floats partially retracted

Plate 7 Sunderland Mk III at moorings

Plate 8   Sunderland Mk III in flight

Plate 9   Sunderland Mk II riding on the step

Plate 10   Sunderland Mk III on the slip at Pembroke Dock

Plate 11   Sunderland Mk I at moorings. Dinghy for transporting crews in foreground. Note also height of fin

Plate 12 View inside bow compartment, showing anchor and winch

Plate 13 The galley, showing primus stoves and starboard galley hatch

Plate 14 Pilots' cabin. Forward companionway hatch was aft of engine controls seen in picture

Plate 15 Navigator's position. Note Dalton Computer to left of navigator's left hand

Plate 16 Wireless operator's position, showing R1155 radio receiver (top of picture) and R1154 transmitter

Plate 17 Flight engineer's station. Dials on panel were for cylinder head temperatures, oil pressures, etc. Levers were cocks for selecting fuel tanks

Plate 18 Interior view from tail, showing rear bunks on lower deck, waist hatch gun positions on upper deck (Mk I)

Plate 19   Mid-upper or dorsal turret with twin Browning .303 guns

Plate 20   The rear turret, with 4 Browning .303 guns, popularly known as the sting in the tail

Plate 21 View from rear bunk area towards tail. Rear hatch on left, fitter's bench on right

Plate 22 Mooring a Sunderland. The 2 wire hawsers coming up from the buoy were the mooring pendants; the coir rope was the short slip. The portable ladder was often needed when shackling or unshackling the keel bridle

Plate 23 Interior view of Catalina, showing cramped conditions

Plate 24 The flight deck, looking forward from the main spar (foreground). Pilots in centre, wireless operator on left, navigator and engineer on right. Note Very cartridges behind 2nd pilot's seat

Plate 25 Sunderland attack on U-boat. From the submarine's track, it clearly tried to take avoiding action by turning to starboard

Plate 26 204 squadron photograph, 1943. The CO, W/Cdr C E W Evison, is 9th from the left, front row

Plate 27   Sunderland Mk I on convoy escort duty

Plate 28   Sunderland Mk II beached on Scottish coast after severe gale

Plate 29 Engineers working on port inner engine of H204. Sgt Price (FE/AG) left and Sgt W Borrowman (FME/AG)

Plate 30 Crew of Sunderland A204, February 1944. Back row, left to right: W/O R B Murray (Canadian), air gunner; F/Sgt C V Woods, WOM/AG; F/Lt FN Johnston, captain; the author, 2nd pilot; F/Sgt H T Swaffer, WOP/AG. Front row, left to right: F/Sgt J P M Hogan, FE/AG; F/Sgt A Young, FME/AG; Sgt T Moore, WOP/AG; W/O H Hulse(American), WOP/AG

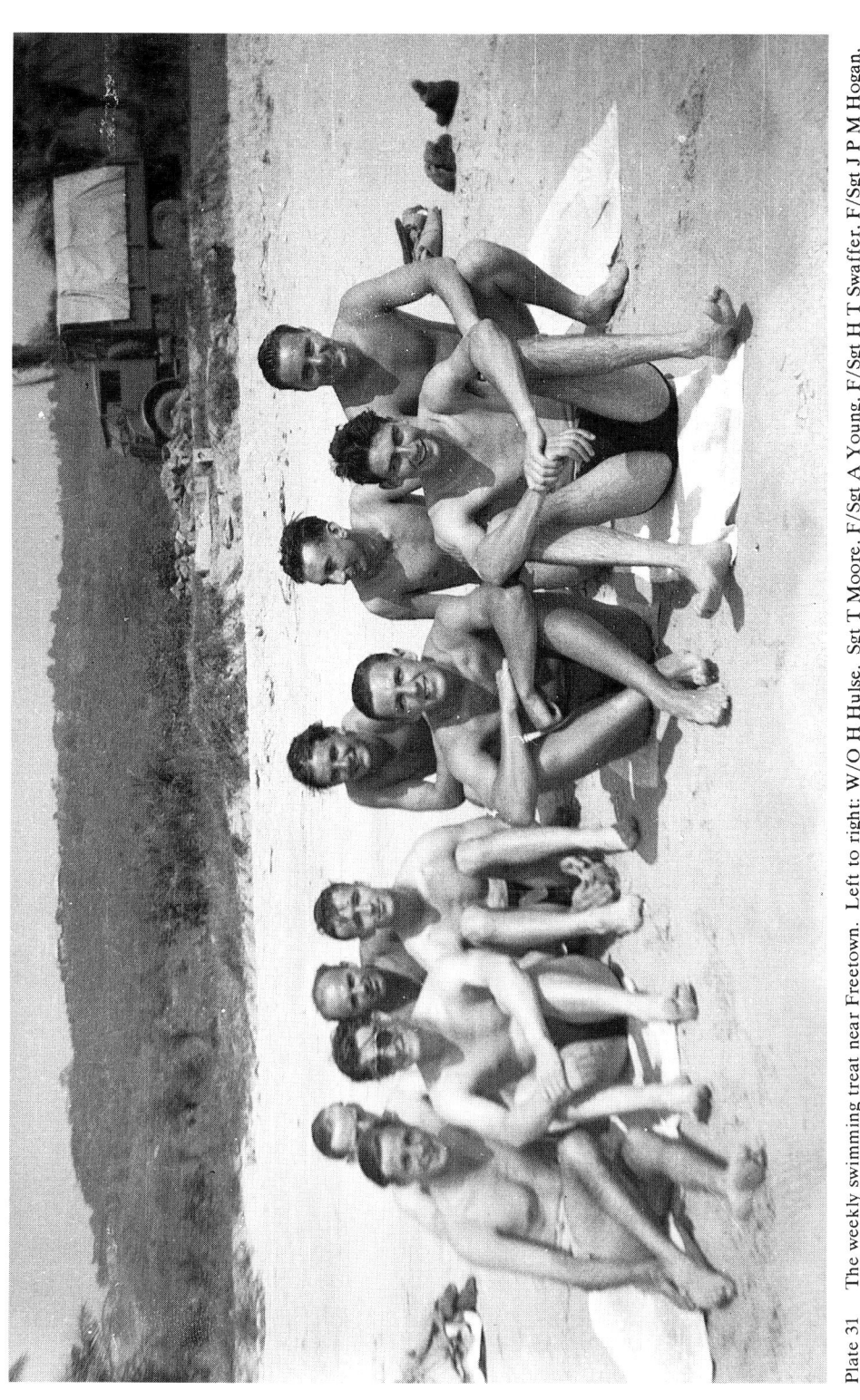

Plate 31 The weekly swimming treat near Freetown. Left to right: W/O H Hulse, Sgt T Moore, F/Sgt A Young, F/Sgt H T Swaffer, F/Sgt J P M Hogan, F/Sgt W Borrowman, the author, F.Sgt C V Woods, F/Lt F N Johnston, W/O R B Murray

Plate 32 Negotiating a flat calm.

Plate 33 Sunderland Mk V over convoy

Plate 34 The author's first crew at 131(c) OTU, Killadeas, NI. Back row, left to right: Sgt R G Smith, Sgt G Torobzoff, Sgt D Brien, F/Sgt W R Mansfield, Sgt G Osborn; Front row: Sgt H B Burton, F/Sgt D Ryan (Aus.), the author, F/O G Moffitt(NZ), Sgt T J Martin

Plate 35 Sunderland Mk V in flight. Note centimetric radar blisters under wings

Plate 36 Sunderland Mk III with centimetric radar

Plate 37   The camp at Fanara (Kasfareit), Egypt

Plate 38   The jetty at Penang, Malaya

Plate 39   Author's crew at start of Far East tour. Back row, left to right: Sgt H B Burton, F/O G Moffitt(NZ) F/O P N Young, the author, Sgt G Torobzoff; Front row Sgt R G Smith, F/Sgt D Brien, Sgt T J Martin

Plate 40   Syriam, Burma. The River Pegu is in the top right hand corner

Plate 41 The trots at Koggala, Ceylon with Mk V Sunderlands

Plate 42 Beached Mk V Sunderland at Koggala

Plate 43   Crashed Liberator N355 in Burma

Plate 44   Dropping a Bircham Barrel to Liberator crew with supplies and messages

Plate 45 The author and engineer awaiting arrival of Liberator survivors

Plate 46 Dinghy bringing Liberator survivors aboard Sunderland D240

Plate 47   240 Squadron photograph, March 1946. The CO, W/Cdr C B Gavin Robinson AFC, is 16th from left in front row

movements were extremely sluggish, making them look quite sinister. They were clearly doomed and we almost felt sorry for them.

Sure enough, the following day very few of them were moving. As we set about clearing up the aircraft and refuelling it in preparation for our next sortie, we counted our blessings that we hadn't had the misfortune of flying into them as we landed. Apart from their obvious effect on the pilot's landing visibility, they could easily have caused engine failure by choking the air inlets. We took care to remove any that might present such a problem before we took to the air again. The fish rapidly devoured the corpses as they hit the water.

In September 1943, I joined another crew at Bathurst, flying as second pilot to F/Lt F N Johnston in A204 (*see plate* 30). Johnny Johnston was a tall, lean, friendly man, with whom it was a pleasure to work. He recognized the need for me to get plenty of practice at take-offs and landings and so gave me every opportunity, not only on local flights but also on operational sorties. This meant that I was now able to experience the feel of taking the boat off with a full load, something which offered a greater challenge than simply getting her into the air for a one-hour air test.

It was also good experience to have to land the aircraft after a tiring tenor twelve-hour sortie. It brought home to me the need to be on my toes at all times when in control of the boat, regardless of how I might be feeling. My first flight with Johnny was a local one lasting just over an hour, when we had the new CO, W/Cdr H J L Hawkins, for company. On this brief trip we air tested the aircraft and carried out air firing and photography practice.

At the end of the same month we spent nearly twelve hours in the air escorting the US tanker Empire Meadows. Although there was no excitement of any kind on the flight, it was satisfying to know just how important this type of sortie was. In those days, Britain obtained all her oil from overseas. Ensuring that the tankers got through was crucial to the war effort. Without large quantities of fuel, we would have been unable to discharge our military commitments and would certainly have lost the conflict. The Germans knew this only too well and did all they could to prevent these vital supplies from reaching their destinations.

The following month began with a new tragedy. The Australian skipper, Clem Mayberry, now acting F/Lt, was on his way from Bathurst to PE in G204 when he was recalled after about two hours flying because of the weather conditions. Attempting a night landing, he found that he was overshooting the flarepath. He had opened the engines to go round again when the aircraft suddenly crashed. Six members of the crew were rescued, including the second pilot, F/Sgt C (Charlie) Todd, while the captain and two others were posted missing believed killed. Charlie was unaware of what had caused the crash. He only recalls being shot out through the cabin window, ending up in the murky water amongst a pile of debris.

Night take-offs and landings in Sunderlands called for special procedures and precautions. We were not able to have conspicuous flarepaths to assist us in seeing the alighting area clearly. We had to operate with only three flares, equidistantly positioned along what was considered to be a safe stretch of water. This was regularly swept by a launch of the marine section, to remove any flotsam which might be a hazard to the aircraft. Hitting foreign objects in the water at a hundred miles an hour could do a great deal of damage.

The drill on take-off was to start just before the first flare and try to get airborne by the second. If we passed the second without coming unstuck, we had to make an instant judgement as to whether the boat would get off by the third. If we were unsure about this, it was imperative that we throttled back, returned behind the first flare and tried again.

When landing, we aimed to put the aircraft down between the first and second flares, so giving us the distance between second and third in which to come off the step and slow down. The flares were really provided to mark out the alighting area. The illumination from them was of limited value in judging our precise height above the water. We therefore had to adopt a blind flying technique, which meant a powered approach.

After gliding down to about three hundred feet, we partly opened the throttles on the outer engines and began to raise the nose, applying power from the inner engines until the rate of descent was about two hundred feet a minute. The aim was to put the aircraft into a normal landing attitude at a controlled rate of descent, so that the point at which she touched down was not critical...provided, of course, that it was between the first and second flares.

This procedure was intrinsically safer than the normal landing method, but demanded greater skill of the pilot. Simultaneously flying on instruments and observing the flarepath through the cockpit window could present problems of coordination. Judging distances and seeing hazards in the dark were also much more difficult than in daylight.

Early on the day following Mayberry's crash, acting Warrant Officer Malcolm Yendell in C204 was trying to take off from the flarepath at PE with a full load. He made two unsuccessful attempts to get airborne within the specified limits and had to abort the take-off and go back and try again. The third time the aircraft swung to port, running up the beach and turning over onto her back.

The navigator, F/O R E Dunn, received fatal injuries, but the remainder of the crew had a miraculous escape. We arrived at PE later in the day and were told that the pilots had been catapulted through the cabin windows and were found sitting in the sand looking slightly dazed some distance ahead of the wreck.

Over the next four weeks we spent much of our lives in the air. We completed eight convoy escorts and anti-sub sorties totalling over fifty-eight flying hours. There were also local flights for air tests, day and night practice circuits and bumps, air firing exercises, a compass swing and low flying practice.

In addition, we carried out a reconnaissance flight to the Cape Verde Islands. This archipelago, lying over three hundred miles WNW of Dakar, consists of fifteen volcanic islands, the highest of the peaks being Fogo, which rises to 9281 feet. The group is spread over a wide area, the greatest distance between the islands being nearly two hundred miles. This meant that we had to be selective about how many islands we visited. More than half our flying time of twelve and a half hours was taken up in reaching the nearest one and in returning to our base at Bathurst after carrying out the reconnaissance.

The purpose of the flight was to establish whether or not the Germans were secretly making use of the islands again in order to be within easier striking distance of the West African convoys. They had used them earlier in the war for refuelling purposes. We flew over each of the major islands in turn, carefully scanning every corner for evidence of the enemy presence and taking innumerable photographs. Nothing sinister was seen. In view of the long distances covered on the outward and homeward legs, we were able to combine the recce duties with an anti-submarine patrol.

Several days later, we tried to carry out convoy escort duties in the most appalling weather conditions. Arriving on station after nearly three hours flying against a stiff breeze, we found ourselves being buffeted about in squalls which threatened to tear the aircraft apart. The cloud base was little more than a hundred feet above the water and the visibility such that we were not able to see the ships until we were right over them. The sea was in turmoil. A heavy swell was running and the spume was being blown from one crest to the next and beyond.

The escort ships, normally busying themselves around their charges like sheepdogs, were being tossed about as though out of control. To add to the discomfort of flying under these conditions, one of our engines started playing up. The oil pressure dropped significantly and we had visions of having to shut the engine down and suffer the consequences. Johnny wisely decided to turn for home, after apologizing to one of the escort vessels. Helped by a tail wind, we reached Half Die and were waterborne two hours later, happily all in one piece.

Conditions like these did, of course, make life difficult. There were two major problems. First, however much we might have felt that the show must go on, there was no future in it if we were unable to carry out our tasks effectively. As previously mentioned, reasonable visibility was important to us if we were not to get lost in that vast area of the Atlantic. It was also necessary if we were to stand a chance of making contact with our quarry and be in a position to attack him. Flying at nought feet in bad conditions made it almost impossible to use the radar. The noise produced on the screen by reflections from a heaving sea would completely swamp any responses from U-boats, or even surface ships. We were fortunate to have been able to make contact with our convoy in the first place. If we had left it in order to go off on an A/S patrol, the chances were that we might not have been able to find it again!

A second consideration was the ability of both aircraft and crew to stand up to such turbulent and stressful conditions for any length of time. For the first hour or so the crew might be able to cope with it satisfactorily, always in the expectation that conditions would improve. After that, every minute would be an increasing trial...there was always that long haul back to base.

The fact that Bathurst offered little by way of local entertainment meant that the Sergeants' Mess was frequently the scene of drinking parties. There was never any difficulty in finding an excuse to have one. Once the grounds were established and the party got under way, the reasons were soon forgotten and nobody would be able to say how it all started.

During one of these parties, I was thoroughly enjoying myself drinking my pints of beer and watching some of my colleagues passing out and being transported back to their beds by those who could still stand up. By this stage in my service career I was confident that I could hold my beer with most of my pals, but I hadn't reckoned on some clot slipping a double whisky into it. Feeling suddenly tired, I got to my feet and set course for the exit, bidding goodnight to the few survivors. I didn't reach the door, but collapsed in a heap and had to face the ignominy of being carried back to my own bed.

The morning brought a trauma such as I have never experienced before or since. I awoke on the concrete floor beside my bed, tightly wrapped in my mosquito net and with my head in a small pool of blood. I felt as though I had been felled by a sledgehammer. Crawling with great effort into my bed, I asked F/Sgt Cyril (Woodsy) Woods, our wireless operator mechanic (WOM), to let the skipper know that I wouldn't be fit to report for flying duties that day. I then spent a painful day nursing a solid head and being unable to take even a glass of water without nausea.

The following morning brought no relief, so I reported sick. After spending forty-eight hours in the sick bay as a suspected malaria case, I was examined by the MO who pronounced, "I think you can go now, sergeant. We all know what your trouble was, don't we?" I gave him a look of mock bewilderment and went back to my hut.

When I arrived there, I was surprised and a little put out to see a copy of my local newspaper on the opposite bed, which belonged to Woodsy. Without giving him time to say or do anything, I treated him to a long and vehement speech of censure for rifling my locker. He was greatly offended. "What do you mean? That crack on your head didn't do you a lot of good, did it? This paper was sent out to me by my mum, if you want to know."

"Oh yes? You'll be telling me next that you come from Weymouth."

"I do." Although we'd been flying together in the same crew for a number of weeks, neither of us had known that we were from the same home town. I was unable to look Woodsy up after the war. Sadly, he died in an air crash when operating from Lossiemouth in Scotland.

Chapter 15

One of our major worries in flying aircraft prone to engine trouble was that they might let us down on take-off when it was too late to abort. This was bad enough on a local trip when the aircraft's weight was at a minimum, but the danger was greatly multiplied when she was at full load.

A204 was setting off on an A/S sweep scheduled to last about twelve hours. We were carrying two thousand gallons of fuel which represented considerable weight, necessitating a fairly lengthy take-off run. No sooner had we left the water than one of the inner engines began to splutter.

F/Sgt A (Geordie) Young, the flight mechanic, yelled out over the intercom from the galley that oil was pouring out of the coughing engine and running along with the slipstream on the underside of the wing. F/Sgt J P M (Johnny) Hogan, the flight engineer, sitting at his panel watching the oil pressure dropping, said almost nonchalantly, "You'll have to shut that engine down soon, skip." Johnston had opened up the other three in order to gain height as quickly as possible, which was top priority.

It was a touch and go business. The windmilling fan on the faulty engine was causing substantial drag and the other engines, which by this time should have been throttled back after the exertion of getting all that weight off the water, had to be operated at full power to give us any chance of gaining sufficient height. Johnny Hogan's calm, down-to-earth voice with the Manchester accent came over the intercom again, "Can't land with all this fuel on board..."

"You're right, Johnny," replied the skipper, "but I daren't let any of it go here. We're too close to the coast. At least we're still gaining height slowly, so I'll head out over the sea."

The phlegmatic engineer had not finished. "Engines are overheating. Can't you throttle back yet?"

"We're at twelve hundred feet now, so I suppose I can. When we've got rid of some of the weight, it'll make it a bit easier for them. Prepare to jettison fuel."

"OK, skip. Soon as you like."

We discharged several hundred gallons of fuel over the sea and, temporarily setting aside the danger we were in, I was thinking about those poor devils on the tankers who'd had to run the gauntlet of enemy submarines and surface raiders in order to make this fuel available. It was heartbreaking to see it all going to waste like this. I didn't know at the time that I would later have to take similar decisions when I was captain of my own aircraft.

The jettisoning operation completed, we turned for home. The skipper was able to reduce power on the three engines after the loss of weight and the engineer reported that the cylinder head temperatures had begun to fall again. Johnston called up the tower to put the Ops people in the picture and we were given immediate landing permission. As a precaution, the fire tender took up its position close to the alighting area. Johnston put the aircraft down safely as though nothing untoward had happened.

Flying boat pilots had to come to terms with the many moods of the sea. Although alighting areas were fairly well protected from the powerful forces of the open ocean, it was not uncommon to experience quite heavy swells when taking off and landing. On one visit to the Free French port of Dakar, the appreciable chop on the surface of the water, caused by a fresh wind, masked an underlying swell. From what we could see from the air there was no reason to suppose that the landing conditions were anything but ideal. The skipper made a conventional glide approach, touching down in the normal way.

Then things started to go wrong. The boat bounced into the air again, only to hit the next roller with a resounding smack. Everyone expected the aircraft to stick this time, but she repeated the performance again and again. As we slowed and the controls became less and less responsive, so the pilot had to wrestle more and more with them to try to keep the boat on an even keel. When at last she came off the step and settled into the heaving water, I found that I was gripping my seat as if my life really depended on it. We'd bounced fourteen times.

We were to return to Bathurst later the same day and were not looking forward to taking-off again in these conditions. It was hoped that things would improve before we had to go. They didn't. We bounced fourteen times again on the take-off run. The skipper's exertions in averting disaster took a lot out of him. His shirt was wringing wet and the perspiration stood out all over his face. He grinned nervously after we were safely airborne and then asked me to take over the controls. Someone rushed a cup of tea up to him from the galley. A double brandy might have been more appropriate.

When we returned to Half Die, we decided that it would be prudent for the maintenance men to take the boat up the slip for an inspection of the hull in case it had sustained any damage. It says much for the immense strength of the Sunderland hull that they could only find a couple of sprung rivets, not enough to cause a leak of any real significance.

Although it was questionable that they would have contributed to the particular problems we'd experienced at Dakar, the hull was found to be covered in barnacles which had to be laboriously chipped off by the maintenance staff. It was no good leaving them there as they could cause unwanted drag on full-load take-offs.

Surprisingly, the hull did not often suffer from leaks, but it was important to monitor the situation regularly. If water did get into the bilges, it could increase the take-off weight markedly. Since the bilges were in separate compartments between the bulkheads, it could also upset the trim of the aircraft. Consequently it was part of the procedure before taking off for the riggers to check that the bilges were dry. If they weren't, the APU or a stirrup pump would be used, depending on the volume of water to be shifted.

By now the Free French Air Force had a squadron of Sunderlands at Dakar and they shared our detachment facilities at PE. Once when we were returning there at night after an A/S sortie, we were making our customary left-hand circuit to land when two navigation lights came towards us on the crosswind leg. We managed to take avoiding action in time and the other aircraft whipped past less than fifty feet above us. It turned out to be a French boat doing a right-hand circuit.

Later the same night, one of our boat guards heard a loud metallic crunch when he was on duty. Looking out of the galley hatch in the direction from which the sound appeared to be coming, he discovered that the French boat had broken her moorings and run aground, damaging her tail when it collided with an overhanging bluff of rock. We concluded that either the crew didn't believe in boat guards or theirs were asleep on the job.

To maintain continuity and effective teamwork it was, of course, desirable for crews to keep together and for each crew to be responsible for its own boat. Many things conspired to prevent this from happening for very long, one of them being that there was a continuous traffic of people being posted in and out of the squadron. Nevertheless, crews were in general trustworthy when it came to looking after their aircraft. They took a personal pride in them and went out of their way to keep them clean and shipshape.

It was common practice, no doubt frowned upon by the powers that be, to use aviation fuel to clean the bulkheads and decks, because duralumin responded very favourably to this treatment. At one time, when we were spending several days at PE, the engineer decided that he wanted to clean up his position and he climbed out onto the wing and siphoned off some petrol into a can. The hatch above the galley was closed, so no one down below knew what he was doing. For some reason I took it into my head to climb the companionway from the galley to the flight deck.

Not realizing that the petrol can was overlapping the hatch, I swung the latter open and sent the can flying, upsetting its contents over the flight deck. One of the riggers was using a primus stove in the galley and when I yelled a warning that petrol had been spilt, he had the presence of mind to grab the lighted stove and hurl it out of the galley hatch. It made a loud hissing noise as it hit the water and sank to the bottom.

We watched the petrol running down the bulkhead behind the remaining stove and realized what a close shave it had been. People got medals for flying prowess. Our rigger should have got one for action beyond the call of duty.

The squadron entered 1944 with no appreciable change in its activities or its fortunes. We continued to carry out our convoy escort work and A/S patrols with diligence and hope, indeed blind faith, but little measurable success in our eyes. It was not easy at the time to come to terms with the idea that we were still doing a good job by keeping U-boats down, when we weren't even privileged to see them. Nevertheless, the now published records of the battle of the Atlantic, especially those of the U-boat commanders themselves, confirm this.

When escort ships were in short supply and air cover was not available, the U-boats had free rein to carry out their dastardly work. The presence of an aircraft, whether or not it was able to press home an attack, had a marked effect on keeping the enemy away from his intended targets. The damage was often done after the aircraft had to return to base and when there was no relief to take over from it. Many ships were also sunk in mid-Atlantic when the convoys were outside the range of Allied air patrols.

Early in the New Year, our expectations were raised when a US aircraft operating from Morocco made a sighting report and signalled that a U-boat was proceeding southwards into our area. As we were driven out to A204 in the dinghy, we speculated on being able to attack our quarry this time. We were a very hopeful crew when we took off from Bathurst in mid-afternoon. After being in the air for ninety minutes, we received a second sighting message and the excitement mounted. Everyone was on his toes and searched the area eagerly. We didn't want to miss this one... but again we did. When we eventually landed at 3.30 the following morning, all we were able to report seeing was a large shoal of fish.

Later in the month, the squadron moved to Jui, Freetown, over 400 miles further south, while retaining Bathurst as a detachment/maintenance base. By this time there had been changes in the command of the squadron. W/Cdr H J L Hawkins had taken over from W/Cdr Evison in September and the following month S/Ldr A Frame DFC, a New Zealander, had joined as Flight Commander.

My own modest promotion to Flight Sergeant did little to boost my morale since it was automatic and, as far as I could see at the time, unearned. It did carry an increase in pay, however, which was gratefully received and duly earmarked for what I hoped would be an impending wedding. Such was my youthful arrogance that I was confident that my proposal would be accepted, despite the fact that Mary and I had spent so little time together. It was to be some months before the question could be popped and over a year to the big event.

The entertainment in Freetown did not appear to be any great improvement over Bathurst's. However, some miles away on the Atlantic coast there was a beach where the natural amenities, albeit basic, gave us considerable pleasure. Commissioning a truck once a week to take us there, we occupied our leisure time swimming in the surf, sitting on the beach sunning ourselves (*see plate* 31) and consuming large quantities of bananas bought from a nearby plantation.

We learned that there had been a serious spate of petty theft from the camp and were advised to guard our personal possessions carefully. On one of the days we were due to go to the beach, I searched in vain for my swimming trunks. Convinced that I'd left them hanging over the bedrail at the foot of my bed, I called my native houseboy and asked him where they were. He shook his head wearily from side to side, muttering, "Donno, sah, no see 'em."

"Are you sure?"

"No see, sah."

"What about the other boys?" Getting no response, I went outside again to question them. One was sitting on the step sporting the missing trunks, his face the picture of innocence. "Where did you get those?"

"From your boy, sah," he said confidently, seemingly unaware that he was a receiver of stolen goods. When I questioned my own boy again, I was rewarded with a flat denial of his having had anything to do with the theft.

Marching both the boys down to the guardroom, I explained the situation to the duty sergeant, who said he would have a quiet word with them. He retired to another room with my boy and after a few minutes returned to announce that he'd confessed to stealing the trunks.

"Do you want to prefer a charge in the civil court, Flight?"

"I think I should, don't you? This thing's getting a bit out of hand."

"Afraid so. These chaps cause us a lot of bother. I don't think they should be allowed to get away with it. Next hearing's on Thursday. Can you get there?"

"Doubt it. I'll probably be flying then."

"OK. I'll have your statement typed up and get you to sign it later in the day." That evening he sought me out in the mess and got me to sign the statement.

Not having heard anything more by the Saturday, I visited the guardroom to find out what the verdict had been. The sergeant told me that the boy had been found guilty and sentenced to six weeks' detention. "He had quite a nice little hoard of RAF types' possessions, including watches, cigarette cases and lighters. Proper magpie, he was."

"Was he, indeed? Then it's a good thing he was caught. Perhaps it'll deter the others. Now, can I have my trunks back, please?"

"Well, er..." the sergeant began with ominous hesitation, "I'm afraid they were whipped from the court during the hearing."

Chapter 16

Although I had disciplined myself long ago to trust my instruments when flying, there were certain systems in the aircraft which I treated with extreme caution and with good reason. I didn't believe they could be relied upon to operate faultlessly at all times. One such device was the autopilot.

When spending many hours in the air, often having to concentrate on detailed searches of a wide expanse of sea, it was very convenient to be able to switch George in and let him do the donkey work. It would have been foolhardy to have left the pilot's position to attend to other things, believing that this mechanical device would deputize for you with complete safety.

On one of our transit trips from Bathurst to Freetown, we were transporting the staff of a naval hospital being moved to a new location. I was in the captain's seat, with George in, and we were flying at about three thousand feet. In the second pilot's seat was a nurse who had come up from below "for the view". She watched the control column making its small corrections apparently unaided and was intrigued that I could be flying the aircraft so ably with no hands.

"Who's flying now, then?"

"George, the automatic pilot."

"Oh... I've heard about that. I'm told you can leave it and go downstairs for a cup of tea or a nap or something."

I looked suitably shocked. "In theory you could, but that would be pushing it. I certainly wouldn't risk it. You can be let down by technology sometimes."

The words had hardly left my lips when the nose of the aircraft suddenly dropped and we were hurtling towards the sea in a steep dive. The airspeed indicator needle began to rise and the altimeter was unwinding rapidly, while the noise of the slipstream was quite alarming.

The nurse screamed and pressed her hands over her eyes. I reassured her as I put George out of action, pulled the boat out of the dive and increased the engine power to climb back to our cruising altitude. She wouldn't believe that the incident was quite unplanned.

Only a month after I had sewn the crown above my sergeant's stripes, I learned of my commission as a Pilot Officer. At the inevitable farewell party in the Sergeants' Mess, I was on my guard against having my drinks spiked again and I successfully stayed the course. My entry into the Officers' Mess, however, was not without incident.

As I proudly stepped over the threshold, my toe caught in the doormat and I sprawled headlong across the floor. One or two officers sitting in armchairs looked up in the manner of elderly gentlemen whose afternoon nap had been disturbed in the peaceful chambers of their London club. I struggled to my feet and made my way hurriedly to the bar for a glass of Dutch courage, already ordered by an amused Johnny Johnston. I was soon to learn to my regret that he was on the point of being posted, having completed his operational tour in West Africa.

Fortunately, I did not know then that I would have only one more brief meeting with Johnny several months later. He was tragically killed the following winter on an operational flight from RAF Alness on the Cromarty Firth, ten days after I arrived on the unit for a radar course. He had been awarded the DFC for his work on the Coast.

I returned to flying with D204, captained by Tom, now F/Lt, Hibberd towards the end of February. S/Ldr Frame took the crew out on a twelve hour U-boat hunt and I remember thinking to myself at the time "If he can't find a bloody U-boat, nobody can! After all, he must have got the DFC for something." But it wasn't to be. After fourteen to fifteen hundred miles of searching, we returned to base with nothing to show for it. It evidently happened to the best of us.

Before long I had the pleasure of flying with John Paré again, this time for night circuits and bumps. By now I was confident in my ability to handle the boat under most conditions and I believed I acquitted myself reasonably well on this occasion. I don't know what John Paré thought about it, but he too was awarded the DFC at the end of that month. He was possibly being rewarded for his fortitude in the face of such danger! Clearly I was considered safe enough, as was another second pilot, F/Sgt Charlie Nears, because we were allowed to take F204 up together to practise day take-offs and landings.

A few days later the CO took the aircraft to Liberia with captains F/Lt R J (Rob) Foulds, F/Lt C A Bayley, a Canadian, and W/O Malcolm Yendell to investigate Fisherman's Lake as a potential diversion base for flying boats. Now that we were operating from Freetown, it was desirable for us to have somewhere further south where we could put down in case of emergency. I went there on only one occasion two months later and had no reason to remember it with affection.

On 14 March, Sgt N J (John) Bowman joined D204 as third pilot. John was to take over from me as second dicky when I eventually returned to UK for my skipper's course.

An incident that caused us some concern occurred when F/O F W H Stevens was on a bombing exercise with F204 and one of his depth charges detonated as it hit the surface of the water, doing some damage to the airframe. The pistol was presumably incorrectly set and an immediate investigation took place. All the other DCs on the squadron were checked and fortunately found to be in order.

Another reported sighting, this time of several U-boats, by a US aircraft operating out of Morocco caused excitement and frenzied activity in 204 squadron. A signal from AHQ ordered all serviceable aircraft to return to

Bathurst at the beginning of April with the objective of concentrating their efforts on tracking down the enemy submarines and hopefully attacking them. For a whole week, everything we had was put into the air and flown virtually around the clock. When an aircraft returned to base after a sortie, it was checked, refuelled and sent out again with a fresh crew. I was in the air for five out of the first eight days of April, flying a total of fifty hours, equally divided between night and day. It was a mammoth operation, showing what could be done when the occasion demanded it.

The excellent support that the maintenance crews gave us during this period deserves special mention. They kept going day and night without very much rest and the standard of their work was extremely high. It is regrettable that the efforts of all who were involved in the operation were not better rewarded with some kills. Our failure to find any trace of the enemy in spite of such saturating coverage suggested that they headed out deep into the Atlantic and well away from our area. Although we did not know it at the time, US Navy escort ships were having greater success west of the Azores, fifteen hundred or more miles away from our nearest base.

On one of the above flights which I made in D204, F/Lt D W Pallett was the skipper. A few days later, he took off in K204 on an A/S sweep and developed engine trouble after about two hours in the air, resulting in his having to ditch in the sea. A launch was sent to take off the crew and it damaged the bow of the aircraft while carrying out this task. A pinnace successfully towed K into Bathurst with a skeleton crew aboard.

This and the increasing number of mechanical failures suffered by our boats on the Coast caused much anxiety. The re-equipment of the Sunderland with more reliable power units, and props capable of being feathered, was considered to be long overdue. Evidently we were not the only people who had shown such disquiet, because a new Mk V was indeed on the way. Experiments were being conducted both by Shorts and 461 Squadron RAAF to replace the Pegasus engines with the Pratt and Whitney Twin Wasps used with such success in the Catalina and the Hudson. The power was thus increased and the installation of Hamilton Hydromatic airscrews effectively dealt with the problem of being unable to feather the props. The new version did not enter service until the following year, however, too late to make any impact on the outcome of the war.

My last flight with Tom Hibberd in D204 was an escort mission, accompanying a tanker with the unlikely name of Balls Bluff. About two thirds of the way into the trip, we developed engine trouble and had to head for home. We concluded that the engine must have been bluffing too, because the oil leak did not prove to be serious and we landed at Freetown without any problems.

One of the hindrances to our work about this time was the weather. It was so bad that we found it extremely difficult to carry out our operations effectively. If you were simply trying to get from A to B with no time restrictions, it was not too important whether you went direct or by some roundabout route. When you had to thoroughly reconnoitre an area without missing any part of it, however, the whole exercise became abortive if you were constantly changing course or altering height to avoid storms or turbulent cloud. Such was our problem and we wondered whether it was worth risking valuable crews and aircraft in such conditions when they were unable to carry out their commitments.

Our feelings were evidently made known to AHQ. The Air Officer Commanding, Air Vice Marshal R Graham, decided to see for himself. Tony Staffiere, now a skipper, was detailed to take him out on an all-night A/S patrol. I was asked to join the crew for this trip and we took off from Jui at 21.15. The mission was to carry out a CLA anti-submarine search (*see page* 65) in a south-westerly direction from Sierra Leone. This entailed flying parallel tracks in a north-west/south-east direction, the distance between successive tracks depending on the radar visibility.

The whole flight of nearly twelve hours was a nightmare, but we diced on regardless. The low clouds were constantly illuminated by lightning flashes. These were uncomfortably close and we found ourselves dodging them all over the sky. At no time was it possible to complete a single leg of the flight plan without taking avoiding action. Coupled with these problems, the turbulence was so violent at times that I wondered if the aircraft would remain in one piece. The only consolation for us was that the top brass experienced the same discomfort! The flight was completely abortive in terms of finding the enemy. The radar had detected nothing.

I was relieved when Tony called for a homeward course. The AVM, who showed no reaction about the trip, had asked to be taken to Liberia, so we made for Fisherman's Lake, landing there at about 8.30 in the morning. When we went ashore to arrange our sleeping accommodation, we discovered that we were in an American camp. The first evidence of this was a strategically placed Coca-Cola machine. I remember making a facetious remark about it being an essential part of the Yanks' front line equipment.

We stayed at Fish'Lake for two days. When we went aboard the aircraft for the return flight to Freetown, the lake was like a mirror and we anticipated problems in taking off. In a flat calm, a flying boat hull tended to stick like a limpet and some means had to be found of breaking the suction under the hull. A method that was sometimes quite effective was to porpoise the boat. When she reached a speed at which there was some positive response to the controls, the control column was rocked backwards and forwards to get the bow to rise and fall rhythmically. If this failed, it was advisable to throttle back, allowing the engines adequate time to cool off before trying again.

Contrary to popular belief that a flat calm (*see plate* 32) should provide ideal conditions for taking off and landing a flying boat, both operations could in fact cause problems. When making an approach, for instance, it was impossible to judge one's height above the water with any degree of accuracy. It was therefore asking for trouble to attempt the customary glide landing, because the aircraft could hit the water before you had decided that it was time to level out. The accepted procedure was to adopt a night landing approach, that is with power. The last two or three hundred feet were not so critical, since the aircraft would be letting down gently in a safe landing attitude (*see page* 82).

Tony opened the throttles and the boat moved laboriously forward. The drag from the still water was immediately obvious. It felt almost as though someone had put the drogues out. Over half the permitted take-off time expired and the aircraft showed no sign of getting onto the step. The skipper tried to porpoise her in an attempt to get her to ride up on the keel but she stubbornly refused. As a last resort, he lifted the gate, a hinged stop which enabled maximum power to be called on in an emergency, and pushed the four throttles through it. Even this seemed to have little effect, except to increase the roar of four engines pushed to their very limits.

I looked out of the cabin window and imagined that the engine cowlings were white hot. Turning towards the engineer, I could see that he was getting anxious about his precious engines. The recommended time for operating them at full power ran out and Tony glanced at me with a questioning expression in his eyes. I shook my head, wondering why he didn't throttle back and allow the engines to cool down again.

I was beginning to feel a trifle panicky when at last the boat left the water and staggered into a weary climb. The engineer called the skipper on the intercom to tell him that the engines had overheated and to ask him to throttle back as soon as possible. The port inner was "looking dodgy" and he "wouldn't be surprised if we have some bother with it." Tony pulled back the throttles to climbing boost and wiped the sweat from his brow.

This take-off was particularly puzzling. Although the physical conditions were not very good, we didn't have a heavy load because we had no passengers and we were only carrying enough fuel for the ninety minute flight ahead of us. She should have come unstuck quicker than that. I asked the engineer if the engines had actually been delivering full power. He assured me that they had. There had been nothing wrong with them on the take-off run, but he wouldn't say the same now. They'd had a hell of a caning. I couldn't understand why it had been such damned hard work, unless...could it have been water in the bilges?

I threw myself down the companionway into the galley and asked a rigger if the bilges had been checked before we took off. He said that they hadn't, because this had been done before we left Freetown. That was the answer, I was sure of it. Convinced that we were carrying excess weight in the wrong places, I helped to take up a deckboard in each compartment to check whether there was any water in the bilges. We drew a blank in the galley and the wardroom, but gallons of water were sloshing about in the bow compartment.

When I returned to the flight deck to report what I'd found, Tony was understandably annoyed, though not entirely persuaded that this was the sole cause of the trouble. It was certainly easy to discount the effect of water in the bilges, because when you saw it lying there the quantity was very deceptive. It was not until you had the job of pumping it all out that you realized just how much there was. Bearing in mind that every gallon weighed at least ten pounds, the extra weight was significant, especially if in the wrong place relative to the centre of gravity.

As soon as we arrived at Freetown, the aircraft was hauled up the slip for a thorough inspection of engines and airframe. The normal procedure for bringing a boat ashore was to tow it in to a buoy near the slip and then to bolt two legs with wheels to the sides of the hull underneath the wing (*see plate* 10). A trolley was secured to the rear end of the keel and a tractor towed the aircraft backwards up the slipway. Edward Hulton, until recently owner of the last remaining airworthy Sunderland, once commented that a boat on beaching gear looked like a man on crutches. The Sunderland flying boat was certainly ungainly when perched on the hard standing, but when in the water we thought of her as a graceful white swan. There were obvious advantages in carrying out any major engine work on dry land where all the facilities and spares were readily available and where the mechanics were not hampered by the moods of the sea.

Two weeks later, I flew with Tony on a trip which was scheduled to be an anti-submarine sweep. We reached about a hundred feet after a perfectly normal take-off when the port inner engine cut and the skipper was forced to operate the other three at full power again. Thanks to his skill, he brought the aircraft down safely and I was very relieved to be in a position to celebrate the rest of my twenty-first birthday in the bar.

Chapter 17

When Operation Overlord, the so-called second front, was launched in June 1944, the Allied progress in Normandy posed an immediate threat to the Landwirt Group of U-boats operating from the Biscay ports. They were about to be cut off from their bases. Of the 36 boats in the Group, only 9 were fitted with the snorkel (or snort) breathing device. Production of this equipment had been greatly hampered by Allied bombing of the factories where it was made.

The snorkel was designed to extend the time a U-boat was able to remain under water. The boat drew air through this tube while at periscope depth, so that the diesel engines could be run to charge the batteries without the need to surface. There were, however, operational problems with the device. One of these was its telltale wake which, like that of the periscope, was unmistakable from the air in daylight. Another snag was that, in anything but calm conditions, the automatic valve kept opening and shutting to prevent water entering the tube. This restricted the air intake for the engines and resulted in their using up vital oxygen inside the boat, at the same time filling it with poisonous exhaust fumes which could not get away.

The crews thus suffered not only from greatly varying pressure on their eardrums, but also from breathing foul air for longer periods than anticipated. They were not prepared for coping with this situation, since shortage of manpower in the U-boat service meant that they were being sent to sea without adequate training. The enemy had hoped that this new device would make it possible for their U-boats to breathe at any time of the day or night. Instead they found that the time still had to be carefully chosen.

The new 1621-ton type XXI, or Electro-boat, on which U-boat Command had pinned its hopes, had also suffered a number of setbacks and had not appeared in service until well into 1944. The need for the advanced boat to become operational was urgent, but the Germans were bedevilled by technical, production and operational problems.

The Electro-boats were of modular construction, sections being manufactured in over thirty inland factories and then transported by canal and brought together in Hamburg, Bremen and Danzig. Production was being severely disrupted by Allied bombing of the aqueducts on the canals, the assembly shipyards and the component factories. The Allied invasion of France also concentrated massive anti-submarine forces in the Channel and its approaches, giving the U-boat commanders very little chance of deploying their new boats against us. The war was virtually over for them.

On the twelfth of June 1944, less than a week after D-Day, I stepped aboard the sloop HMS Lowestoft for the voyage home to do my skipper's course. F/O Don Grant and I were guests of the wardroom and looked forward to the trip immensely – until we learned that the ship would be escorting an eight knot convoy! It was a salutary experience for us both to find ourselves in an escort ship which was fussing around a slow convoy like those we'd so often escorted from the air. Whatever the crew's feelings might have been about their own vulnerability, everyone on board was in good spirits and seemed to go about his duties with a will. The men looked forward to some home leave at the end of the voyage, but that was almost three weeks away and we had to get through the Bay of Biscay and the Western Approaches before then.

The ships being escorted steamed doggedly on day after day and no doubt there were times when their crews wished they could get a move on. It was obviously frustrating for those on board ships capable of a good turn of speed to have their progress limited to the speed of the slowest vessel in the convoy. The sloop herself was not so restricted. She was free to weave about at a much higher speed and her limited overall rate of progress was therefore not so evident. In a way, it was reassuring to see her foaming wake streaming out behind us. It *looked* as though we were really going places, even if this was something of an illusion.

From time to time there were alerts and calls to action stations. The ship's company rushed about in a businesslike manner, all appearing to know what they were doing. It was rather disconcerting, therefore, to discover that the aircraft recognition skills of the gun crews left a lot to be desired. From time to time, aircraft were sighted in the distance and reports to the bridge as to their identity were often grossly inaccurate. Happily, no harm was done since they were all ours, but we began to wonder how the gunners would distinguish between a Ju88 and a Beaufighter. More to the point, did they know the difference between Allied and enemy flying boats?

This alarming discovery had Don and me greatly worried, because we were now west of the Bay of Biscay and likely to come across enemy aircraft. We had a word with the first lieutenant, who agreed that something should be done about it. "How about giving them the benefit of your own knowledge?" he suggested.

Don looked across at me with raised eyebrows and I nodded. "We'd be glad to," he said. There were two gun crews, so we each took one of them and instructed them in the finer points of aircraft recognition. It proved a revelation – not only for them, but also for us. We set about teaching them the differences between friendly and enemy aircraft which were similar and particularly difficult to tell apart. We hoped that our efforts would avoid any unnecessary risk in the future. As it turned out, we were miraculously unmolested. The alarms, due to both submarine and aircraft contacts, came to nothing and the convoy arrived in the UK intact.

Of the two weeks leave I was given, the first was spent with my parents and the second with Mary, who was able to take her annual holiday from work. The bond between us was reinforced during this leave and the ultimate outcome of our liaison was a foregone conclusion to everyone who knew us. We had a blissful week, visiting many of the beautiful places within easy reach of Glasgow. We went 'doon the watter' by Clyde steamer to Dunoon, by 'bus to Edinburgh and also to Balloch where we hired a rowing boat and spent several hours on Loch Lomond.

We were hoping to be able to savour the beauty and peace of this Scottish loch, in those days untouched by commercialism. It therefore surprised us to hear the strains of the then popular song Kalamazoo wafting across the wide expanse of calm water, which was broken only by what appeared to be an unmanned dinghy. As we approached it, all we could discern were the oars which were neatly stowed. Drawing alongside, we were able to see the occupant, a uniformed sailor, lying on his back in the bottom of the boat playing a mouth-organ.

As we strolled past a naval shore establishment at Helensburgh, the guard came smartly to attention and saluted. This took me completely unawares, as I'd been used to far less formality about this sort of thing on the Coast. Some adjustment was necessary to the more customary service procedures at home. Embarrassed, I hurriedly released Mary's hand so that I could return the salute.

The day after I was due to report for my captain's course in Northern Ireland was Mary's twenty-first birthday. To miss this would have been something of a disappointment, to say the least, so I decided that I'd apply for an extension of leave. It was a long shot and none of us really believed that there was a chance. I sent a telegram, without giving any reason for the impertinence, and this made the family even more doubtful of its success. Much to everyone's astonishment, not least my own, a reply was received within twenty-four hours extending my leave by another two weeks. Although the family thought I had a bit of a nerve, no one complained.

I reported for duty at 131(c) Operational Training Unit at the beginning of August 1944. It was based at Killadeas, near Enniskillen, County Fermanagh, on the eastern shores of Lough Erne, a few miles from the border with the Republic. Here I was to have my own crew for the first time (*see plate* 34) and we were to be trained together as an operational unit.

Although I personally found the setting idyllic and would have enjoyed exploring the countryside if I'd had half a chance, the crew did not entirely share my enthusiasm. They complained about the conditions being extremely wet. They'd heard that the camp had originally been built for the Americans who'd refused to occupy it and had moved to higher ground near Omagh. The huts were equipped with paraffin stoves for heating, but these were useless to begin with because no paraffin had been supplied. The crew eventually managed to get themselves warm and dry when our ever-resourceful Irish member located the storage tank and some five gallon jerricans.

Within a few days of my arrival at Killadeas, my promotion to Flying Officer was announced. The only other commissioned member of the crew was the second pilot, F/O A G (Graham) Moffitt from New Zealand. The navigator was F/Sgt D (Dave) Ryan, an Australian, and the three wireless operators were F/Sgt W (Reg) Mansfield (WOM/AG), Sgt T J (Terry) Martin (WOP/AG) and Sgt H B (Benny) Burton (WOP/AG). Sgt F T (Frank) Osborn and Sgt G (George) Torobzoff were flight engineer (FE/AG) and flight mechanic (FME/AG) respectively. The first air gunner was Sgt David (Paddy) Brien (St.AG), a native of County Fermanagh, whose home was conveniently within a few miles of the base.

The second air gunner allocated to our crew did not last very long. He seemed to be out of step with the others. They very soon summed him up as being an idle character and before long were whispering their doubts about him in my ear. I'd already made my own assessment and concluded that I'd have to take some action. The first move was to speak to him. It was something of a pep talk, centred on the idea that no operational crew could be effective without the active contribution of every member. His contribution was well below standard and his continued presence on the crew was in question. He listened impassively, shrugged his shoulders and told me that he was not worried, because he was in no hurry to go on ops. He was evidently twitchy about getting involved in the fighting. I was glad to have found out then, rather than at a time when he might have endangered the lives of the rest of us.

The way was now clear for me to speak to the adjutant. "I've no intention of taking this chap on operations. He'd be a liability and it wouldn't be fair to the rest of the crew. I'd like you to replace him."

"That's no problem, old man. Here's a list of gunners who are on leave at the moment. Pick one of them and I'll recall him."

I had a sudden twinge of conscience. Having doubled my own leave, here I was about to curtail someone else's. Shifting the responsibility onto the adjutant, I told him, "But I don't know one from another. I'll have to rely on you to find the right one for me."

He didn't argue but selected a Sgt R G Smith (St.AG) who was to report to me two days later. When he turned up, he didn't have to introduce himself. We had been at school together. Reg met with the approval of the crew and flew with us until demobbed about eighteen months later. A willing worker, he proved a reliable asset to the team.

The captain's course, which was very enjoyable, lasted nearly three months. Our first few flights were for familiarization purposes and involved exercises lasting four or five hours with ex-operational instructors, including the Officer Commanding C Flight, F/Lt H Feilding. One of their tasks was to assess my suitability as a Sunderland captain, so I felt that everything I did was being carefully scrutinized.

This did not trouble me unduly. I'd had so much valuable experience on the Coast, thanks to competent and helpful skippers, that I had reasonable confidence in my ability to do what was required. I didn't expect a high rating for my performance, but I consoled myself with the thought that one doesn't have to be brilliant to be acceptable. In fact, Feilding and his fellow instructors judged me average (whatever that might mean) for the record. For me it was sufficiently satisfying to be considered safe by the crew.

The training flights covered day and night circuits and bumps, emergency landings and operational flying exercises, which included long range navigation, A/S techniques, bombing and gunnery, escort work and so on. The various skills were then practised without an instructor and the real training began. One had to develop one's own style of captaincy and the ability to mould the crew into an effective team. I can't remember being given much help with that. My instinct was to try to set an example, by demonstrating that I was an active member of the team who concerned himself with getting to know as much as possible of everyone's job. On the longer flights I sometimes took turns with other crew members in their various positions in the aircraft. I would relieve the navigator, the wireless operator, the engineer or gunner in an attempt to acquire a general, though clearly not detailed, understanding of their jobs by first hand experience. It paid off in my getting to know what was or was not practicable and also in terms of gaining the crew's confidence.

Although I thought at the time that I'd established a reasonably friendly working relationship with them, I have since wondered whether my outwardly serious nature created the wrong impression. It certainly surprised me to learn recently that several of them believed me to be much older than they were, while in fact I was one of the youngest members of the crew. Terry told me jokingly that he wouldn't have flown with me if he'd known that in advance!

For some curious reason, and this is not in any way a criticism of our mechanics on the Coast, I did not expect to have any engine trouble on my skipper's course. Such naïvety was impossible to explain. We were flying the same type of aircraft, the Mk III, so why it should have behaved any differently in Ireland is hard to imagine. In the event, there were at least four occasions when we had to return early from an exercise due to engine trouble. In two of them, the problem arose immediately after take-off and we landed again within half an hour. In the others, we stayed in the air for an hour and a half and two hours.

Several of the instructors, including F/Lts R A Brown and L Silburn DFC, had served on 204 squadron when I was there. I learned from one of them that the day after I left Freetown on the sloop, F/O D Pearson had a blowout in one of the cylinders of his port outer engine when taking off in M204. He had to make a forced landing immediately in Freetown harbour and he made such a good job of it that he was commended by the AOC.

I also found out that towards the end of my tour on the Coast, the boffins in the UK had suggested that the introduction of planned maintenance would improve the reliability of our aircraft. The theory was that engine performance, etc would be continuously monitored and breakdowns anticipated. If any components were suspect, they would be changed before they caused any real problems. This would not only improve safety but also give crews greater confidence in their machines. At the time that we were asked to implement this policy, our squadron serviceability, which had been running for some time at between 50 and 60%, had reached a record high of nearly 70%. Soon after the change to planned maintenance was made, it dropped to just over 40%!

Some unhappy news which reached me from someone newly returned from Freetown was that Tony Staffiere, who had taken G204 to Bathurst for an overhaul two days before I left, had crashed there on 13 July with the loss of the entire crew. Six of them had been members of the crew which I'd joined two months earlier for the flight with the AOC. This was the second 204 squadron boat with the designation G to be written off dramatically in the space of nine months or so. The superstitious would have said that there was a jinx on G204. The information set me back on my heels and I fell to making assumptions as to the reasons for the mishap. I was convinced that the aircraft must have had engine trouble, remembering the problems that we'd had with her when I flew with Tony a few weeks earlier. No other possibility had occurred to me. Thirty-nine years passed before I found out what really happened.

The squadron records revealed that the boat had been taking off on a long range A/S patrol from Bathurst. There was a heavy swell running, creating difficult conditions. As a wing dropped, the float was ripped off and the mainplane was quickly awash. When the crew tried to escape and right the aircraft by scrambling out onto the other wing, the depth charges exploded. This shattering news made a deep impression on me.

Chapter 18

One of our operational flight exercises from Killadeas was scheduled to be a night patrol over the Atlantic. Three Sunderlands and two Catalinas were airborne on similar tasks. The conditions for take-off from Lough Erne were calm, but the weather forecast promised a front eventually moving into the area from the west. We were briefed to carry out as much of the sortie as we could; when we encountered the front we were to return to base. Moderate winds and a ceiling of over one thousand feet were expected.

Our initial course took us out over Donegal Bay and we hugged the coast past Sligo Bay and Downpatrick Head. To stay below cloud, we had to keep losing height until we were flying at about seven hundred feet. Although it was a dark night, it surprised me to be able to see spume blowing off the crests of the waves.

"This is no moderate wind," I said to Graham, who was craning his neck out of the second pilot's window. "I'd say a gale's blowing up. Have you been able to check it, Dave?"

"It's certainly changed and freshened, skipper. Reckon it's backed to two-thirty degrees. Must be about forty knots..."

"I wasn't expecting anything quite like this, were you?"

"No, skip. We've been given some duff gen."

"Forty knots? That's about force 7 or 8. If that's not a gale, I don't know what is."

The ride was far from comfortable. It was now raining heavily, the air had become turbulent and the aircraft was being heaved about in all directions. Another half-hour of this and I decided it was time to pack it in. I looked at Graham. "It's no good going any further in these conditions, is it?"

"Shouldn't think so. Looks as though we've hit the front already."

At that moment, Reg Mansfield reported that he'd picked up a message from another Sunderland whose skipper had decided to return to base.

"Wise man... We'll do the same. Let them know we're aborting the exercise, Reg. Course for base, please, Dave."

After about twenty minutes on a new easterly heading, the navigator came up on the intercom again.

"Things have gone completely mad, skip. We've been blown way up north of Ireland. Your course is one-seven-five, confirm one-seven- five."

"OK, one-seven-five it is, but I just don't believe it!" I glanced across at Graham, who looked equally puzzled.

"True enough," Dave confirmed. "I've made a radio check. The wind's southerly now and I reckon it's well over forty-five knots, gusting to fifty-five at least."

I started worrying about the height of the land that we had to avoid on the way home. "What height do we need to get over the hills?"

"Highest peak I can see on the map is about seven-fifty. Reckon a thousand will be OK."

"Just as I thought. We'll be in bloody cloud again." I climbed to a thousand feet and confirmed my course, height and airspeed with the navigator.

The intercom clicked on again as the wireless operator reported "F/O Hallisey's kite's in trouble, skipper. Something to do with the exactors."

"Poor old Denis. What a time to get exactor trouble. Ask base to give him landing priority. We'll go in later."

"They've already told him he's first in the queue. They're actually talking him down now."

Our progress was painfully slow. We were struggling directly into wind and our speed over the ground was only about half what the airspeed indicator was telling us. Visibility was nil and I had to concentrate very hard on the instruments. Eventually base made contact to the effect that they were about to start the approach procedure. They gave us a course to fly and made several adjustments to it until, after what seemed an interminable time, we passed slowly over the Lough.

Still in cloud, we were unable to check our position visually. We had to put our trust in the stalwarts on the ground. I began to wish we were down there with them. They instructed us to continue for some miles beyond base on a southerly heading and then turned us on to the downwind leg as part of our normal circuit. With the wind behind us, we found ourselves back over base again in no time at all and were told to begin the descent, turning to port on to the approach heading. We broke cloud at six hundred feet and there in front of us was the flare-path.

"Thank you...visual contact now." I began to carry out a standard powered approach.

"One thing about it," said Graham, "the touchdown speed won't be too great in this wind..."

My eyes were locked on the flare-path ahead of us. We seemed to be hanging in the air, our progress towards the alighting area being astonishingly slow. All the time the boat was being buffeted about and seemed to be unresponsive to the controls. I wasn't looking forward to the touchdown. Although fairly sheltered by hills to the south, the Lough looked pretty angry. The only consolation was that it wasn't the open sea. The real danger was sudden gusting on the point of touchdown and immediately afterwards.

The flares kept disappearing in the troughs of the waves. The turbulence wasn't abating; we were still lurching erratically in all directions. Rain was hammering against the cabin windows, greatly reducing visibility and making landing prospects even more hazardous.

I juggled with the throttles to control our descent, briefly thinking of

Denis Hallisey. I didn't envy him having to make his landing with the added complication of faulty engine controls. He would be having problems manipulating the throttles, making a powered approach extremely difficult.

Our aircraft was now tossing about so much that I realized that a safe touchdown was not simply dependent on my skill, but also a matter of luck. Should the big boat lurch at the critical moment of touching the water, who knows what would happen? I was mesmerized by the spume which I could see in the feeble light from the flares and kept telling myself that I must not be distracted. I must concentrate...

Then suddenly the waves came up and hit the bottom of the hull with a resounding smack. I wasn't expecting to connect so soon. The aircraft bounced as I struggled to keep her going straight and to hold her wings level. As she made contact again I eased back on the throttles. The waves threw the boat off once more and she shuddered as she dropped into a trough. This time the bows dug into a huge wave and I pulled back on the control column trying to keep the hull level.

Thanks to the strong wind, the boat rapidly lost way, as Graham had predicted. Before long she was actually moving backwards, heaving about in the rough water and threatening to shed her floats, which were visibly vibrating. She hadn't even reached the second flare. I was almost powerless to control her in these conditions. Opening the outer engines, I made for the trots. As the bow rose and fell, columns of water splashed up over it and I wondered how Reg Smith and George Torobzoff would get on when they wound the front turret back for the mooring up operation. It was normally open by now. They were obviously putting off the evil moment.

The strong wind helped me in making the final approach to the buoy, since in these conditions it was easy to stop the aircraft dead to order. There was no need to use the drogues. Terry has since told me that he and Benny, on duty in the galley, would have been hesitant about releasing them anyway, due to the power of the waves "piling past the hatches". The drogues could easily have been ripped from their mountings.

The men in the bows had a hair-raising time, first of all getting swamped by the waves breaking over the hull as they wound back the turret. It was a miracle that we didn't sink, because in a very short space of time we shipped a considerable volume of water through the open turret hatch and into the bilges. When Reg and George tried to moor up, the aircraft and the buoy kept swinging up and down in the water, tantalizingly moving in opposite directions. After several minutes of such fun and games, the boat was finally secured, the bilges were pumped out and the crew had only to brave the journey back to the shore in a tossing dinghy. On the way, we identified Denis Hallisey's aircraft at her moorings and breathed a sigh of relief that he and his crew were down safely.

For some reason, Paddy was not flying with us on this eventful trip. He was in his home town at the time and in conversation with some of the locals he learned that one of the aircraft airborne that night had only just cleared a 600 foot hill to the south of the Lough. We shall never know which aircraft it was!

I was feeling unsteady on my feet and was not sorry to be on dry land again. Terry recently mentioned that his map of the area bore the legend "Lough becomes rough in strong winds", something of an understatement for the night in question. We all agreed that it had been a most uncomfortable trip and we were anxious about the safety of the other aircraft caught out in these conditions, especially the Catalinas. They would have found things particularly difficult, because their cruising speed was little more than ninety knots. The Ops Room reported that four out of five of the boats were down. The pilot of one of the Cats, unable to make progress against the wind, decided to make for Sullom Voe in the Shetlands, where he landed safely.

The other Catalina skipper was the Hon. Colin Buckmaster, who has recently confirmed the appalling conditions of that night. He recalls the "strange, almost yellowish colour" of the sky as he made his way out across Donegal Bay. Very soon the wind freshened and raindrops began to smear the windscreen. Conditions rapidly deteriorated and over the next two hours the turbulence increased and the rain became heavier. He was fascinated by the phosphorescent glow of the water as it broke on the tops of the enormous swell, to the extent that he gradually lost height until he was in danger of hitting the sea. He suddenly realized that in flying from a high to a low pressure area his barometric altimeter was giving him a falsely high reading. Happily he was able to take swift action to avert disaster.

By this time he and his crew hadn't the faintest idea where they were. To add to their trauma, "water had got into the W/T set, the radar, the loop aerial and we were totally and utterly lost in the centre of a storm which, even by North Atlantic standards, was of an extraordinary ferocity." Colin decided to fly back and forth, west and east, until daylight, when he hoped to be able to fix his position. With only four hours fuel left, the prospect looked grim. Then someone called out that he could see a light, which turned out to be from Belleek, situated between the Bay and the Lough. Shortly afterwards, they landed safely at base. Their flight time had been nine hours and forty-five minutes. Those on the ground who had waited anxiously for the Catalina's return (we in our Sunderland had only been airborne for four and a half hours) were more or less resigned to their having crashed into the hills.

My stay at 131(c) OTU at Killadeas was on the whole very agreeable. I recently discovered that two pages of the unit's operational records for the period were headed Killadead, but concluded this was a genuine typing error and not to be taken seriously. The friendships developed there were most enjoyable, if transitory. The majority of my colleagues were to be like ships that pass in the night and I regret not having renewed acquaintances after the war.

When I had completed my training in Northern Ireland I was given over two weeks leave. I lost no time in making my way to Glasgow and another reunion with Mary. This time I was determined to put our engagement on the agenda if at all possible. We decided to go down to the south coast together to stay at my home for a few days and we set off on what was to be a most tedious and uncomfortable train journey. The weather was atrocious, trains were packed and we had to wait for hours on bleak railway stations for our connections. This was par for the course in wartime Britain. In the mood we were in, however, we were prepared to go through anything just to be together.

In both our family camps there were mixed feelings about our wish to get married, not because we were in any way considered unsuited to each other, but because we were seen to be rushing into things before we'd had the opportunity to spend much time together. We believed that through our letters we'd got to know each other extremely well and were mature enough to be able to make the decision ourselves. Becoming unofficially engaged in Weymouth, we then returned to Glasgow, bracing ourselves for the final hurdle.

The Old Man, as Mary's father was affectionately known throughout the family, was concerned about the hurry and wanted to know why it couldn't wait until the end of the war. We said we didn't know when that would be, because the war in Europe was not yet over and then the Japs had to be defeated. At first he was worried about the risk of his daughter becoming a war widow at a tender age and then he asked me about my post-war prospects.

Having anticipated this question, I was able to tell him that I hoped to get a permanent commission. His next question was quite unexpected. Did I think Mary would like that sort of life? I didn't really know the answer to that one, although I had a sneaking feeling that it was in the negative. Indeed, I wasn't sure that it was the kind of life I wanted for her.

Gradually he seemed to come to terms with the idea of our getting married, because he asked me when we were planning that this event should take place. I said that it couldn't be for some time, since I was expecting to go abroad again and the last time I did so it was for twelve months. He digested this information for an interminable minute and then announced, "Very well, it can be when you come back from overseas."

Chapter 19

After completing their courses in Northern Ireland, crews went to RAF Alness, Scotland, commanded by Group Captain D M Gordon, to learn about and practise a new technique for attacking submarines at night. The difficulties experienced by flying boats in tackling U-boats in darkness were worrying us all and the advent of the radio altimeter enabled a new approach to the problem to be developed.

The advanced instrument depended upon bouncing a radio signal off the water, or whatever the boat was passing over, and measuring the time it took to be reflected back again. Since the speed of travel of the signal was known, the distance of travel was readily computed. This distance represented the aircraft's height above the water or ground.

The calculation was instantaneous, so could be read off the altimeter dial directly as in the barometric version. The accuracy of the latter, however, was seriously affected by (often unknown) changes in sea level pressure. Since the radio altimeter did not suffer from this disadvantage, it was now possible to fly blind much closer to the water with reasonable safety.

The chances of being able to surprise a U-boat on the surface were greatly increased. The remaining problem was being able to see the target clearly enough when the aircraft arrived over it, so that a successful attack could be made. This was overcome by installing in the after compartment a flare chute through which a succession of small flares could be released.

A buoy in the Moray Firth was used as our target for training purposes. It was located by ASV and the boat then dropped down to between fifty and one hundred feet on the radio altimeter ready for the final run-in. About a thousand yards or so away from the target, a crew member pumped small flares into the chute as fast as he could to provide illumination for the strike, which was then made as if in daylight.

A good deal of skill was needed in getting the timing just right but, thanks to the new altimeter, crews felt more confident about not ending up in the drink trying to fly too low. When I first started to practise this technique, there was an undetected low bank of stratus cloud over the target area. As the flares flooded it with a brilliant white light, a huge outline of an aircraft appeared on the cloud above us. Instinctively taking evasive action, I discovered to my embarrassment that I was looking at a silhouette of our own boat.

Life on the camp, which was on the northern shore of the Cromarty Firth, was cheerless. It was winter time and a thick blanket of snow covered everything. The crews lived in Nissen huts and, as a more pleasant alternative to spending their free time sitting around their coke stoves shivering, they attended dances in Alness and frequented a friendly café in Dingwall.

There was no real incentive to explore the surrounding countryside in this weather, attractive as it might have been in warmer seasons.

Graham was like a cat on hot bricks and was impatient to do something, although he wasn't really sure what. One day he decided to amuse himself making what he hoped would be a working model of a flying bomb. Gathering together some odd pieces of dural, he fashioned something which looked vaguely like a flying bomb and filled the tube along the top with powder from a Very cartridge. The model was duly set up on an improvised ramp outside the hut and Graham announced to the crew that he was about to launch it.

We congregated outside to witness the great event. Graham made sure that no one was in the line of fire, lit the fuse and then retired to a safe distance. There was a dramatic *whoosh* as the gunpowder flashed and clouds of smoke rose from the model. The tube containing the propellant slowly melted and drooped wearily like the end of a burning match. The bomb did not move an inch.

"I'll bet none of Hitler's do that," taunted Paddy.

"Well," Graham retorted with a grin, "he's got slightly better facilities at his disposal, hasn't he?"

As recorded earlier, I was to meet Johnny Johnston again briefly soon after my arrival at Alness. He was busily carrying out operational flights from the Cromarty Firth and on his last mission he developed engine trouble soon after take-off and radioed that he was returning to base. He crashed and the DCs went up. No one survived. There was speculation among the other crews that his control surfaces froze up as he tried to land in the extreme weather conditions, but to my knowledge there was no evidence to support this.

Some good news reached us before we left the Alness unit. The RAF had taken delivery of the first batch of the long-awaited advanced version of the Sunderland. It promised to be more reliable and more lethal...to the enemy, that is. The Mk V (*see plates* 33 and 35) was equipped with four Pratt and Whitney Twin Wasp 1830-90B 1200hp engines, a great improvement on the existing Pegasus units. The Hydromatic propellers could be feathered in an emergency and could thus be prevented from windmilling in flight.

The armaments were also greatly improved. In addition to the .303 Brownings in front and rear turrets, there were two free .5 Brownings in the waist hatches. Numbers 10 and 461 squadrons RAAF had been experimenting with swivel-mounted K-guns in the galley hatches and four fixed pilot-operated Brownings in the bows. The latter installation became standard in the Mk V (*see appendix* A). This devastating additional firepower could be brought to bear on the target as the pilot lined up his aircraft for a DC attack.

The ASV had at last been uprated, the new boat being equipped with the equivalent of H2S used by Bomber Command. The latter had always contended that it could do more damage than Coastal Command to Hitler's

U-boat fleet by bombing its shipyards and component factories. It therefore demanded higher priority for the new centimetric radar and, sadly for Coastal Command, got it. Although some later Mk IIIs were fitted with it (*see plate* 36), it came much too late for us. Had we been equipped with it in West Africa, our success in intercepting U-boats might have been greatly enhanced.

The display on the Mk VIC radar was on a planned position indicator (PPI) which had a trace scanning through 360 degrees. When a signal was received from a target, a luminescent response appeared on the screen as the trace passed over it. The response retained its luminosity briefly, being reinforced when the trace scanned it again one revolution (two seconds) later. The result was that the screen resembled an illuminated map, all land masses, ships, aircraft, etc within the equipment's range showing up very clearly in their true positions relative to the aircraft.

The PPI display provided much more detailed information and enabled more accurate bearings and distances to be read directly from the screen. The equipment also suffered less from the swamping of signals by unwanted responses, or noise, as had been a problem with earlier types of radar. The scanning of the area through 360 degrees was made possible by the use of constantly rotating directional aerials (scanners) housed in blisters under the wing-tips (*see plate* 35).

We were introduced to the Mk V at 302 FTU Oban, where we had to undergo a short conversion course. I thought the new aircraft was superb. When the throttles were opened, I felt as though I was being kicked in the back and the general feeling of power was incredible compared with earlier versions. There were greater revelations to come. Charlie Nears (now Warrant Officer) and I were airborne with F/Lt Peter Moffatt for an hour and a half, learning about the new features. The next month was spent getting used to the aircraft, swinging the compasses and the loop aerial and generally preparing the boat for delivery to a squadron.

The value of being able to feather the propellers was ably demonstrated to us on the brief flight with Peter. First of all, he shut down the port inner engine after stopping the propeller. Straight and level flight at about 112 knots was easily maintained by operating the other three engines at maximum continuous weak mixture power and adjusting the aircraft's trim.

"Incredible."

"You haven't seen anything yet." He stopped the port outer engine. The aircraft yawed appreciably this time as it lost all its power on one side, but it settled down again when Peter put on full rudder trim and increased power on the other two engines. We were still maintaining height at over 112 knots with maximum climbing power. "If you've lost all your power on the port side like this, you need to apply a lot of rudder in addition to maximum trim to keep her going straight. This shouldn't be as pronounced if the power loss is on the starboard side."

"I just don't believe it. She wouldn't do this with a full load."

"Hardly, but she'd cope all right up to 50,000 lbs. You can in fact get by on one for a short time if you've only got a light load, but you won't find that in the handbook!"

Peter also gave us a practical demonstration of evasive action during a simulated submarine attack. This required violent manoeuvres in a mad twisting dash down to the prescribed 50 feet attack altitude. Although our own exercise went off without incident, he has since told me that when going through the same procedures with two other pilots later that day, the manoeuvres almost resulted in disaster. At times they were so violent that the engines kept cutting out due to the fact that the small quantity of fuel being carried was swilling about in the tanks.

On the same flight "...the flap over the control locks (behind the pilots' seats) had not been shut and in the wild excitement of the attack a Verey cartridge fell out of its rack, rolled over the floor and fell into the control locks and jammed them! Fortunately the cause of the jammed controls was quickly realised and the Verey cartridge was freed using the fire axe before we hurled ourselves into the Firth of Lorne!" Peter reminded me that the fire axe "...had many uses, from opening the baked beans to sharpening the navigator's pencil, but none more useful than this one!"

I found the demonstration of the new engines both impressive and encouraging and I could see from the expressions on the faces of the other members of the crew, particularly the engineer, that they agreed. What an asset this would have proved if it had been available to us earlier. Much anguish would have been avoided and our efforts would have been a good deal more effective. This was an oft-repeated cry from all branches of the services starved of up-to-date equipment during the war. It was a constant battle to keep ahead of the enemy on technical developments and to provide new equipment in sufficient quantity to meet the needs. It is sad to reflect that the peak of such human ingenuity and enterprise seems to be reserved for man's self-destruction.

Another great attraction of my being at Oban was that it was within reasonably easy striking distance of Glasgow by train. Because of RAF commitments I was unable to go there myself, but one weekend when Mary had the Saturday off from work she came to Oban. She arrived on the afternoon train when we were airborne on a local flight. We escorted the train into the station by circling above it. When Mary was installed in her hotel overlooking the harbour, she watched us flying low over the town and landing among the vessels in the sheltered sound between Oban and Kerrara Island.

We were itching to take this new boat on ops, but we learned that we were shortly to ferry it out to 209 squadron based at Mombasa, East Africa. In the interests of security, of course, we had to keep this information to ourselves. Although Mary knew that we were about to go overseas, she was not aware that we would soon be back again. I couldn't wait to see how the OM would react when I returned unexpectedly early from my overseas 'tour', demanding to take the hand of his daughter in marriage as agreed only a few weeks ago!

The weather at Oban in early March 1945 did not favour a full-load take-off for several days. The harbour was surrounded by high ground, making it risky to attempt a take-off when the cloud base was low and visibility poor. The RAF would not have wanted this brand new weapon written off before it was able to prove itself on operations.

The delays really got me down and I became exceedingly irritable. My forthcoming marriage became a preoccupation, seeming to overshadow everything else. I thought of the crews in Africa who needed these boats to continue their fight against the Japanese. I was getting my priorities confused again.

At last the weather cleared. On 15 March, we were airborne for Gib at first light. Although over three hundred miles longer than my previous flight to the Rock, the trip only took about half an hour more, thanks mainly to favourable winds. One of the engines started to play up on the last leg of the journey and we found ourselves adopting an almost complacent attitude towards it. After all, we were confident now that we could manage perfectly well on three engines, if necessary. However, the repairs took some time and resulted in our spending two extra days at Gib.

During this time Frank, a stickler for keeping the boat shipshape, became very annoyed with the gulls which took a liking to it and smothered it with their droppings. He climbed out onto the mainplane with a stiff broom and a bucket of water and set about scrubbing it down. The rest of us were highly amused. "Don't be daft, Frank," mocked Reg Smith, "those birds are just waiting for you to finish and they'll be back to cover up your good work again."

Nothing daunted, the engineer finished the job, leaving an expanse of immaculately clean wing. As he re-entered the aircraft, the raucous screams of dozens of gulls proclaimed their return and Reg's prophecy was fulfilled.

Chapter 20

The next leg of our journey was across the Mediterranean to Sicily. By this time, the war in Europe was as good as over, the Allies being poised for the final assault on Berlin. This did not mean that there was no longer any chance of coming across enemy U-boats or aircraft. They were certainly still at large and had we been able to make contact with them we would have expected them to give a good account of themselves. In general, German morale was known to be at a low ebb, but there were some indomitable optimists among their airmen and U-boat commanders who were still eager to continue the fight. We therefore had to remain vigilant although, since we were only on a transit flight, the atmosphere on board was almost as if we were going on leave.

As it turned out, we were to see nothing. When we eventually flew over Sicily, we recalled that the Allied troops had landed there less than two years earlier, but there was no longer any evidence of this from the air. Going ashore at Augusta on the east coast, within sight of Mount Etna, we became more aware that this island had been caught up in the war. The town looked derelict and the inhabitants demoralized. People approached us for cigarettes and other commodities in short supply there, offering local wines and other drinks for barter. "I wish I'd known about this before," groaned Paddy, "I'd have stocked up with Woodbines in Gib."

After our eight and a half hour trip from Gibraltar, we refuelled and stayed the night at Augusta, setting off the following morning for Kasfareit (or Fanara) on the Great Bitter Lake in Egypt (*see plate* 37). Making a landfall north of Benghazi in Libya, we then followed the coast eastwards, at times flying very low to get a good view of the debris from the North African conflict. Over two years after El Alamein, it was still possible to see the rotting shells of tanks and other vehicles used in the desert fighting.

The day after our arrival in Egypt was spent preparing the aircraft for the following day's journey south into the Sudan. The engine repairs carried out at Gibraltar had been satisfactory, so the customary daily inspection was the only mechanical attention she needed. She was refuelled and the least reluctant crew members took on the job of cleaning her.

On the flight to Khartoum the next day we followed the course of the Suez Canal for about twenty minutes and had good views of the shipping passing through the narrow international waterway. From then on it was across country for about six hours, with occasional glimpses of the meandering River Nile. It was extremely hot and the haze restricted visibility. Much of the terrain was desert, with green vegetation confined to the fertile river banks, on which most of the settlements were clustered. On arrival at our destination, we landed on the Nile and after mooring up arranged for refuelling right away so that we'd be ready to move on early the next morning. There was no time to explore Khartoum. We turned in early to prepare ourselves for the challenges to come.

Our next port of call was Kisumu, at the eastern end of the lake of that name, which adjoined Lake Victoria. There was more desert in the first part of the trip, but as we moved further south this gave way to savanna and forest. Since most of Uganda was at an altitude of between three and five thousand feet, we had to fly above this and were glad to get some respite from the excessive heat. The lake itself was over three thousand feet above sea level so that we did not have far to let down for the landing.

Kisumu is on the equator and this was certainly evident when we went ashore there. It was oppressively hot, dry and airless. Once again we busied ourselves with the necessary preparations for an early take-off the following day. There was no real encouragement to stay in Kisumu when within a few hours we could be enjoying the sea breezes on the coast.

I'd been looking forward to the last leg of the trip to Mombasa, but it did not quite work out as expected. The take-off from Lake Kisumu was itself something of a novelty for us. At over three thousand feet up the engines, equipped with single speed superchargers, would not develop their full power in the rarefied atmosphere.

An added problem was that the flat calm conditions hampered the take-off, which was laboured and proved longer than we'd become used to in the Mk V. This time, however, a few seconds with the throttles through the gate did the trick. I was grateful for the increased power of the Twin Wasps and wondered how many attempts the earlier versions of Sunderland would have had to make in these conditions.

The greater part of the flight was to be over the Kenyan plateau, which varied in height from about three to over six thousand feet above sea level along our proposed track. On either side of us there would be isolated peaks, several of which reached over 8000 feet. Mount Kilimanjaro, rising to 19,340 feet, was expected to be at a safe distance to the south of our route. Dave wanted to know what our ceiling was and since I wasn't sure, I put the aircraft into a climb until it was only just able to maintain a cruising speed of 115 knots with the throttles right through the gate. The barometric instrument registered fourteen thousand feet.

I was told that we'd be all right if we stayed on track, but we couldn't afford to stray too far from it. There were no suitable radio aids in the area so we relied entirely on dead reckoning navigation. This meant that we needed to see the ground, firstly to measure drift and so calculate the course to fly and secondly to take visual fixes periodically to check our actual position. For the first twenty minutes or so we were able to do just that and Dave reported that we were on track. Then we flew into cloud and all visual contact disappeared.

I hoped that we'd not be in this situation for too long. The very presence of cloud after a relatively clear sky could mean a movement in the weather pattern, with a possible change in wind direction. We no longer had any means of finding out if the wind had veered or backed, or if it had increased or decreased in strength. We needed to be able to check it soon to be sure that we were not deviating from our track.

I asked the navigator if he was confident that he knew our exact position. He'd checked it just before this happened, but couldn't guarantee that the wind hadn't changed since then. I wanted to get below the cloud so that we could confirm our position. Dave thought that we could go down to ten thousand feet in reasonable safety for not longer than fifteen minutes.

After taking George out, I throttled back for the descent and concentrated hard on keeping the boat on course. The turbulence made this a little difficult, but I was conscious of the importance of not wandering from our intended heading. Not being absolutely sure of our position, we did not know how much scope we had for varying our course or our height.

We levelled out at ten thousand feet and were still in cloud. I swore to myself and asked the crew if anyone could see anything. Several voices chorused "No." We were no better off down here than we had been at fourteen thousand and were possibly more at risk. I raised my eyebrows at Dave who was now standing between the pilots' seats. He responded with the suggestion that we could probably go down another thousand feet, but no more.

We had to use the barometric altimeter in this situation because the radio altimeter only indicated the aircraft's height above the ground immediately below it. Neither instrument, of course, was capable of giving us any prior warning of a sudden increase in the height of the land. The ASV was also of limited value because of the misleading signals received from such varied terrain. The barometric altimeter, which in effect measured pressure, was more useful to us in establishing our actual height above sea level, provided the sea level pressure had been accurately set at the last opportunity and that it hadn't changed significantly meantime!

Before levelling out at nine thousand feet, we briefly broke cloud and saw a large bird flying straight at us. Neither aircraft nor bird had time to take evasive action and the inevitable collision occurred just outside the starboard outer engine. A hole about eight inches in diameter suddenly appeared in the leading edge of the wing. Within minutes we were in cloud again and Dave warned that we could not stay at this height with safety any longer.

As we climbed to our ceiling again, I asked if he'd managed to get a fix during the brief period that he could see the ground. He hadn't, since there had been no recognizable landmarks. He'd managed to take a drift, however, which had confirmed that things hadn't changed materially, so we could be hopeful that we were still on track. He calculated that after another fifteen minutes it would be safe to let down again.

Those fifteen minutes were an eternity. Flying through cloud over inhospitable country and not being sure how close you are to the obstacles is no picnic. The tension was clearly evident. Whenever anyone spoke it was in short, staccato bursts. I could see Graham shifting nervously in his seat, but he said nothing. We just had to keep calm and hope that Dave had got his sums right. A small error could be fatal for all of us.

At last we broke cloud again to find that the ground was now very much further below us than expected. We caught a glimpse of Kilimanjaro about ten or twelve miles away on our starboard bow. The panic was over and everyone relaxed. Tension was relieved by animated conversation. The navigator slumped onto the main spar with obvious relief.

As we circled Mombasa, we were surprised at the size of this important port and the extent of the shipping activity in its natural harbour. The town itself, built on a coral island, was joined to the mainland by a bridge. The sheltered flying boat alighting area was fringed with brilliantly green palm trees. A number of aircraft, both Catalinas and Sunderlands, were bobbing about gently at their moorings. Once we had landed, the sun beat down on us, but the sea breeze that we had looked forward to made the heat tolerable. Areas protected from the wind were uncomfortably hot.

The first thing I wanted to do when the aircraft was safely moored up was to examine the damage done by the bird. I climbed out onto the wing and lay on my stomach, hanging over the leading edge. The poor creature had gone right through the dural skin, coming to rest in a badly battered state against a spar inside the wing. Graham remarked that it was lucky the slip-stream hadn't torn the wing open like a sardine can. The damage was repaired with a patch rivetted over the hole.

We were accommodated at the camp at Port Reitz. About a mile away was the Port Reitz Hotel, which some members of the crew lost no time in locating. They walked to this welcome hostelry where they were introduced to what was, and still is, known as a John Collins; a lethal mixture of gin, brandy and angostura bitters, topped up with lime juice.

During the few days that we were at Mombasa, I made the acquaintance of Squadron Leader W E Ogle Skan who was Flight Commander of 259 squadron based at Dar-es-Salaam, 200 miles down the coast. The unit was converting from Catalinas to Sunderlands and, while we were awaiting our return to the UK, instructions came through that they were to cease training. At the end of the month (March 1945), they transferred to 209 squadron, based at that time at Mombasa. I was to meet the Squadron Leader again a year later when I spent a brief period on 209 squadron at Hong Kong and Singapore.

For the first part of the journey home to the UK, the crew flew as passengers on BOAC flying boats. A Short C-class boat, the Carpentaria, skippered by a Captain Colvin, took us as far as Kisumu. From Kisumu to Khartoum and then to Cairo, we flew with Captain R F Caspareuthus in a G-class boat, the Golden Hind. It was a new experience to travel by civil flying boat. We felt at a loose end not having to carry out our normal duties during the flight.

For some unexplained reason, the officers and NCOs were split up for the remainder of the trip home. The latter languished for a while at a transit camp at Heliopolis, where conditions were so basic that not even civilized equipment like knives, forks and spoons, or 'irons' as they were known in the RAF, were available to them. Eventually they left from Almaza Airport, Cairo, on a Dakota, calling at Castel Benito and Istres (Marseilles) en route for Hurn Airport.

Graham and I were unaware of the conditions they were suffering. For myself, I'd thought it a comedown to be told that I was going to make the rest of the trip, from Cairo to Augusta and then to Poole, Dorset, as a passenger in a Mk III Sunderland. What ignominy, after flying the Mk V!

My unexpectedly early arrival in this country caused a considerable stir in Mary's household, but her father had said that we could marry when I returned from overseas and he was true to his word. The wedding took place on 17 April, eleven days after I had landed at Poole. During the ceremony, I became a little confused when the vicar asked me to take Mary's right hand in mine. If he had said starboard, I'd have known exactly what he meant.

Chapter 21

After honeymooning in the highlands of Scotland, during which I succeeded in falling into Loch Earn fully dressed in my best blue uniform, I reluctantly returned to number 302 Ferry Training Unit. In my absence it had moved from Oban to St Angelo, which was not far from Killadeas, Northern Ireland. I therefore had much further to go to rejoin it. It was arranged for me to take the train to Stranraer and then complete the journey as a passenger in a Sunderland.

My parting with Mary at the railway station was probably one of the worst moments of my life. We'd had to accept that the first year or so of our married life was likely to be spent apart, with no opportunity even to speak to each other on the telephone. It was 7th May 1945, the eve of VE Day. The British population, tense with pent-up excitement, anticipated tomorrow's announcement of the Allied victory over Germany and the end of hostilities in Europe. Huge bonfires were lit, despite warnings that active U-boats were still operating around our coasts. People were understandably impatient to start their celebrations. No one without relatives serving in the Far East seemed to give a thought for those who still had to bring about a Japanese surrender. Although it was not known for certain, the Far East was where I expected to end up. I couldn't imagine that all this training would not be turned to good account.

It was a miserable journey to Stranraer. The thought of not seeing or hearing my wife for the next year or possibly more was intolerable. I toyed with all kinds of solution to my problem, but one by one rejected them. Reporting sick would only be a temporary expedient which would simply prolong the agony. Feigning illness long enough to prevent myself from going abroad would be difficult in any event. Going absent without leave would create more problems than it would solve. I might be drummed out of the service with ignominy. What good would that do to my future? I would just have to pull myself together and press on regardless.

I boarded the flying boat at Stranraer in a daze, but the familiar surroundings and the preparations for take-off going on around me helped to take my mind off my personal problems. I asked the skipper if I could spend the trip on the flight deck as I felt a bit out of it down below. He agreed and I stood between the pilots' seats for take-off.

The wind was from the south-west, which meant that the take-off path would bring us directly over Stranraer itself. As the aircraft left the water with plenty of space to clear the town, the pilot held her down a few feet above sea level as she gathered speed towards the built-up area. My grip tightened on the seat backs as the town loomed larger and larger ahead of us. I was convinced that if the pilot didn't pull the boat up soon it would be too late. I looked briefly at his face. It bore a sadistic grin as he revelled in this foolhardy amusement.

At the very last moment, when it looked as though we were going to make a dramatic entrance into someone's front room, he hauled back on the control column and the aircraft roared over the rooftops, no doubt putting the fear of God into the people on the ground. I swore that we were within inches of the houses rather than feet. I had been exposed to all kinds of flying risk before this but had never felt quite so scared, knowing all the time that I was helpless to do anything about it.

The danger in this kind of manoeuvre was that the aircraft would tend to mush-in, continuing momentarily in the same direction due to gravity before it finally took up the flight path intended. How we avoided disaster at Stranraer I would never know. All I did know at the time was that the sooner I got off that aircraft, the better I'd be pleased.

This incident reinforced my feelings about a captain's responsibility towards the other people on board. When at the controls and able to direct the aircraft's every movement, a pilot can experience an exhilaration which might easily lead to arbitrary and reckless action. In a single-seater aircraft he only has himself and the machine to worry about, but when he carries a crew and possibly passengers, he needs to spare more than a passing thought for their safety and comfort. They're powerless to influence his behaviour and have to trust him, hoping that he's aware of the substantial weight of responsibility that rests on his shoulders. I always tried to remember to get my crew's agreement before executing manoeuvres which put their welfare or safety in jeopardy. I can't truthfully say that I always kept to this self-imposed rule, but any lapse was on my conscience for a very long time afterwards.

At the end of May we returned to Oban and a week later took delivery of a new boat. After spending nearly three weeks familiarizing ourselves with her and carrying out the necessary checks, we left Scotland for the Far East. Two members of the crew, Dave Ryan and Reg Mansfield (now Warrant Officers), were due for release from the service and did not accompany us. I was disappointed that these changes had to be made so soon after the crew had been trained so successfully together. As it turned out, only one replacement was forthcoming for the transit trip to India. F/O P N (Peter) Young joined as navigator (*see plate* 39) and he remained with me until the end of my Far East tour.

We were not happy about losing our WOM. Wireless operator mechanics had more technical training than other wireless operators. They were expected to be able to isolate faults in the equipment and repair them, provided that this did not require the use of a fully equipped workshop or sophisticated test gear. In some situations, this skill could be a valuable asset.

The first leg of the overseas trip was intended to be Gibraltar. When within two or three hours of our ETA, we received a message to say that the landing conditions were unfit due to the notorious Gibraltar swell and we were diverted to Port Lyautey in French Morocco, north-east of Rabat. There we landed and moored up in the river estuary. We were delayed a whole day awaiting clearance from Gib and two other Sunderlands flew in from the UK.

Before we set off for Gib the following day, the three captains (hopefully having conferred with their crews!) decided to beat up the beach where American servicemen were sunning themselves. Flying in tight V-formation, the three boats swept across the crowded shore at fifty feet. The leader failed to see a child's kite, which wrapped itself around the leading edge of his aircraft's wing. It was fortunate that it didn't hit one of the fans. It could have caused serious damage, if not disaster.

Augusta being the next port of call, several of the crew could not resist the temptation to buy cigarettes in Gib to barter for drink in Sicily. The drink, which included the island's speciality Marsala, was stored in the bilges to keep it cool. We were looking forward to having a party when we reached our final destination.

The following day, we were flying along the North African coast and were about halfway to Kasfareit when the unpleasant smell of overheating electrical insulation reached me. "Something's burning, Graham. Go and find out what's happening." The second pilot unplugged his intercom and disappeared aft, returning shortly to report that the long-range radio wasn't working. During their investigation, Benny and Terry had discovered that the accumulators were flat, so they'd disconnected the leads and coupled them up to the spare bank of batteries. This gave rise to a nice display of arcing, but didn't cure the real problem. The radio equipment's power supply had failed.

"Well, can they do anything about it?"

"'Fraid not. It's put an end to any further radio contact with anyone."

I got him to relieve me at the controls while I went aft to see what damage had been done. The power supply unit was burnt out, but mercifully nothing else appeared to be seriously affected.

"What's the score?" I called out to the rear end of a wireless operator.

A red-faced Benny emerged from under his desk to confirm that "The only damage seems to be to the power pack, but without a supply we can't operate the radio any more." He looked pleased at the prospect of not having to work for the rest of the trip.

"What does Kasfareit know about us, Dave?"

"We sent them a message to say we were airborne at Augusta and our estimated time of arrival would be 15.15 their time. I've just had to revise the ETA to 16.03, but I haven't been able to tell them."

"So they'll start twitching when we don't show up at three fifteen after several hours' silence?"

"Probably, but there isn't much we can do, short of going back to Augusta, is there?"

"No thanks, anything but that."

When Graham, Dave and I finally entered the Ops Room at Kasfareit for debriefing, we were treated to an inquisition about what had happened to us and why we were late. The Ops Officer seemed a bit put out by our apparent inefficiency, until we were able to explain the true position to him. His anxiety turned out to be justified, because he'd been trying to contact us for about three hours to warn us of an impending sandstorm over the base. Had we not been late we would have flown right into it.

Replacement of the power supply and accumulators took some time, so we were forced to spend several days at Kasfareit. It was one of those outposts where there was very little to do and when we considered going into Ismailia to look for the high spots, it was suggested that we carried our service revolvers with us in case we were attacked. There had been reports of people being waylaid after dark by unidentified brigands who were not averse to planting knives between their shoulder blades. Despite the warnings, the NCOs hitched a lift to the RAF Maintenance Unit at Fayia, four miles south, and managed to get a few pints of the local beer and a film for Terry's Brownie camera.

After three days at Kasfareit, we took off again thankfully for Iraq, only to return two hours later with a faulty compass. The instrument was replaced and we air tested it the next day. Our second attempt to get away was successful and we set course for Habbaniya, about 50 miles due west of Baghdad.

Circling the lake there, we experienced heat which was even more intense than at Kisumu on the equator. As we taxied to our moorings, Terry and Benny made their way to the galley to take up their drogue stations. They agreed that they would soon get some fresh air through the boat when they got the galley hatches open. They were dismayed to find, on sticking their heads through the open hatches, that the blast of air that met them was "akin to a furnace".

When we'd finally moored up to our buoy, we set about refuelling. The upper surface of the mainplane was so hot that we could scarcely stand on it, even when wearing thick-soled shoes. Refuelling was hastily completed and we were glad to get ashore and have a long, cool drink in the mess. The resident officers were very amicable, though we were suspicious when they offered us dromedary sandwiches. The meat was so delicious that we did not want to show our disbelief about its source and undermine our friendship. I recalled my feelings at Port Étienne when I first discovered that the Bedouins ate camel meat.

The leg between Habbaniya and Bahrein in the Persian Gulf was not completed at first attempt. We had flown about two thirds of the way when we had a radio message from Bahrein asking if we'd ever landed there in a sandstorm. Since we hadn't had this pleasure, they wanted us to return to Habbaniya, because Bahrein was in the middle of a sandstorm and it was not known how long it would last.

We were not very happy about going all the way back to Habbaniya. Pete checked to see if there were any suitable diversion bases reasonably close to our route. There were none ahead of us, so we turned north again and made for Basra. Our information was that they were able to cater for boats as well as landplanes. On arrival, we were slightly disconcerted when instructed to land on runway two! After circling the area and pinpointing the mooring buoys and landing stage, we put down on the Shat-el-Arab river.

The Shat-el-Arab was a large waterway reminiscent of the Mississippi. Like that river, it had sizeable tributaries, notably the Tigris and the Euphrates. It was also very fast flowing and carried a good deal of silt out to the Persian Gulf. After landing as near to the buoys as possible, I made an embarrassing error of judgement. Signalling for the drogues to be deployed, I then wondered why we were drifting backwards at about five knots!

I have since learned that, while I'd been concentrating on my approach procedure, several of the crew had been watching a number of dhows being towed upstream. On the river bank, something like a hundred Arabs were pulling away on ropes to move the boats against what Benny described as "a hell of a current". He and Terry took up their positions at the galley hatches and, with serious reservations, carried out my instructions to deploy the drogues. In no time at all the cables were "humming like bow strings." Try as they might, the disillusioned wireless ops were unable to trip the drogues and they both expected the hawsers to snap.

The only way that it was possible to make any progress towards the buoy was by using the outer engines at fairly high revs and risk tearing the drogues from their mountings. As luck would have it, the worst did not in fact happen and we were able to reach the buoy without damage. I told Graham that I'd never made such a mess of mooring up before. His expression clearly conveyed the message that it was perfectly obvious what a damnfool thing it was to use drogues in an eight knot current.

Refuelling was not necessary this time, because the trip to Bahrein the following day would only take about two and a half hours and there was plenty of fuel in hand. The officers and NCOs had to part company since no officer accommodation was available in the nearby RAF camp. Graham, Pete and I were therefore put up in the Shat-el-Arab Hotel. It was here that we sampled Turkish beer and thoroughly enjoyed it, until we saw the bill next morning. At the sterling equivalent of seven shillings and sixpence for a half-pint bottle, it was a luxurious pleasure indeed.

The oppressive heat continued unabated. It was extremely difficult to find any effective means of cooling off. Terry thought that by filling a bath with cold water and then dragging it under a slowly revolving fan, he would crack the problem. In his own words "result – soaking wet and still sweating freely."

Chapter 22

The landing conditions at Bahrein had greatly improved by the time we arrived there. As we went ashore in the dinghy, the water around us seemed to be a solid mass of jellyfish. Our discomfort due to the heat was made worse by very high humidity and we were grateful that we didn't have to stay there for more than one night. We were kept awake all night by a cacophony of howling dogs throughout the island. First one started barking, then another and another, until the chorus was taken up by every dog within a radius of several miles.

I tossed and turned in my tent, unable to rest as I lay on my bed soaked in perspiration. Some of the crew found the conditions so sticky that they chose to sleep under the stars. We wished that we'd gone the whole way from Basra to India in one day. There would have been little difference in the flying time involved.

We arrived at Korangi Creek, near Karachi, the next day, 14 July, and spent two days there before taking off again for the final leg of the journey to deliver the aircraft to an operational squadron. Most of the time, when we were not refuelling or cleaning up the boat, we were resting on our charpoys or socializing in the mess. We were still having some difficulty getting accustomed to the changing climate and welcomed the opportunity to take it easy for a few hours.

We were well entertained by the residents in the officers' mess. One of the stories told was of an occasion when some of them drove into Karachi for a dinner party. On the long straight road they came upon a caravan of camels, tied head to tail and making slow progress towards the city. The driver on the leading camel was fast asleep. The RAF party stopped and turned the procession round. When the party returned to camp again after dinner, they passed it continuing in the wrong direction, the driver still asleep up front. Whether true or apocryphal, the tale was so well told it had us all in stitches.

We had been officially posted to 240 Squadron, based at Redhills Lake near Madras. Having been reformed from 212 Squadron and the Special Duty Flight of the former 240 Squadron at the beginning of July, it was busily converting to Mk V Sunderlands from Catalinas. The Officer Commanding was Wing Commander C B Gavin Robinson, the Flight Commander Squadron Leader A M Ruston and the Training Officer Squadron Leader L Hoare. Known as the Vikings, the squadron had a crest showing a Viking helmet. Its motto in Icelandic 'Sjo Vordur Lopt Vordur' meant 'Guardian of the sea, guardian of the sky'.

The boat that we'd flown out from the UK had to be delivered to 240's detachment base at Koggala in Ceylon, not far from Galle on the south-western shore of the island. It became N240 and I was to fly it again on only two other occasions several months later. The Catalinas were being taken out of service and over the next five months they were flown to the Korangi Creek scrap heap.

We accompanied F/Lt Coulson on one such trip at the end of July 1945 and it took us over sixteen hours. The same flight by Sunderland in the reverse direction ten days previously had taken less than eleven hours. The Catalina flight was the only one I remember during my RAF service on which I felt queasy. This was not due to airsickness, but to exhaust fumes from the APU which seemed to hang about in the restricted space of the fuselage for hours on end.

Just before leaving Korangi Creek for the second time, we learned that the atomic bombs had been dropped on Japan. My own feelings about this were mixed. While the prospect of an end to the war was naturally welcomed, I would have preferred that it had not happened in this way. The action was being justified on the basis that the alternative would have meant an even heavier loss of life among our own people. The carnage had to be brought to an early end.

I suddenly felt redundant, but then assured myself that there would be plenty to do before we were finished in the Far East. There would be many prisoners of war to get home for a start. I hated to think what sort of life they'd been leading in the Japanese camps.

I arrived in Madras on 10 August in Sunderland F240 captained by F/Lt J Donaghy. The NCOs spent five days and six nights travelling across the subcontinent by rail, via Hyderabad, the Sind Desert, Lahore, Delhi, Agra, Nagpur and then down the east coast to Madras. When at Lahore and Delhi they stayed overnight in transit camps, otherwise they slept on the train. Despite the roundabout route and the discomforts of the journey, they seemed to enjoy this new travelling experience.

When a new captain joined an RAF squadron, it was the custom for the Flight Commander to fly him over the area surrounding the base and acquaint him with local procedures. Three days after my arrival at Redhills Lake, Madras, the Squadron Leader took me up in M240. No doubt he also had to satisfy himself as to my skills as a pilot and captain of aircraft. By this stage I had completed a full tour as a second pilot on Sunderlands and had also flown them on training units and transit flights, clocking up a total of over a thousand flying hours on the type. I could not resist an arrogant smirk when the Flight Commander overshot the lake at first attempt and had to go round again.

Had they been present, my crew would have been greatly amused by this episode, but they had not yet arrived in Madras. They began flying with me again two days later when we air tested J240. The same night, we were airborne again with the Flight Commander for night circuits in K240, the first Sunderland to be delivered to the squadron. About this time we welcomed a new WOM, F/Sgt J (Mickie) Crowther, to the crew. He had previously flown with Charlie Nears, whom we'd last seen at Oban. I was also pleased to meet up with an old friend from training days, Cliff Short, who was now flying L240.

One of the penalties of having past experience in flying Sunderlands was that one sometimes had to assist Catalina pilots to convert to the new aircraft. We had some anxious moments at Redhills when they were practising circuits and bumps. The problem was that the hull of a Cat was considerably shallower than that of a Sunderland, so that its cabin was several feet nearer the water. Thus, when making a landing approach in the bigger aircraft it was necessary to level out from the glide much sooner than in a Catalina. Some pilots with many flying hours on the latter could not get accustomed to this and I found myself nervously taking over from them in time to prevent the boat from diving into the sea.

The poor Sunderland took quite a thrashing during training sessions. Terry Martin reminds me that the crew greatly disliked these exercises. One of the WOPs would have 'drawn the short straw' to be included in the crew for them. Terry has vivid memories of standing on the platform under the astrodome as the aircraft slewed all over the place on take off. He was always relieved when she finally got off the water. The landing would have been even more alarming as seen from the astrodome!

The squadron was responsible for weekly meteorological flights. Because of the long range of our aircraft, it was possible for us to observe and record weather conditions over a very wide area. This met data was of vital importance both to our shipping and to our own aircraft. Obtaining it was, however, a very tedious duty and these first trips did not give us much encouragement. We were introduced to the activity by S/Ldr Ruston, who flew with us on two occasions, once in K240 and then in L240. Ironically, we had poor weather conditions throughout the first flight, which lasted twelve hours. The cloud base was low, the visibility limited and the sea rough enough to make a safe landing, if needed, well nigh impossible. On the second trip, the port inner engine sprang an oil leak. As we were several hundred miles out into the Indian Ocean at the time, I was grateful that we were not flying a Mk III. We had our first real experience of feathering a propeller of necessity and completing the flight on three engines without too much embarrassment.

Round about this time, F/Lts J Cowle and J Donaghy had a backfiring starboard inner engine in A240 and had to cut it and feather the prop. They radioed to base that they were prepared to carry on with their assignment for a further four hours until a relief was sent. How times had changed.

Needless to say, losing an engine was not entirely without problems. As previously mentioned, the dangers of being unable to stay airborne with reduced power had been virtually eliminated in the Mk V, but there were other complications. Most of the aircraft's main services were provided by the inner engines. They each drove a 1500 watt, 24 volt generator, which charged the accumulators and also supplied power to such electrically driven equipment as engine starters and fuel pumps, automatic controls, radio, lighting and instrumentation. The port inner was also fitted with a vacuum pump for the wing de-icing system and the starboard inner drove one of the three hydraulic pumps which operated the gun turrets. Two other such pumps were driven by the outer engines, which at the same time provided the power for vacuum pumps to operate the blind flying instruments. Thus failure of any engine involved the loss of one or more of these services.

Although the war in the Far East was theoretically at an end, we were warned to be on our guard against possible attack by the Japanese. Their forces were still well distributed across South East Asian territory and it was on the cards that some, particularly those in the more isolated islands, might not have heard of the cease fire. We were therefore rather tentative about removing our armaments. The .303 guns were taken out, but we retained the .5s in case we at any time needed to protect ourselves.

The Special Duty Flight, under the command of S/Ldr J C Parry DFC, dropped agents and freight by parachute in certain remote areas of Malaya, Siam, Indo-China and the Andaman Islands. The remainder of our aircraft were used for reconnaissance of occupied or recently yielded territory, for delivering urgent supplies to Singapore and for returning prisoners of war who were being repatriated.

Detachment bases were opened up at Rangoon and Penang (*see plate* 38) and a regular courier service was set up between Madras, Koggala, Penang and Singapore. The air-sea rescue service was, of course, continued both by Sunderlands and Catalinas. On one such flight, a Catalina sent out in search of a missing Dakota discovered after several hours in the air that the latter had never taken off.

September 1945 was a memorable month. The enemy formally surrendered in Tokyo on the second and the Allied victory was celebrated. Our squadron had already had a Victory Parade in Madras on 20 August. Everyone was given two days leave and several activities were organized. Among these was a football match between numbers 230 and 240 Squadrons. We won 2-0. Fortunately for 240 I had not been asked to play or the result might have been very different.

Our crew took over D240 which was named Odin from Scandinavian mythology. We became particularly attached to her, because she virtually remained ours for the rest of our tour. Indeed, I took her with me when I transferred to 209 Squadron the following April. The name Odin seemed somewhat enigmatic in describing our much-loved aircraft. I could come to terms with the idea of a supreme god and creator and, of course, the god of victory. The god of the dead, represented as an old, one-eyed man, albeit of great wisdom, did not fit! I always thought of her as a boat rather than an aircraft, entitled to be treated as a member of the opposite sex. She was therefore never referred to as Odin – although the more favourable features of that style were naturally assumed – but simply as 'D'.

Early in September, we flew her to Rangoon on detachment, landing and mooring the aircraft on the Pegu River at a village called Syriam (*see plate 40*), the site of an oil refinery. The buildings in which we were housed ashore were substantially made and still intact, but they had been completely ransacked by the retreating Japanese. The plumbing had been wrecked and all that was left of the electrical installations were bare wires hanging from the ceilings and protruding from walls. Lighting for us was strictly by candles. Bath tubs had not been removed, but the means of getting water into them had to be improvized. We rigged up sheets of corrugated iron so that they deflected the rain water from the roof. Bath day was thus reserved for when it rained and then there was a mad rush to get one's bath in before the rain stopped.

These problems did not trouble us unduly. In fact, we really enjoyed our detachments at Syriam. The RAF's restoration of normal services began with the officers' mess and the bar, so I felt that they were getting their priorities right. The NCOs, after several nights ashore, were so disenchanted with the sergeants' mess tariff, which was mainly M & V (canned meat and vegetables), that they decided to sleep on board.

They traded with the locals, offering M & V etc in exchange for eggs and other commodities, and prepared their own breakfasts in the galley. Drinking water, which was obtained from the camp, was doctored with purifying tablets when they wanted to brew up. For washing and shaving, dirty brown river water was collected in a bucket trawled from the galley hatch. The unsavoury liquid was liberally laced with Dettol before use.

There were one or two anxious moments when the river was running at six or seven knots. A considerable quantity of debris raced past the boat as she swung heavily from side to side, threatening to break her moorings. Terry Martin slept on one of the after bunks, above which a canvas cover had been rigged to prevent water dripping on him from a leaking mid-upper turret fairing. The cover soon sagged with the weight of water collected and had to be regularly emptied.

Our first operational flight from Burma was to Bandon Bay in the Gulf of Siam. The briefing informed us that there would be several Dakotas proceeding southwards from the Bay along the west coast of the Malayan peninsula and we were to give them ASR cover. We were airborne for over eleven hours but no contact was made. As will be described later, this was to be the first of a number of abortive flights to this area, in which we had been asked to provide other aircraft with some support.

Two days after the frustrations of the above trip, we were carrying out an air test from Rangoon when we quite unexpectedly came across a crashed Spitfire some miles inland. We'd received no information that one was missing, so the encounter was purely by chance. The pilot was safe and we were able to relay his position to base. We also dropped cigarettes to him. It was fortuitous that we spotted him when we did, because he no doubt got back to his unit very much quicker than he would otherwise have done.

Chapter 23

On the evening of 16 September 1945, Graham, Peter and I were having a drink in the mess at Syriam after a satisfying curry dinner. The discussion centred around the recent departure of our first-rate engineer, Frank Osborn, who was returning to the UK on release from the RAF. We were all very sorry to lose Frank but were agreed that his successor, F/Sgt R (Taff) Stapleton, was already settling in well.

A new crew member's arrival always gave rise to some apprehension, until the others got to know him and he earned their acceptance. A Sunderland crew was a closely-knit group in which everyone was expected to pull his weight. There was no room for anybody who wasn't prepared to contribute his fair share to the team's activities.

About eight o'clock, we heard a large aircraft flying very low over the camp. Rushing out into the darkness to identify it, we were only just in time to see navigation lights disappearing into the far distance. We spent some time speculating as to what it might be, since none of our own aircraft was airborne and we were not expecting any from Redhills. We returned to our drinks and a couple of hours or so later turned in, the mystery still unsolved.

The following morning we were wakened very early. An apologetic NCO shook me into consciousness and told me there was an emergency. We had to make a dawn take-off to look for a crashed aircraft. I stirred myself, rapidly got dressed and freshened up, then joined my colleagues in the mess. A hasty breakfast disposed of, we made our way to the Ops Room for briefing.

A Liberator of 355 Squadron based at Salbani, 90 miles west of Calcutta, had carried out a supply drop over Saigon airfield in Indo-China and on its return had made a forced landing. The reason was not clear. Various D/F bearings had been given before the crash and a single fix was obtained by radar, but the results were conflicting and the crashed aircraft's position was not known with any degree of accuracy. Our scanty information suggested that it was somewhere in the coastal region of the Gulf of Martaban, an extensive area south of the Sittang estuary. The coastline here ran north-eastwards from the Rangoon River mouth.

The weather for take-off was reasonably good; wind south-westerly force two, sky overcast but ceiling at three thousand feet... Some deterioration was expected later. The wind was likely to be increasing, possibly to force five, cumulonimbus cloud building up, turbulent conditions... There was no time to lose, so we set off for our boat without delay.

It was first light when we became airborne and began the first leg of a CLA search (*see page* 65) on either side of the coastline north-eastwards from the Rangoon River. Since we were fairly certain that the crashed aircraft was the unidentified one which flew over the camp the previous evening, we felt that it was more likely to have tried to put down on land than in the Gulf. The Liberator was known not to have a particularly good reputation on water. I suggested to Pete that the search should provide equal land and sea coverage. The crew dispersed to their stations and were briefed to report anything at all that might be considered relevant. We hoped that I'd taken the right decision as to the area we should sweep and that we'd soon be in a position to see any signals that the Lib crew were able to send up.

Three hours into our search, one of the waist gunners reported what was thought to be a smoke puff when we were on the fifth south-easterly leg of our CLA. Graham, who was flying the aircraft at the time, altered course to investigate. We found nothing, so resumed our flight plan. Twenty minutes later, Reg Smith saw red Very cartridges on the port side and this time we homed successfully onto the crashed Liberator N of 355 squadron (*see plate* 43).

It had made a first-class belly landing in a paddy field two miles from the coast and had cut a long swathe through the vegetation, coming to rest facing thirty degrees to port of its original track. Five members of the crew were standing on the wing, apparently unharmed, and they were surrounded by more than fifty of the indigenous population, many of whom were crawling all over the aircraft.

A message was sent to base confirming the contact, giving the position of the wrecked aircraft and asking for instructions. While waiting for a reply, we flew low over the scene to ascertain the condition of the crew and to take photographs. A Bircham Barrel was dropped containing, among other things, medical supplies, cigarettes and a request for information about survivors (*see plate* 44). On our next run in they indicated that one of them had an injured arm.

The information was passed to base, together with a description of the surrounding country. Since the terrain was unsuitable for any type of aircraft to make a satisfactory landing and get off again, we asked permission to put down in the Gulf. After flying to the coast to inspect the condition of the sea, we returned to the Liberator to find two Beaufighters circling it. When the pilots learned that things were being taken care of, they flew off again.

The Ops Officer informed us that there was a naval motor launch (ML) due south of us, but it would only be able to patrol beyond a ten mile limit. The waters were uncharted further in and the Navy was not prepared to risk the boat in these conditions. Our charts confirmed that the waters were potentially dangerous, but I felt that we could reasonably land about ten miles out, beyond the uncharted area, and taxi in with care, taking soundings from the bows as we went. The crew were consulted over the intercom and their response was unanimously in favour. They seemed to be looking forward to the possibility of a little excitement. After training and met flights, this kind of activity would be a welcome change.

The terrain between the Liberator and the coast was hostile, much of it consisting of dense undergrowth and deep mud. Nevertheless, it was a fair assumption that, with the help of some of the Burmans, the survivors would be able to get to the coast. We dropped a message putting the proposition to them and saying that we would indicate the direction in which they should travel and would land in the sea and pick them up. They agreed without question.

We certainly didn't envy them their journey. The weather had become distinctly unpleasant, the wind having freshened as forecast. Heavy showers were becoming more frequent. We wondered whether the survivors would get bogged down in the mud, preventing them from reaching us.

Putting our plan to base, I fully expected to be refused permission to carry it out because of the unsuitable landing conditions. Instead, I was gratified to receive a reply allowing discretion. Thanking my friend in the Ops Room, who subsequently got reprimanded and posted to another unit for his pains, I told him that we were going down and would be keeping radio silence while on the water. So that he would not get in too much of a flap should he not hear from us for a long time, I promised to call him in an hour, an undertaking which, in the excitement of the moment, I failed to keep. We had little idea how long this job was going to take us and we all got so totally involved in the immediate problems that we tended to forget everything else.

A quick survey of the coastline revealed that we were not far from a small river estuary or creek. We decided that if we made for that we might be able to anchor in a moderately sheltered position to await the arrival of the survivors. Plans were made to land in the sea. It was looking pretty choppy, the air conditions were becoming slightly more turbulent and I estimated the wind to be about force four, that is up to 18 knots.

It was not difficult to assess wind direction in such conditions. When the surface of the water was sufficiently disturbed by the wind, parallel streaks of spume were clearly seen running with it. The behaviour of the waves themselves would indicate whether the wind was blowing from the direction of the streaks along which you were looking or from its reciprocal. The DR navigation should, of course, provide a check on this information.

To save time I decided not to make a normal circuit but to go straight in, once the aircraft was lined up with the streaks. The landing signal was sounded and everyone braced himself for what promised to be a rough ride. It proved not to be as bad as we'd thought, which suggested that at least there wasn't a heavy swell running – yet. We began to taxi towards the shore and the ten mile trip seemed to take an interminable time at a speed considered safe.

The riggers went on watch in the bows looking for hazards. As luck would have it, the water was remarkably clear and they claimed that they'd be able to give reasonable warning of any obstructions which might endanger the aircraft. Using an improvised plumb line – a fitter's vice at the end of a rope! – to check the depth of water from time to time, they kept the rest of us informed on the intercom of the results they were getting.

Happily, no obstructions were found. Steadily, but with increasing urgency, we progressed towards the creek. Very cartridges were fired to guide the survivors in our direction. Once in the comparative shelter of the estuary, we were quickly able to find a suitable anchorage. The riggers shackled the anchor to the anchor chain, paying it out until the flukes dug themselves firmly into the river bed. The engines were cut and everything went astonishingly quiet.

I called for four volunteers to go ashore in the dinghy to make contact with the Lib crew and get them aboard, suggesting that Graham should be in charge of the operation. Strongly built and thoroughly reliable, he was just the man to handle this situation. He jumped at the chance, seeing an opportunity for some real adventure at last. Pete, Reg and Paddy volunteered to be the other members of the landing party. Service revolvers were strapped on, the dinghy was inflated and the four set off for the shore. They took a Very pistol with them so that their position could be indicated to the Lib crew from time to time.

In the dinghy, the tensions were clearly evident. Graham was smoking like a chimney. Pete has recalled his own apprehensions as the four paddled ashore in total silence. Looking back at the flying boat, he had visions of D ending up on a sandbank because the anchor wasn't properly secured, or of her drifting out to sea because the engines wouldn't start. What if she wasn't there when they eventually got back? He imagined the shore party paddling their dinghy all the way back to Rangoon, which would have been no mean feat in adverse tidal conditions. He worried about what wildlife they might encounter, because the crew were never briefed about what to expect if they came down in unknown territory. They might even come across the odd Japanese or two who didn't yet know that 'the show was over.'

On the Sunderland, preparations were made to receive the survivors. The bunks were covered with blankets. Food and drink were got ready. It was not known in what state the men would be found. Indeed, our own landing party were to some extent at risk, so we were prepared for anything. For those of us left on board it was an anxious time (*see plate* 45).

Eventually distress signals from the Lib crew were seen. The shore party, which had been moving along the coastline awaiting a clue as to what direction inland it should take, intercepted them after forty-five minutes. They were making very slow progress and it was another hour or so before they reached the aircraft. The terrain was such that they had to board the dinghy nearly two hundred yards downstream from the anchorage and this meant paddling frantically against the current for this distance (*see plate 46*).

The shore party had all its work cut out to make any way against the tide and but for Graham's brute strength might not have succeeded. Benny Burton was on the aircraft's port wing, using the F24 camera to take photographs of the operation for the record. When Paddy realized this, he stood up in the dinghy to pose for his picture, while his companions paddled with renewed vigour.

At last the dinghy's occupants were on board, two hours after the rescue party had gone ashore. The Lib crew members consisted of F/O Tom H Blackburn (captain), P/Os Ken J F Watson (second pilot), Don H Lamb (navigator) and J Pat Winch (another pilot flying as engineer), and Sgt Jock Paris (wireless operator). Not surprisingly, they were exhausted and thoroughly dishevelled, so they were dried out, made comfortable and given hot refreshment.

We learned that they had been making for their squadron's forward base at Pegu, nearly 50 miles north of Rangoon. The radio was believed to be unserviceable, as they had not received any response to their signals. The fuel gauges showed near empty tanks and they had to fly at 50 feet to get below the cloud in order to try and obtain a visual fix. Coupled with these problems, the skipper realized that there were pagodas at Pegu rising to 300 feet. He contemplated abandoning the aircraft, but climbing high enough through the dense cloud, rising to tens of thousands of feet, in order to bail out might have resulted in their parachutes being swept upwards in strong air currents. He had visions of everyone suffering from oxygen lack and freezing to death before they reached the ground. To attempt a forced landing, albeit in the dark, seemed to be the better option.

The other wireless operator, F/Sgt Gordon Shawcross, who had dislocated his arm in an unfortunate accident with the waist hatch over the target area earlier in the flight, was not in fact in the party as expected. Nearly two hours before D arrived, he had left the crashed aircraft with the Scottish bomb-aimer P/O Jock McGowan and some native volunteers to seek medical attention. Many uncomfortable hours were spent on a river in a single-oared boat before an Indian Army Post at Thongwa was reached, from which arrangements could be made for them to be picked up. An ambulance was then summoned from 30 miles away. Gordon's arm had been dislocated for forty-eight hours before it could finally be operated upon.

Back at the creek, a message was sent bringing base up to date with developments and preparations were made to weigh anchor. I looked around to assess conditions for take-off. As the met report had warned, the weather had deteriorated markedly and I concluded that it would be suicidal to try to take off in the open sea, which was now looking angry.

Discussing a plan of action with Graham and Pete, I suggested that there was really only one course open to us. We must try to taxi further up river and then come belting down at full power in the hope that we might be able to get off by the time we hit the swell in the uncharted waters of the Gulf. I was unaware at that time that the Sittang River had a bore not unlike that of the River Severn at home. Whether prior knowledge of this would have affected my decision it is hard to say. I was firmly convinced that there was no other solution to the problem.

There was a certain amount of scepticism about the plan but no one was able to suggest a practical alternative, short of staying where we were overnight. I felt that the survivors needed to be returned to civilized conditions at the earliest opportunity. The proposal was put to the rest of the crew, who all agreed. When I told Tom and his crew what was being considered, they too raised no objections. After what they had been through they were game for anything, if the odds were on getting back to normality fairly quickly.

They had not enjoyed their walk to the coast. They had waded laboriously through a "glutinous mass of mud", at times up to their thighs. The going was so bad that one of their number had to be carried part of the way by the natives. Snakes were in evidence and a persistent one was killed by one of the Burmans. The survivors could not speak too highly of these people. Although there were early difficulties of communication, sign language proved adequate in the circumstances and the natives' skills in coping with conditions familiar to them were greatly valued.

After weighing anchor, we began taxiing up river. Keeping to the centre of the channel, I occupied myself with the thought that as it was narrowing all the time, I had to make sure that I left enough room in which to turn D round. Because of the freshened wind, I knew that our turning circle would be greatly increased. When I judged that we could go no further with safety, I opened the port outer engine to almost full power to swing the big boat around in the smallest possible distance.

It was then that she ran aground. This was all we needed. We were literally up the creek. I asked Graham if he could see what the obstruction was. He looked out of the cabin window, screwing up his eyes in concentration, and said he couldn't, but it hadn't felt like anything hard – probably only silt. Throttling right back on the engines, I contemplated the problem, wondering what we could do to get out of this tricky situation. As luck would have it, my ingenuity wasn't tested. Thanks to the strong current, the boat was suddenly lifted off the sandbank without any help from us. I allowed her to drift a few yards down river again to make sure we were clear of the obstruction. The procedure of trying to swing her round was repeated, this time with success. The port float missed the bank by a couple of feet at most.

The stiffened breeze was now coming from the south, which meant that the aircraft was about 45 degrees out of the wind when lined up with the channel. This introduced new difficulties. Under normal take-off conditions, there was plenty of water on either side of the boat and drifting a few degrees to port or starboard did not create any real problems. Here the channel was narrow, so one had to keep slavishly to the centre of it, making constant compensation for the fact that the boat was straining into the wind. There was no margin for error.

Because of the greatly restricted take-off run, I decided to open all four engines at once. D surged forward, but then she checked again as her bow dug in. We'd hit another sandbank. Fortunately, she pulled herself free and was soon hurtling down river gathering speed. I struggled to keep her on an even keel and prevent her from swinging to starboard and ending up on the muddy bank. The course of the river itself was not entirely straight, so corrections had to be made for that, too.

Pete was standing in the astro-hatch, fascinated as he watched the foam-crested bow waves fanning out and lashing at the banks on either side of us. The estuary was now coming up fast and I prayed that D would get up on to her step in time. I didn't like what I saw out to sea, but I couldn't abort the take-off now. Conditions had got very much worse since we'd been anchored in the creek. Under a leaden sky, the Gulf was whipping itself up into a frenzy and in the distance I could clearly see the spume blowing off the surface of the waves.

At last, the boat started planing on her step, but still more power was needed to lift her off the surface before we got into the rough water. Pushing the four throttles to their full travel through the gate, I could feel the added thrust in my back as the full four thousand eight hundred horsepower of her four engines took effect. At last, D hit the swell in the open sea at just under eighty knots. She lurched into the air, appearing to hang there momentarily as if trying to make up her mind whether or not to drop in again. Mercifully she stayed airborne and as she gained speed and height we were able to throttle back to climbing boost and revs. I looked first at Graham and then at Pete, who was now standing between the pilots' seats. They both smiled. The ordeal was over and the tension subsided.

Flying back over the wreck of the Liberator to check that the other crew members had not returned to it, we could only see natives sprawling over the doomed aircraft. We radioed base to tell them that we were safely airborne with our five charges. Giving them our ETA, we asked for dry clothes to be made available for the survivors to change into before they left the aircraft. In less than half an hour, we had landed at Syriam. The whole operation from take-off to landing again at base had taken ten hours.

Not long after this episode, I had a visit from an RAF Officer who requested full details of the rescue. I was hesitant to tell him the whole story, seeing him as a reporter rather than someone who needed the information for official record purposes. I suggested that he would simply splash it around in the papers just to fill space now that the war was over. In actual fact, I was more concerned that any report that did appear in print should be an accurate one. In the event my reservations proved justified.

He assured me that he was not 'a journalist', but was an Intelligence

Officer. He was required to get the official account for Air Ministry records and there his responsibilities ended. He had no personal wish to publicize it, but he could have no influence over what his superiors might choose to do with it when submitted to them. He departed with a carbon copy of my official report.

Only days later, I discovered that the episode had received very wide coverage in the media. It had been reported on the 8am BBC radio news at home, in the Far East forces newspaper SEAC and in the local paper of every member of the crew. Our WOM Mickie Crowther was from Jersey and my father-in-law, also a Jerseyman, sent me a copy of the Jersey Weekly Post containing the report. My mother first heard about the episode from a Dorset Daily Echo reporter and was somewhat bemused by it all. The story soon spread around the grapevine at home, with varying degrees of accuracy from paper to paper. Mary obtained a transcript from the BBC because she hadn't heard the broadcast.

Until then, the rescue had seemed almost a personal thing between Tom Blackburn's crew and mine and I greatly valued the letters I received from him and from Pat Winch several weeks later. Now it had been reported in full on the other side of the globe, suddenly becoming public knowledge worldwide.

Chapter 24

Lying between Burma and Sumatra are two archipelagos known as the Andaman and Nicobar Islands. When the Japanese overran most of the Far East, they occupied these islands, their most important military concentrations being around the towns of Port Blair in the Andamans and Nancowry in the Nicobars. On 20 September, eight days after Lord Louis Mountbatten, Supreme Commander, South East Asia Command (SEAC), had formally accepted the Japanese surrender in Singapore, we took off from Rangoon on a reconnaissance flight to the islands. Our instructions were to find out all we could about the installations at the two ports.

The Japanese were reputed to be past masters at camouflaging such sites and it was with some satisfaction that we were able to produce a detailed report on gun positions, radio stations, fuel installations, military buildings, etc. Our information was later confirmed and it appeared that we had missed nothing of consequence.

Flying very low over the military establishments at Port Blair, we saw Japanese soldiers in their khaki tropical uniforms running out into the open to see what was going on. Suddenly, one of the air gunners yelled into the intercom that they were shooting at us with small arms. He wanted permission to retaliate. I flatly refused, reminding him that the war was over, even if the news hadn't filtered through to the island. The soldiers' behaviour was probably just a reflex action because they'd been caught off guard.

Later, while circling Nancowry, we came upon a Japanese minesweeper which was under way. As we passed over her just above mast level, several of her crew were seen jumping overboard, seemingly believing that they were under attack. A Sunderland flying boat could be a frightening sight if it arrived over you unexpectedly at nought feet.

Our operation completed, I asked Pete for a course for Penang, a newly acquired detachment and transit base off the west coast of Malaya. The Royal Marines had landed there two weeks earlier, immediately following the Tokyo surrender. We refuelled and stayed the night, taking off for Rangoon the following day with instructions to recce Mergui on the way. During this trip I learned that certain members of the crew had not been able to resist the temptation of dropping some empty beer bottles on the Japanese camp at Port Blair the previous day. The whistling noise produced the illusion of falling bombs and the crew evidently revelled in seeing the Japs running for cover in all directions.

Long-range communications in Sunderlands required the use in flight of an aerial which trailed below the hull. After take-off, a long tube known as the fairlead was assembled in the galley which enabled the wireless operator on the flight deck to run out his trailing aerial through the bottom of the hull. It was part of the landing drill always to ensure that the aerial was wound in and the tube dismantled before touchdown. Some crews on the squadron had been lax about this, had landed with their aerials out and consequently lost them. This was becoming costly and also an embarrassment, since there was some difficulty in getting replacements. A notice signed by the CO appeared on the squadron notice boards threatening a heavy fine on skippers who lost their aerials in this way.

When we arrived over Mergui, a Burmese settlement on the west coast of the Kra Isthmus, we located the airfield and I dropped down low to investigate it. It was deserted, but a number of Japanese Zero fighters were to be seen on the apron and one had come to an unhappy end in the middle of the runway. It was clear that it had either been shot up or bombed while trying to take off or land.

As we flew along the runway a few feet above the ground, a cry of anguish came over the intercom from Terry, whose signals had suddenly died. Contrary to normal practice, I hadn't warned him about this manoeuvre and he hadn't therefore been able to wind in the aerial. It had wrapped itself around the Zero on the runway. Remembering the CO's threat, I was resigned to having to shell out for the lost aerial when we returned to base. However, no more was heard and I was puzzled to discover that a replacement aerial had been installed before our next sortie. I asked no questions about its source.

While on detachment in Rangoon, I first learned how to drive a motor car. Over twenty years later, a Harvard professor acquaintance of mine simply could not believe that I had learned to fly a 'plane before I could drive a car. A jeep was at the disposal of visiting crews at Syriam and I persuaded F/O Dave Banton, a fellow skipper who had become a staunch friend, to give me some lessons, so that I could take full advantage of it.

When trying to do a hill start after stalling, I inadvertently engaged reverse instead of first gear, let in the clutch and shot rapidly backwards down the hill, ending up in a ditch beside the road. Dave exploded into uncontrollable laughter which did little to reassure me. I was visibly shaken and was concerned that I might have done some damage to the vehicle. As it happened, it had hit a soft earth bank and was unscratched.

Once I felt competent to do so, I took the jeep out on my own and visited neighbouring villages to make contact with the residents. Most of the womenfolk, certainly the older ones, seemed to spend their time sitting on their verandahs, or simply on the dusty earth outside their houses, smoking enormous hand-rolled cheroots which looked more like leeks than cigars.

The children were very appealing with their straight black hair tied in a knot on the top of the head. They enjoyed being given rides in the jeep. Their parents showed no outward concern and I was surprised that they could be so trusting. Little did they know what a sprog I was at this driving game.

On one of the occasions when alone in the car, I came across a dead dog being stripped by three or four vultures alongside the dirt track. Without thinking about nature's way of controlling disease, I took instant exception to these ugly birds and kept driving the jeep at them to disperse them. I hadn't counted on their hunger or their tenacity. At each sally, they launched themselves on their huge wings and settled again only a few yards away, returning to their prey immediately my back was turned.

The memorable September ended with our first flight to Singapore to take part in the courier service. We followed the Malayan coast down through the Malacca Strait, a route with which we were to become very familiar over the months ahead. Passing over Port Dickson and Port Swettenham, two of the easily identifiable landmarks on our flight, we were oblivious of the fact that these were the two ports at which Mountbatten had intended to land his forces to recapture Malaya only a few weeks earlier.

The dropping of the atomic bombs on Japan had brought about a suspension of these plans, called Operation Zipper, and the invasion forces, which had already crossed the Indian Ocean, were now lying off the Nicobar Islands awaiting further instructions. After the capitulation, they were scattered over the expanse of reoccupied territories to enforce the surrender and carry out policing duties.

We were approaching our destination at about 16.30 hours local time and we learned the hard way that this was a time to be avoided for a landing at Singapore during the rainy season. A violent thunderstorm was centred over the area and we were told later that you could almost set your watch by the daily phenomenon at this time of the year. We had to fly around in the Malacca Strait killing time until the cumulonimbus cloud had moved on. A mental note was made to time our arrival better on future trips.

The flying boat base at Seletar was on the north side of Singapore Island, not far from the notorious Changi gaol, where many Allied prisoners of war and others had been incarcerated by the Japanese. The take-off and landing area was in the Johore Strait between the island and the mainland. It was a substantial stretch of reasonably sheltered water, providing an ideal flying boat base, and it had been in regular use before the war.

The following month proved as frustrating as September had been satisfying. After a round trip to Koggala via Redhills, we found ourselves back at Rangoon with several days of inactivity. We then took off on an ASR flight for Bandon Bay, on the eastern side of the Kra Isthmus, where we were to cover a sortie by some Thunderbolt fighter aircraft. Since they were very much faster than we were, we needed to be in the air several hours before they were due to take off from their airfield in Burma.

We were airborne at 06.00 hours and headed south along the Burmese coast. An hour out from Syriam, we received a message to the effect that cover was no longer required and we were to return to base. Asking for clarification, we were told that the fighters hadn't taken off. The operation had been postponed.

I was livid and petulantly called for a course for Syriam. Not only was this fiasco a sheer waste of everyone's time, but it would also prove extremely costly. I was not prepared to land at Syriam with an almost full load of fuel, so we would have to jettison some of it. I asked Taff the engineer what he felt about the quantity of petrol that would have to be discharged into the sea.

We'd started with nearly two thousand gallons in the ten tanks in anticipation of a trip lasting about twelve hours. We'd be landing within two and a half hours of take-off. There'd still be around seventeen hundred gallons on board, representing a dead weight of well over five tons. Having to land with a heavy load immediately after take-off due to engine failure was one thing, but doing so in these circumstances simply wasn't worth the risks. We agreed that several hundred gallons had to go. It was a painful decision.

A week later we were briefed for the same operation and were in the air again at 06.00 hours. After a little more than half an hour's flying, Terry announced over the intercom that the trip had been cancelled again and that we'd been recalled. My anger began to affect my flying, so I handed over to the second pilot. When we arrived at the Ops Room, I stamped in and demanded what was going on. That was twice within a week that we'd had to come back because the Thunderbolts had not taken off. What game did they think they were playing?

The Ops Officer looked stupefied. He didn't know. He was just told the whole thing was off, so we'd be wasting our time going down there. I suggested that we should protest to AHQ in the strongest possible terms. While we were clearly not in a position to prevent the Thunderbolts from aborting their operations in the future, we did manage to come to an arrangement with them. We would not take off again until we received definite confirmation that they were going.

The following day we tried once more and it turned out to be third time lucky. We carried out our patrol west and east of the Kra Isthmus in southern Siam, taking in Phuket Island and Bandon Bay. By now we had christened the latter Abandon Bay. We had to leave by midday because of the build up of monsoon cloud, which was almost down to the deck over much of the area. After flying blind for about thirty miles across the isthmus, we then had to fly at a low level under the cloud for the remainder of the trip home.

In the next few months, many of the flights we made were passenger- and freight-carrying trips on the courier service between India, Ceylon, Burma, Penang and Singapore. Needless to say, the end of the war gave rise to comings and goings of both civilians and servicemen. High ranking officials and service officers were on the move across South East Asia almost continuously and flying boats provided a convenient and not too uncomfortable mode of transport. D was modified to carry VIPs. The bunks were converted into upholstered bench seats and blue curtains covered the portholes in the wardroom, in which a cocktail cabinet was also installed.

One of our problems was that since so many passengers, sometimes over twenty, had to be carried, a mixture of ranks was usually represented and it was not always possible to provide special arrangements for the more senior officers. They seemed to understood the position and I don't recall having difficulties with anyone pulling rank. On the contrary. On one flight from Koggala to Singapore, I had to explain the situation to Air Marshal G C Pirie. I told him that I was in something of a quandary, not being able to offer him the wardroom for his personal use. He smiled and told me not to worry. He had come prepared, having brought an airbed with him. All he wanted was a "quiet spot" where he'd be able to sleep and he assured me that he'd be no trouble! Since the bow compartment was unlikely to be used during the flight, he was able to have it entirely to himself and could rest undisturbed. Blowing up his airbed, he got his head down and within minutes was fast asleep.

On another occasion, I discovered that my entire passenger list was made up of WAAF officers and other ranks, sixteen in all. It seemed to be tempting fate to throw them into a confined space with my crew for over twelve hours. I needn't have worried. They all enjoyed the company and behaved impeccably (as far as I know!). This was Graham's last flight with us and he said that he couldn't have thought of a better way of spending it than with sixteen WAAFs. With the end of the Far East war, Colonial servicemen were being repatriated. Graham, now a Flight Lieutenant, returned to New Zealand. He was sadly missed. A very popular second pilot, he had been a great asset to a crew in which high standards were expected of everyone. His successor, F/Sgt Ray Morgan, a Pensacola trained pilot, was very much aware of the void he had to fill, but he got over the initial barriers without too much difficulty.

The last of the squadron's Catalinas went to the Korangi scrap heap on 2 December, when I was commencing a welcome spell of leave. With some colleagues, I went to Ootacamund in the Nilgiri Hills, a popular holiday resort about three hundred miles south west of Madras and over six thousand feet above sea level. It provided a cool, relaxing climate, a much needed respite from the heat of the eastern plains. The steep ascent into the hills was made by rack railway, in which a pinion driven by the engine engaged with a rack laid between the lines. The train climbed laboriously through the eucalyptus plantations and the gradient could be checked periodically on wooden markers placed at intervals alongside the track. One of my friends, Maxie Beaumont, a former Catalina skipper now on Sunderlands, either had a touch of the sun or was suffering from oxygen lack, because he amused himself by letting fly at the markers with his service revolver.

Not content with this, when we arrived at the Kingscliffe Hotel in which we were to stay, he had to be restrained from using an ornamental brass plate over the inglenook fireplace for target practice. When asked why he'd brought his pistol with him on holiday, he said that he'd been told that there were man-eating tigers in the hills and he wanted to make sure that he could protect himself.

During my restful stay at Ooty, my growing interest in classical music got the better of me. I agreed to share the cost of a gramophone with Dave Banton and bought several new records. Back at Redhills, I instructed my Indian servant in the operation of the machine, then languished in my bath listening in ecstasy to Tchaikowsky's Fifth Symphony, as the boy changed the records and rewound the motor of the HMV portable. The latter became my sole property when Dave was posted and I bought out his share.

We were all very happy with the Mk V boat and often our conversation got around to extolling its virtues. On the way out to D in the dinghy for an air test one day, we were discussing the aircraft's cruising speed. Several members of the crew wondered why, with the substantial improvement in engine performance over earlier versions, the cruising speed was not much higher. We concluded that the bulky two-decked hull, capable of being taken off from and landed on water, could not be sufficiently well streamlined. Since stepping up the power by a mere 14 per cent was not going to overcome this difficulty, one could not expect a significant increase in speed.

This was one reason why the flying boat could not look forward to a future in post-war civil flying, although there was so much scope throughout the world for landing on water and no expensive runways were needed. We hadn't really found out what our own boat's maximum speed was and I told the crew that I should like to put it to the test in a dive. Since we only had a light load for this trip, now was the time to experiment. I did not expect them to think much of this suggestion, so I was somewhat surprised when they all agreed to go along with it.

When we had completed the necessary flight checks, I climbed to six thousand feet, then pushed the nose down steeply, throttling back to about a third open on all four engines. The needle on the airspeed indicator began to climb... 130, 140, 150, ... The noise of the slipstream past the huge hunk of metal increased in volume. I looked out at the wings. They seemed to be flapping up and down like a bird's and the aircraft was vibrating from stem to stern as if shivering from cold. I began to wonder how much she would be able to take of this.

The needle went on climbing until it reached 180 knots (207 mph) and there it stopped. It was clear that I couldn't push it any further and I was running out of height, so gently pulling out of the dive I allowed the speed to fall back to normal cruising before applying the power again. Calling the crew on the intercom, I told them that we had only reached 180 knots, which was "no great shakes". The hoots of laughter which greeted this statement told me that I hadn't chosen my words very carefully.

Chapter 25

By Christmas 1945, the Andaman and Nicobar Islands had been evacuated by the Japanese and we learned that D was to go to Port Blair on the night of 27/28 December to prepare the port for a visit of the Viceroy of India, Lord Wavell. He would be landing in a Sunderland from another squadron for a tour of inspection of the area.

There was only one change in our aircrew, that of the flight engineer. Taff Stapleton had left us and his replacement was John Haigh, a popular NCO who was well received by the others. We also took with us a maintenance crew of eight in case the VIP's boat needed servicing or repair. Landing at Port Blair at dawn, we were led to some moorings which the Japanese had laid for the use of their small seaplanes. As we moored up to one of the tiny buoys, I wondered whether it was capable of holding a four-engined flying boat and I warned the crew to keep a constant watch for any shifting.

A launch then took me ashore to a meeting of the top brass over breakfast, while the crews reluctantly remained on board. I met senior officers from each of the three services and they indicated that their knowledge of Sunderlands was very limited. They were therefore happy to leave the arrangements for receiving the Viceroy's aircraft entirely in my hands, promising me whatever practical support I might need.

The main requirements were for the preparation of the landing area and the provision of suitable mooring, refuelling and dinghy facilities. I had serious reservations about using an unproved seaplane buoy for the VIP's Sunderland. The risk of the moorings breaking loose was too great. In any event the trots were considered to be too far away from the intended landing point. The Royal Navy was therefore requested to lay a buoy which would provide greater security for the aircraft and easier access to and from the jetty.

I also explained that, shortly before the Sunderland was due, the alighting area would have to be swept so that there was no risk to the boat of damage from floating debris. The visitor intended to take off from Port Blair again at 03.00 hours the following morning, which meant that a flare-path would have to be laid. Such facilities had not been in use there before, so we had to set about improvising them. Clearly, the Rangoon ASR launch could be used as one flare, but what could we use for the other two? After some deliberation, it was finally decided to hang hurricane lamps in two whalers moored in appropriate positions!

While occupied with supervising the laying of the flare-path, I was told that someone on my aircraft was trying to attract attention by flashing an Aldis lamp in our direction. Acknowledging the signal, we learned that D was leaking in the galley and the pumps weren't coping. This was an unexpected and unwelcome complication. I already had my hands full with my preparations and now I could imagine my boat sinking to the bottom while I busied myself with my flare-path.

The launch took me over to D. On board, I found Pete and Paddy paddling in the galley bilges. The navigator, perspiring profusely, was repeatedly filling a bucket and handing it up for emptying through the galley hatch, while the Irishman was using the stirrup pump. The APU was also running, though not very well, and these combined efforts seemed to be making no significant impression on the water level.

Bubbles appeared to be rising from around the trailing aerial outlet in the bottom of the hull (*see appendix* C, *ref*. 125). Lying on my stomach on the deckboards and dipping my arm into almost a foot of water, I felt around the collar of the outlet. This was riveted to the hull bottom in the horizontal plane and to a fairlead tube, through which the aerial was normally run out, in the vertical plane. The water was seeping in around the tube. Several rivets holding it to the collar had sprung, loosening the joint and allowing the water in at a prodigious rate.

In the air it was necessary to slide into the tube a longer one, the fairlead (*see appendix* C, *ref*. 127), which projected below the hull when the aerial was deployed. It was usually a fairly comfortable fit and I asked if anyone had considered using it to try to stem the flow of water. They looked at me incredulously, kicking themselves that they'd not thought of such an obvious solution. The fairlead was duly inserted and the water flow virtually stopped. The level was now going down visibly as the pumping continued and I was able to return to my flare-path laying. As it turned out, most of my effort on this activity was for nothing, because His Excellency postponed his departure until first light and the improvised flare-path was not needed.

During my stay in Madras, I met Mary's elder brother, Murray Simon, for the first time. He was then a Lieutenant in the 2nd Recce Regiment and had been serving in Burma. On his way home on leave, he was held up in Karachi because prisoners of war were given transport priority. He contracted jaundice and spent some time in hospital there. When he eventually arrived home, he suffered a bout of pneumonia, which delayed his return to SEAC. We met in Madras when he was in transit, trying to catch up with his regiment, now in Johore. Our boats were currently making regular flights to Seletar and we agreed to get together again when Murray finally arrived in Malaya.

Early in the New Year, the squadron moved from Madras to Koggala. There were mixed feelings about this at first, but when they had been there for a week or two, people found that it had a lot to commend it, as post-war developers have discovered. It is now an important seaside resort. We were close to the south-west coast of the island near Galle and when sitting on the beach there you could easily imagine yourself on a remote desert island in the Pacific. All that could be seen was golden sand flanked by palm trees, a limitless expanse of dark blue sea and a sun-drenched sky punctuated with puffy white cumulous cloud. It was a tropical paradise.

Apart from the heat, life at Koggala was very pleasant. It was common practice when we were not flying to take a shower and then resort to our charpoys for a siesta in the hottest part of the day. Lying prostrate under my mosquito net one afternoon, I was watching a chameleon on the wall when I became aware of a shuffling noise on the floor near the open doorway. Raising myself on my elbows, I looked down to see a mongoose sniffing its way around the bottom of the wall.

I wasn't quite sure what the normal relationship was between mongooses and humans. I understood the creatures to be sworn enemies of rats and snakes, often getting the better of them. I hoped that put them on my side, because I could see no way of escaping from the room without being cut off by this one. I froze and watched the animal as it made its way systematically along the wall around my bed. It didn't appear to be aware of my presence. If it were, it chose to ignore me. When it arrived at the doorway again after a complete circuit of the room, it started excavating feverishly under the doorpost. Unearthing a frog, it picked it up in its mouth and made off with it.

Just at that moment, my servant boy arrived on the scene, saw the animal and immediately gave chase. I yelled out to him to leave it, but I was too late. The mongoose dropped its prey, by now partially dismembered but still alive, and bolted into the undergrowth. I admonished the boy for causing the frog unnecessary suffering and then got him to put it out of its misery.

I should like to have been able to keep a mongoose as a protection against snakes, which were quite common in the area. My intense dislike of these reptiles was not surprising because some of the local species were lethal. Walking through the camp one day, I came upon our Medical Officer pelting the ground with stones. I wondered whether he'd succumbed to the heat, because from a distance I was unable to see the reason for this violent behaviour. When I reached him, he showed me a small snake which he had just dispatched. I jokingly accused him of being a bully, attacking a poor defenceless little creature like that. He told me that it happened to be the most deadly reptile in Ceylon. It took a regular toll of human beings, so you just didn't stand around waiting for it to be nice to you.

One of my abiding memories of both India and Ceylon was the elegance of the native women. They had a physical bearing not matched by people of any other country I visited. There was a tranquillity about them which did not seem in keeping with the deprivations so many of them suffered. One of the best compliments that their own menfolk could pay them was to say that they walked like an elephant, meaning erect, stately and with a swaying motion.

The flying boat base, on a lake at Koggala, had certain limitations. The mooring area was restricted and the trots were therefore too close together. If you were leaving an inner buoy and the wind was offshore (*see plate* 41), there were problems trying to avoid aircraft in the outer row when turning downwind. It says something for the seamanship skills of our pilots that there were very few taxiing accidents.

Another difficulty was that although the lake provided adequate stretches of water for light load take-offs, full loads could be a bit tricky, because we had to turn a corner in the middle of the run. Since the lake was surrounded by tall coconut palms (*see plate* 42), we also had to make sure that we left the water in good time to be able to clear them. At night this could be a trifle worrying. It was not unusual, when trying to get off with fifteen or more passengers on board, to have to abort the take-off and go back and start again.

The scourge of malaria became more evident to us as we began to reopen bases like Rangoon, where the disease was rife. The drug mepacrine was provided on the squadron as a preventative. Taken in tablet form, it gave rise to a sickly yellow colouring of the skin. A good suntan tended to obscure this, but when the tan wore off on our return to more temperate climes, we appeared yellower than the yellow races themselves. It took several years for us to lose our jaundiced look.

The regular use of Penang as a detachment and transit base required that we set up a command there. Maxie Beaumont became the first officer-in-charge at the beginning of February, 1946. Later in the month he was recalled, because his Class C (compassionate) release from the RAF had come through, and Dave Banton took over from him.

The crews which paid frequent visits to the island on their way to Singapore soon found out that the local Chinese were as hard up for cigarettes as had been the Sicilians. Some took advantage of the situation, smuggling ever increasing quantities of cigarettes and other commodities aboard their aircraft in India or Ceylon and transporting them to Penang. It was not until one of them was seen on the jetty meeting other crews and offering to act as middleman in deals with the Chinese that the practice was firmly stamped upon.

When in Singapore again, I made contact with my brother-in-law and he invited Pete and myself over to his unit at Johore for the day. He took us for a ride in a Bren gun carrier and, although he said the terrain was not particularly rough, I was so violently shaken up that I felt my insides had been shuffled like a pack of cards. I wondered why I'd ever had the nerve to complain about conditions in aircraft. By way of compensation for subjecting us to this discomfort, Murray invited us to dinner and drinks. When I was feeling suitably mellow he asked when we were returning to Ceylon. This gave me something of a jolt, because I'd completely forgotten that we were due to go back the following morning. I told him that we'd be airborne at about 07.00 hours. He expected to be on the parade ground at that time, so we promised to liven up the proceedings for him.

Next morning we took off from Seletar as planned. There were no passengers, but we were to collect some at Penang. I was at the controls and suffering to some extent from the previous night's indulgences. Instead of climbing as usual to cruising altitude, I flew along the Johore Strait at about three hundred feet, dropping down to fifty feet as we passed over the army camp at Johore. The daily parade, which was taking place at the time, was somewhat disrupted by this activity, as everyone wanted to look up to see what was going on. The crew waved to the soldiers from the hatches and I tilted the wings first one way and then the other in greeting. With a noisy burst of power from the four engines, we climbed away steeply and set course for Penang. Conscious of the fact that the standard of my flying was atrocious, I handed over the controls to Ray, asking him to take over before I did something stupid.

This episode worried me because we had a rule, usually conscientiously observed, that if we were known to be flying the next day we would lay off the drink. There was too much at stake for pilots to take chances with their flying due to overindulgence. I discouraged the crew from going out on long sorties at all if they were feeling under the weather for any reason, because I knew that their actions, or lack of action, could endanger their companions and the aircraft.

In some instances this policy, adopted for the best of reasons, could lead to rather extreme behaviour when there was a lull in flying activity. About a month after the Johore incident, a number of us spent a lively evening at the Coconut Grove, a favourite haunt of servicemen a few miles out of Singapore. During the party, someone remarked that Pete was missing. Several of us went in search of him.

Outside, we found that a thirty-hundredweight truck from RAF Tengah had been driven against a palm tree and the engine was being revved up urgently, to no avail. At the wheel was our missing colleague. When he saw us he exhorted us to jump in, undertaking to drive us back to Seletar. I yelled out to him not to be damned silly, told him it wasn't even our station's truck and insisted that he got out before he did some real damage. A spirited struggle ensued and with difficulty we managed to bundle him into a taxi. The following morning he swore that he didn't remember anything about the episode, but complained about a very sore jaw. He refused to believe that he'd received it from his skipper.

The disbandment of 240 Squadron made March 1946 a sad month for us. W/Cdr Gavin Robinson, our popular CO, who had been awarded the Air Force Cross three months earlier, returned to the UK, while S/Ldr Ruston moved to 209 Squadron, based at Hong Kong. Some of the aircraft were transferred to 209 and some joined 230 Squadron. A photograph of 240 Squadron personnel was taken for the record (*see plate* 47), but the Flight Commander did not appear in it, having already moved to his new squadron.

D's crew was broken up and its members were either repatriated or transferred to other units. Ray seemed a little put out when he learned that his former employer had made an application for a Class B (industrial) release for him. He could have avoided it, but knowing that nearly everyone else of his close acquaintance was going home, he acquiesced graciously. Terry joined Dave Banton in O/230 for the flight home from Singapore, while Paddy and Benny chose to make the trip by troopship. Peter and I moved to 209 squadron with D, which was renumbered M209.

Chapter 26

Sarawak, the territory on the north-western coast of the island of Borneo and home of the Dyak head-hunters, had been ruled by the White Rajahs, the Brooke family, since 1841. At the centenary celebrations in 1941, the third Rajah, Sir Charles Vyner Brooke, told his people of his intention to relinquish his absolute powers and substitute a democratic system. There was to be a properly elected Council with a written constitution. He was nearing 70 years of age and wanted to prepare the country for his retirement. He had no male heir, so the succession was uncertain. There was strong opposition at that time to the idea of the country becoming a Crown Colony.

On Christmas Day, the Japanese entered the capital, Kuching. The Rajah was away in Australia and his people, consisting of Malays, Chinese and Dyaks, were shocked and disillusioned. They felt that, after enjoying three generations of secure Brooke rule, they had now been let down by the white man. Towards the end of 1945, Sir Charles returned to a country which had been occupied by the Japanese for forty-five months. He found that the attitudes of a significant proportion of the population had changed. He recommended to the Council that the country be ceded to the British Crown. In May 1946, the Council was to vote in favour, but only by a very narrow majority.

During the Easter weekend of that year, my new crew and I were told that we were to fly Lord Louis Mountbatten from Singapore to Kuching on 22 April. Although we did not know it at the time, the purpose of his visit was to sign a document handing the administration of Sarawak back to Sir Charles. Only two months later, the cession of Sarawak was to become a reality.

It was obvious that there would have to be some tidying up on board M209 before we could entertain the Supremo and his party. I visited the Ops Room and asked if anybody was available to clean the aircraft. Since it was a public holiday on the base, the only people we could find were three Indian labourers. Their services were enlisted and they were set to work on board with cans of 100-octane aviation fuel. When I returned some time later, I was depressed to find that there was no evidence of any improvement. The labourers were stood down and I went back to see the Ops Officer, asking him if that really was the best he could do. He replied that it was, unless I was prepared to go and see the colonel in charge of prisoners in the Japanese compound.

Borrowing a jeep, I followed up this proposal and told the Japanese colonel who our distinguished passenger was to be. He spoke passable English and quickly appreciated the situation. I got the distinct impression that he felt that the Supremo could make life very uncomfortable for him if he did not comply with the request. He snapped an order to an NCO who quickly departed and came back with two soldiers. They were told what they were expected to do and they nodded and bowed. I thanked the colonel and bundled the prisoners into the back of the jeep. On board the boat, they removed their boots and set about their task without delay, working with such alacrity and purpose that one would have thought their very lives depended on it. Within about three quarters of an hour the aircraft was sparkling.

Ashore again, I returned the men to their compound, offering them a full pack of Lucky Strike cigarettes on the way. It transpired that only one of them smoked. He opened the pack, removed one cigarette and tried to return the remainder. I told him he could keep them. When the two prisoners left the jeep, they bowed deeply until it was out of their sight.

The following day we took off in M for the brief flight from Seletar to Singapore harbour at 07.00 hours. S/Ldr Ruston was at the controls and F/Lt Bertram, who had replaced Ray Morgan when I transferred to 209, was our second pilot. The Supremo had moved his headquarters to Singapore from Kandy, Ceylon, the previous October. I welcomed him aboard at Kallang. He was accompanied by his daughter, Lady Patricia, who later succeeded to the title of Countess Mountbatten of Burma. She was in the uniform of a WRNS officer and was carrying a portable typewriter.

Advising the VIP that the trip was estimated to take about three and a half hours, I asked him how he would like to spend it. He said that he and his daughter had work to do and would be happy to shut themselves away in the wardroom. He would like to be called when the aircraft was about to land and perhaps he would then "be allowed on the flight deck."

We landed on the river four miles from Kuching with the Supremo standing between the pilots' seats. After mooring up, we awaited the arrival of a large open boat, equipped with an outboard motor, which was to take Mountbatten and his party ashore. Unfortunately, when the boat was within a hundred yards or so of the aircraft, its engine cut out and it began to drift swiftly downstream. I had visions of having to deploy the aircraft's inflatable dinghies. The Army officer in charge of the reception party, Captain Dudley Morgan of the Royal Welsh Fusiliers, was understandably embarrassed by the breakdown, as I learned twenty years later when we found ourselves working in the same group of companies. He has also told me since that the place at which this incident occurred was appropriately called Pending. Eventually the engine was restarted and the party was safely transported to the jetty.

During Mountbatten's stay in Kuching, an open air military display was arranged in his honour and the Sunderland crew was invited to join the other guests of the Rajah in the 'royal box'. We watched fascinated as the Dyaks, resplendent in full war paint and regalia, performed their spectacular dances. It was comforting that we were on friendly terms with these people. Some members of the Japanese occupying forces had been less fortunate. Their heads had ended up on poles outside the long-houses.

We had to spend the night in Kuching before returning to Singapore. Here we discovered one of the reasons why the Dyak long-houses were built on stilts ten to fifteen feet above the ground. The torrential rain which fell throughout the night turned the whole area into a quagmire and I could understand why Sarawak had been described as a country of swollen rivers, swamps and dense hillside forests.

Although not without experience of tropical rainstorms, I had never seen anything quite like this. The rain fell with such force that it was extremely painful to stand out in it. The weather was still unsettled on the morning of our intended departure and a message was sent to the Supremo recommending a postponement until the next day. He wouldn't hear of it and we were airborne again at 15.00 hours, by which time conditions had improved.

When the passengers disembarked at Kallang, Lord Louis shook hands with members of the crew and thanked them. The next time I wrote to Mary I told her that he was the most impressive man it had ever been my privilege to meet. He was powerfully built and was immaculately turned out in his naval officer's tropical uniform, his broad chest decorated with several rows of medal ribbons. In spite of his natural air of authority, he had a pleasant and friendly manner and I felt that he was someone with whom I could be completely at ease. Those who worked under him said that he demanded the highest standards of his subordinates. I have little doubt that he also inspired them to give of their best.

The following week we moved to Kai Tak, the RAF base at Kowloon, on the mainland across the harbour from Hong Kong Island. We flew in low over the landplane runway and, although Chinese junks were discouraged from using our alighting area in the harbour, we had to take particular care in case any strayed across our path. They were inclined to give aircraft a wide berth, however. Their owners knew that if the slipstream caught them they could very easily be overturned.

I reported to Wing Commander W E Ogle Skan, whom I had first met at Mombasa, in his room. After offering me a scotch, he told me that he wanted me to fly to Iwakuni in Japan the following day. At any other time I would have jumped at the opportunity, but I was suffering from a severe bout of sinusitis and had to decline. F/Lt H S P, now Sir Hector, Monro was then detailed to take my aircraft and crew, but the weather in Japan deteriorated and the trip was cancelled.

When I was fit again, we prepared to return to Singapore on 3 May. Our passengers were twenty members of the Anglo-Polish Ballet Company. The trip proved a unique experience. When the passengers were taken aboard, they were shown what accommodation was available and were asked if they would sort themselves out as comfortably as they could. I hesitated to allocate seats and I was to regret it.

The second pilot was at the controls when we slipped moorings and taxied out to the take-off area. I went below to brief the passengers and was horrified to find everything in a state of chaos. People were milling about all over the boat as though they were in a corridor train; no-one was seated. Members of the crew were standing around looking helpless, their efforts to control their charges having been abortive. They found the situation unmanageable.

With difficulty I tried to marshal the passengers into seats in such a way that the trim of the aircraft would not be unduly affected on take-off. Bertram had reached the take-off area now and was taxiing the boat around, killing time. At last the passengers were seated and I explained that it was important for everyone's safety that they didn't move about until we reached cruising altitude. Returning to the flight deck, I heard the Wing Commander on the R/T angrily demanding to know why the boat hadn't taken off.

After changing seats with the second pilot, I did my cockpit check and was about to open the throttles when one of the crew called out over the intercom that "they're wandering about again." I threatened to take the boat back to her moorings if the passengers did not settle down. This seemed to do the trick and I was told that they were finally under control. We took off to a tirade of abuse from the tower and, with some relief, made our way out over the South China Sea heading for Singapore.

We climbed to an altitude of three thousand feet and I put George in. The second pilot took over while I went below to see how the passengers were faring. Most of them were sitting on their bunks looking very subdued, the expressions on their faces suggesting that butter wouldn't melt in their mouths. The only Pole in the party was imbibing beer at the rear of the aircraft and he tried to induce me to share it with him. Two of the other men sat together on one of the after bunks, locked in each other's arms. Some of the girls in the wardroom made me promise to go to one of their performances of Swan Lake in Singapore the following week, an invitation which I accepted.

When I went into the mess at Seletar again, shortly after my promotion to Flight Lieutenant, I was delighted to learn that my release group had just been announced. Within weeks I expected to be on my way home. The Flight Commander, unaware of this development, was telling me in the bar that he thought it was time I had some leave. I agreed and said that it was already laid on – release leave. This clearly did not please him, since he'd mistakenly thought he was able to count on my staying on the squadron. My permanent commission had not yet come through, but he felt that it was now only a formality. I had to tell him that my top priority was to go home.

I had not yet completely finished with flying. We were to revisit Borneo, but this time it was to be Labuan, a small island off the coast north-east of Sarawak. There were eighteen passengers aboard, mainly Indonesian political prisoners being taken to Labuan for internment. They were far too frightened to give us any trouble. I was nevertheless pleased to hand them over to the authorities in Victoria, the capital of Labuan, and return to Singapore. This was my last flight in M209. She had served me well and I was very sad to leave her. Two final local trips in other aircraft were not a very memorable swan song. They involved giving instruction in circuits and bumps to other pilots.

The final day on 209 squadron was my twenty-third birthday and I transferred to a holding unit awaiting the boat home. It was over three weeks before I stepped aboard the SS Empress of Australia for the twenty-four day voyage. The trip was both comfortable and restful, giving the much-needed opportunity to wind down before starting a new life.

Chapter 27

Reflecting on my RAF service fifty years on, I was tempted to describe it from a present day vantage point, with the benefit of experience and hindsight. As this would have given a totally false picture, I tried instead to write my account through the eyes of a very young man, not through those of an older one looking back on his youth. Many wartime books give the impression that their authors were mature men of the world during their wartime service, rather than impressionable and inexperienced youngsters striving hard to make sense of unfamiliar and rapidly changing situations. It was my first venture into the wide world and I travelled extensively, staying in 23 different foreign countries during my five years in the RAF. My feelings at the time were an integral part of the story I had to tell.

In retrospect, I don't feel that I made the best of the opportunities afforded me by these experiences. Outside my work, which I took very seriously, I paid scant attention to what was going on around me in the various places I visited. One of my biggest regrets is that I was largely unaware of the wealth of wildlife, particularly birds, which surrounded me. I did not become interested in ornithology until the early 1970s and now realize with some disappointment that I missed countless opportunities to study exotic birds during my worldwide travels. It is surprising how blind you can be to things around you when you've no particular interest in them at the time.

The demands of the work on which I was engaged tended to dominate my life. After spending twelve hours in the air concentrating on the job, I did not find it at all easy to summon up the energy to go out and explore the environment. Frequently, as in Port Étienne, the attractions of the immediate vicinity were limited and one had to content oneself with the simplest of pleasures.

Time softens the unpleasant events in one's memory. Looking back on the war years, I would now say that the satisfactions greatly outweighed the frustrations. There were, of course, long periods of inactivity, particularly at holding units, when my impatience to get on with the job knew no bounds. I tended to assume that, instead of sitting idly in places like Moncton, New Brunswick or Harrogate, Yorkshire I could be in training or on operations somewhere else, doing something useful. There would be aircraft for me to fly and all the facilities would be laid on. I was too young and inexperienced then to understand that things were not quite like that. I realize now that the powers that be faced the most difficult logistical problems as they tried to assign our often inadequate forces and equipment to the worldwide theatres of war.

Our frustrations were soon forgotten when we finally found ourselves on operations, although new ones took their place. Single-minded about the task in hand, we were most anxious to make our full contribution to the winning of the war. However, the effectiveness of much of our effort was not easily determined. Just as a fighter pilot's success was measured by the number of enemy aircraft he shot down, so our effectiveness was likely to be judged by the number of U-boats we sank. If this were truly the yardstick, we could not have been seen as particularly successful. The chances of a flying boat crew accounting directly for the death of a U-boat were slender. Only 28 U-boats were known to have been sunk by Sunderlands during the war, although they did share further kills with the Royal Navy and other aircraft.

The majority of Sunderland crews did not have the satisfaction of direct contact with the enemy. There were several reasons for this, the most significant being that the Germans regarded our long-range anti-submarine aircraft as lethal. Much of the time they took every possible precaution against having encounters with them, as surviving U-boat commanders like Peter Cremer and Heinz Schaeffer have since testified. They had to stay at sea for long periods, operating hundreds, often thousands, of miles from their bases. They could not afford to sustain damage and risk being unable to reach port for repairs.

Curiously, the Sunderland was not as lethal as it could, and should, have been. It had considerable firepower, certainly, and could wreak havoc among the crew of a surfaced U-boat if they were caught taking the air. However, straddling a diving submarine successfully with a stick of DCs demanded swift, instinctive action and great skill, as I have described. There was little time to work out how to handle any situation that might arise; the responses had to be instantaneous. The flying boat's depth charges were set for a predetermined depth, usually 25 feet, and if a dived U-boat was not at or near that depth, it would stand a very good chance of surviving an attack.

One of the factors which enabled the enemy to evade our direct attentions was that for some period of time they could detect our ASV radar before we were able to pick up a response from them. Thus they had plenty of warning of our approach and were able to submerge and vanish without trace.

The tactics of the two sides became highly competitive as each sought to wrest the initiative from the other. When we got to know the technical or tactical reasons why we were having fewer contacts, we devised plans which would give us the advantage. Before long the Germans got wind of what we were doing, introduced their own counter measures and the tide turned again in their favour. Thus throughout the conflict the scales tipped first one way and then the other.

It is important to remember that most of the operational U-boats used in the war had to come up to periscope depth in order to launch an attack on the target. They then became vulnerable if any aircraft or escort ships were in the vicinity. What Sunderlands, in common with other Coastal Command aircraft, achieved was to keep the submarines down so that they were not in a position to release their torpedoes. Naturally, we wanted to be more successful in destroying U-boats, but by simply preventing them from making attacks on our ships we achieved the next best thing.

Our aircraft crews suffered much heartache, as they could seldom be given any concrete evidence at the time that they were being effective. They spent excessively long hours in the air, by day and night, escorting convoys, carrying out A/S patrols and chasing radar blips, only to return to base unable to report having actually *seen* anything. This was not good for morale and they had to be constantly reminded that, partly due to their efforts, convoys were getting through and the UK was not being starved out as the enemy had intended.

Our merchant ships were not only carrying food and the normal supplies for survival to the UK. One of their vital roles was transporting troops and military equipment to the battlefields. An interesting observation was made by Maurice Allward in his book *An illustrated history of seaplanes and flying boats*.

The value of an anti-submarine aircraft, he says, "...cannot be indicated by the number of German craft sunk, but rather by the number of Allied merchant vessels it helped to keep afloat. The saving...of even one ship was the equal of winning a significant ground battle in terms of the equipment involved, as indicated by the following figures. A typical cargo for an average 6000 ton merchant ship was 21 tanks, four six-inch howitzers, 44 small field guns, 12 armoured cars, 25 Bren carriers, 2,600 tons of ammunition, 300 rifles, 200 tons of tank spares and 1000 tons of miscellaneous stores."

This kind of information was not, of course, available to us at the time. For much of our operational lives we were working in the dark. We were briefed to escort convoys without knowing what they were carrying or how important their cargoes were. They were all treated as top priority, which in the long run was probably a good thing. Most of our A/S patrols were carried out without any prior knowledge of whether or not there were any U-boats in our area. We were also largely oblivious of what was going on in the war elsewhere. We had our own area to cover and we concentrated on covering it to the best of our ability.

Flying boat crews accepted that they could not expect any sympathy or help from the enemy if he brought them down in the sea during a skirmish. U-boat commanders had strict instructions from Dönitz not to take survivors on board. For one thing they had little enough accommodation for themselves and their crews; for another there would be a risk of disclosing their own position to other aircraft or ships in the area.

I've shown that I was not without fear during my flying experience, whether in anticipation of action with the enemy, mechanical problems or adverse weather conditions. Coping with this was made easier by the rigorous training we received as a closely-knit team. We shared responsibility and danger, becoming totally absorbed in carrying out the tasks set us. Whatever our inner fears, we were careful not to disclose them to our companions, lest they felt that we were not up to the job. We were all conscious of the fact that if we failed to do that job, we'd be failing them. This would not bring us any thanks, particularly if lives were put at risk by our negligence.

The reader may feel that I have overstressed the problems of mechanical failures and aircraft losses during my tour on the West African coast. The fact is that these were persistently recurring hazards and we could not treat lightly the possible loss of anything up to a dozen or so fully trained aircrew in just one accident. Of all the Sunderland crashes and losses in West Africa that I have referred to in this book, not one was due to enemy action. They have been recorded not for the sake of drama, or for historical purposes, but because they all had some impact on my own life and philosophy. They led me to analyse the problems and to work out my own strategies for use should I ever find myself in similar situations.

One of my greatest anxieties was losing an engine on take-off when the aircraft and her crew were at their most vulnerable. Trying to gain or maintain height with a full load on three engines with the fourth producing nothing but drag was a nightmare to me. There was also the worry of possible engine failure when we were hundreds of miles out to sea. At least two crews of my acquaintance had to make forced landings in these circumstances and had lucky escapes. At no time did I blame the ground crews for mechanical failures. They did a first class job in most difficult conditions. Our engines were overworked and obviously prone to certain faults which could not always be anticipated.

In April 1944, the operational records of number 204 squadron made mention of the fact that a new version of Sunderland was long overdue. When I eventually flew the Mk V in the following February, I realized that it was perfection by comparison with its predecessors. There were no longer worries about engine failures on take-off, because in the first place they were rare occurrences and in the second it was not at all difficult now to deal with such problems. The airscrew on the offending engine could be stopped from windmilling, so that its drag was reduced to a minimum. There was nearly always adequate additional power available from the other three engines to get one out of trouble. The Mk V also scored in having improved ASV and a radio altimeter as standard, to say nothing of uprated armaments. We were already trained in an improved attack strategy for which the new boat would have been eminently suitable, but we were never able to use it against the enemy. It would have been a formidable weapon indeed had it been available earlier.

The Germans were at the same time putting their own faith in the new type XXI Electro-boat, but this again did not appear in time to be able to prove itself against its adversaries. This was a greatly improved U-boat which had been under development for many years. The enemy had similar feelings about its exceptional capabilities as we had about the Mk V Sunderland. It will never be known what would have been the result had these two advanced machines been joined in battle.

A unique feature of serving on a Sunderland squadron was that we often lived in our aircraft as well as flying it. Frequently we operated from detachment bases where it was necessary both to sleep and eat on board, suitable facilities ashore being nonexistent or limited. This kind of life called for teamwork and camaraderie of the highest order. It developed in us all an independence which was of considerable value in later life.

A level of responsibility leading to early maturity was thrust upon some of us when scarcely out of our teens. Although a very rewarding experience, to many it proved unsettling when trying to integrate ourselves into a totally different society after the war. We went away to war as callow youths and came home as mature adults.

In the same way that aircrew serving in fighters, bombers and other aircraft were proud of their machines, so we grew to respect our Sunderlands and came to regard them as something very special. The fighter pilot distinguished himself from others by leaving undone the top button of his tunic. The flying boat pilot could be readily identified by the condition of his cap badge and buttons which became tarnished from exposure to the sea spray. I recall an occasion in Scotland when I was most upset at losing my cap overboard from a dinghy. It had been a truly battered and faded specimen, adorned with a very green cap badge which had been weathered by the sea spray for many months. When forced to replace it with a spanking new one, I removed the wire frame, jumped on the cap a few times and then rubbed the gold badge with a typewriter brush in the vain hope of making it look as though it had got some service in. None of us liked to look like sprogs.

The age of the Sunderland flying boat lasted twenty-one years. At the time of its eventual retirement, it was the longest serving operational aircraft in the RAF. In all, 739 aircraft were built, 456 of which were the Mk III version. The Mk V, of which 150 were made, was introduced into service too late to be used offensively in the anti-U-boat war. It nevertheless gave invaluable service in other ways, for example in air-sea rescue work, repatriating POWs from the Far East and transporting large numbers of service and civilian personnel at the end of the war.

The aircraft's post-war service with the RAF was also impressive. It played a significant part in the Berlin Air Lift in 1948 and was the only RAF aircraft to serve in the Korean war in 1950. It was used to combat Communist terrorist activities in Malaya and had an important role in the North Greenland Polar Expedition in the early 1950s. Although it was taken out of RAF service in 1959, the French continued to use 19 boats until 1960 and the Royal New Zealand Air Force were flying 16 Sunderlands in the Pacific until 1966.

On 16 October 1987, which happened to be the 50th anniversary of the maiden flight of the prototype, the last airworthy Sunderland in the world was blown off her beaching trolley and badly damaged at Chatham in the hurricane which hit the southern counties of Britain. Restored to airworthiness by her then owner Edward Hulton, who invested a large sum of money in her preservation, she is at the time of writing still flying and has been sold to an American. I understand she will be joining a private collection of aircraft in the US and will be refitted as a military flying boat.

Once I had experienced the Sunderland life, I soon got over my early disappointment at not being selected to fly fighters. I have concluded that flying boats were the right kind of aircraft for me. They suited my temperament, particularly my stubborn persistence, without which those long hours spent flying over the sea might have been soul-destroying. I always had a degree of optimism which, coupled with the unusual amenities provided on board, made these sorties tolerable. By a curious irony, notwithstanding the dangers from mechanical breakdowns and the capricious moods of the sea, being chosen to fly these magnificent aircraft probably ensured my survival. I was privileged to serve in them.

Area of operation – West African Tour (204 Squadron) 1943/44 and locations of stopover bases on transit flights to Mombasa and Karachi 1945

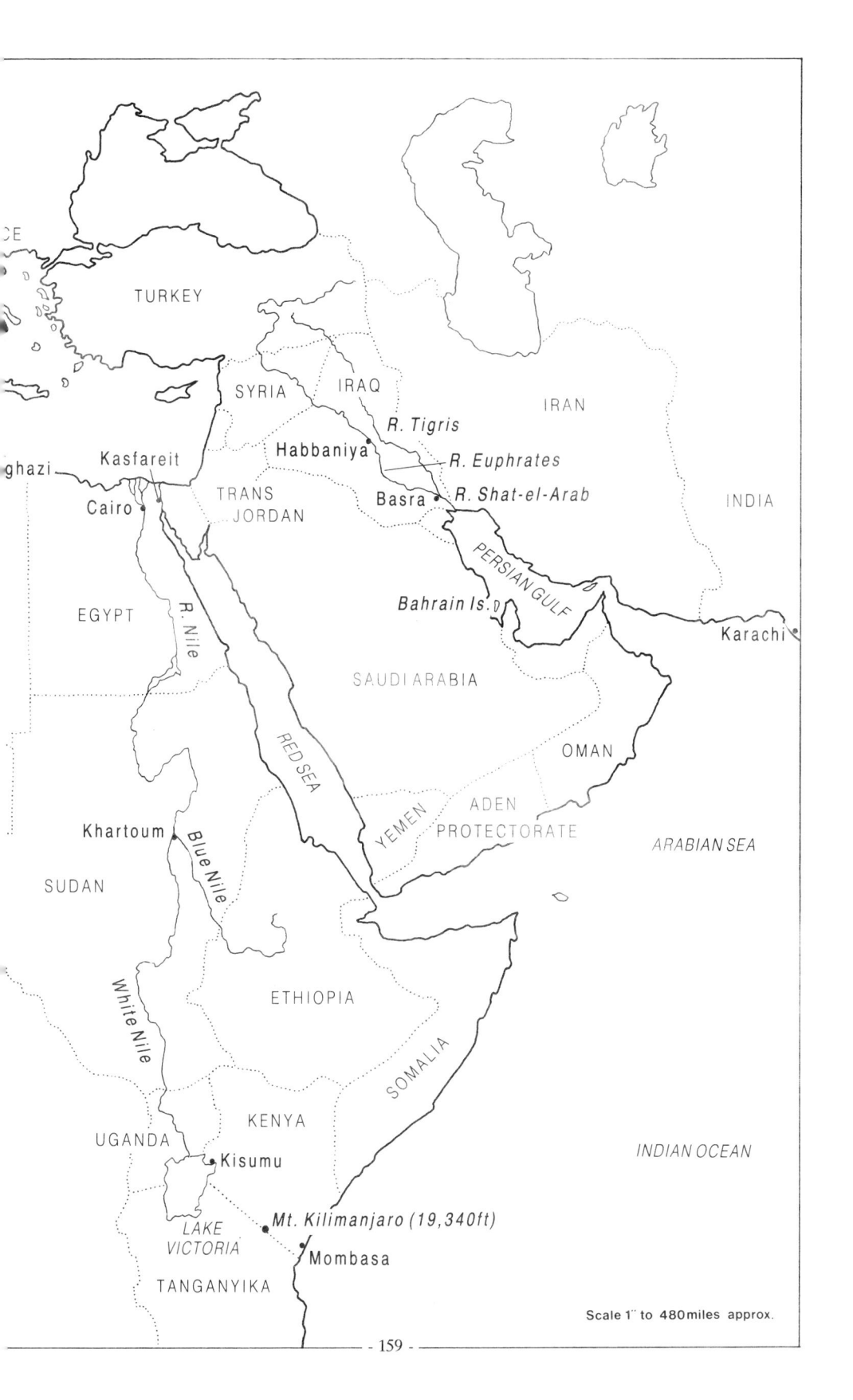

Area of operations in author's Far East
Tour (240 and 209 Squadrons) 1945/46

Map

- CHINA
- Hong Kong
- BURMA
- Syriam (Rangoon)
- SIAM
- GULF OF MARTABAN
- man Is.
- Mergui
- t. Blair
- GULF OF SIAM
- INDO-CHINA
- Saigon
- BANDON BAY
- bar Is.
- Phuket Is.
- Nancowry
- SOUTH CHINA SEA
- Penang Is.
- MALAYA
- Labuan
- BRUNEI
- Pt. Swettenham
- Pt. Dickson
- Singapore
- Kuching
- SARAWAK
- MALACCA STRAIT
- BORNEO
- SUMATRA

Scale 1" to 280 miles approx.

— 161 —

Appendix A1

Comparative Technical Data - Short Sunderland flying boats

(to be read in conjunction with notes given in Appendix A2)

VERSION	MARK I	MARK II	MARK III	MARK V
MANUFACTURE				
number built	90	43	456	150
factory	Rochester Dumbarton	Rochester Dumbarton Belfast	Rochester Dumbarton Belfast Windermere	Rochester Dumbarton Belfast
DIMENSIONS				
wingspan	112'9½"	112'9½"	112'9½"	112'9½"
hull length	85'4"	85'4"	85'4"	85'8"
hull width	10'2"	10'2"	10'2"	10'2"
height*	32'2"	32'2"	32'2"	32'2"
tailplane width	35'9"	35'9"	35'9"	35'9"
wing area (sq ft)	1487	1487	1487	1487
WEIGHT				
empty (lbs)	30,589	33,000	34,500	37,000
maximum take-off (lbs)	50,100	56,000	58,000	65,000
maximum landing (lbs)	50,100	52,000	54,000	57,400
STEP MODIFICATION	No	No	Yes	Yes
SPEED				
take-off (knots) at load (lbs)	83 48,700	75 42,189	75 50,000	80 50,000
take-off (knots) at full load (lbs)	91 50,100	85 56,000	85 56,000	85 65,000+
for maximum climb (knots) at load(lbs) (up to 6000')	125 50,000	125 50,000	125 50,000	125-130 50,000

APPENDIX A1 (contd)

VERSION	MARK I	MARK II	MARK III	MARK V
SPEED (contd)				
optimum climb (knots) varying with height	114-8	114-8	114-8	110-130
maximum permissible (knots)	210	210	211.5	200
cruising for maximum range:				
light load (knots)	120	120	115-120	120
full load (knots)	140	140	125	125
cruising for maximum endurance:				
light load (knots)	105	105	105	105
full load (knots)	110	110	110	110
gliding (knots) varying with height/power	110-120	110-120	95-115	95-120
landing (touchdown) (knots)	85	85	75-85	80-85
ENGINES (4 air-cooled radials):				
type	Bristol Pegasus XXII	Bristol Pegasus XVIII	Bristol Pegasus XVIII	Pratt & Whitney Twin Wasp R1830-90 B & C
cylinders	9	9	9	14
maximum horsepower at sea level	1,010	1,050	1,050	1,200
propellers (3-bladed)	DH 2-pitch (coarse/fine)	DH 20 degree constant speed	DH 20 degree constant speed (early types) or DH 'Rack' con./speed	Hamilton Hydromatic (fully feathering to 88 degrees)
FUEL CAPACITY (100 octane − 10 tanks):				
maximum	2034gals	2034gals	2552gals	2552gals
RADAR	–	ASV Mk II	ASV Mk II (later Mk III)	ASV Mk VIC

APPENDIX A1 (contd)

VERSION	MARK I	MARK II	MARK III	MARK V
ARMAMENT (K = Vickers; B = Brownings)				
front turret	2 x .303B	2 x .303B	2 x .303B	2 x .303B
fixed forward guns	–	–	4 x .303B (some a/c)	4 x .303B
mid-upper (dorsal) turret	–	2 x .303B (later a/c)	2 x .303B	2 x .303B (some a/c)
galley guns	–	–	2 x .303K	2 x .303K (some a/c)
waist guns	2 x .303K	–	2 x .5B (some a/c)	2 x .5B (some a/c)
rear turret	4 x .303B	4 x .303B	4 x .303B	4 x .303B
bombs/DCs	8 x 100lbs bombs	8 x 250lbs DCs	8 x 250lbs DCs	8 x 250lbs DCs

KEY:

*   height to top of fin (on beaching chassis)
+   reduced to 60,000lbs in tropical conditions

Appendix A2

NOTES

1) The comparative technical data table in Appendix A1 was compiled from a large number of sources, as the quantity of information sought was not available in any one place. Most of the manufacturer's records had been destroyed in Short Bros' move from Rochester to Belfast. In some instances the memories of individuals who had been involved in designing and building the Sunderland had to be tapped.

Inevitably there will be inaccuracies, due to conflicting information from different sources, the occasional use of unqualified data and the fact that modifications were being made and performance figures updated over the life of the aircraft type. The author has tried to keep these inaccuracies to a minimum, but would suggest that the figures are accepted as a guide only.

Performance figures quoted in publications without any qualification can be very misleading. Speeds were, of course, affected by a number of factors, the most important of which were engine power, weight (and its distribution in the aircraft), height and weather conditions. All of these would be changing throughout a flight of ten or twelve hours. As the other conditions varied, engine power would have to be adjusted to maintain the airspeed necessary for the required performance, eg maximum range or maximum endurance. It should also be borne in mind that considerable differences in performance were possible between individual aircraft of the same type.

2) The adjustments in engine power mentioned above also gave rise to changes in fuel consumption. The following operating data provided in the pilot's notes for the Mark V may be of some interest. The first table represents climbing conditions and the second cruising conditions:

(a) Approximate total consumptions in gallons per hour in rich mixture at 2,000 ft are:

Boost (lb./sq.in)	R.P.M.	
	2,550	2,325
+5½	440	
+2		250

(b) Approximate total consumptions in gallons per hour in weak mixture at 2,000 ft are:

Boost (lb./sq.in)	R.P.M.						
	2,250	2,150	2,050	1,950	1,850	1,750	1,650
−¼	148	142	134	128	122	118	112
−1	140	135	128	123	117	112	108
−2	131	126	120	115	109	104	101
−3	121	116	110	106	102	−	−

APPENDIX A2 (contd)

As take-off boost and revs per minute to develop 4,800 horsepower (total) were + 9 lbs/sq in and 2,700 rpm respectively (up to five minutes limit), the fuel needed to get the aircraft off the water would have been very much greater than the 440 gals/hour (22 gals for three minutes) quoted for maximum climb conditions.

The engine limitations for combat conditions were + 7½ lb/sq in and 2,700 rpm for a maximum of five minutes, with the proviso that cylinder and oil inlet temperatures remained within recommended limits.

3) The Mk IV version, introduced in late 1944, was named the Seaford. Only 10 aircraft were made at the Rochester factory. It was intended to satisfy the need for a faster boat. The prototype MZ269 was powered by four Bristol Hercules XVII engines developing 1740 hp each, while the production boats were fitted with Hercules 100 units of maximum rating 1680 hp. They all had fully-feathering, four-bladed De Havilland Hydromatic propellers. The hull was widened by 12 inches. It was also longer and the fin taller than in the previous versions by 3'3" and 2'1" respectively. The tailplane area was increased and the mainplane built of thicker metal for greater strength.

The increased weight over the Mk III was 10,500 lbs empty and the maximum all-up weight was stepped up by 17,000 lbs. The aircraft's armaments were uprated, the most significant change being replacement of the 2 x .303 Brownings in the mid-upper turret with 2 x 20mm Hispano cannon. The front and rear turrets carried twin .5 Brownings, while the two waist hatches each had one. There were four fixed .303 Brownings in the hull just aft of the front turret.

Although the top speed was greater by about 25 knots, the overall performance did not come up to expectations. The design was abandoned in favour of the Mk V for post-war operation.

4) Mk III boats operating with West African and some other Sunderland units overseas had the mid-upper turret removed to reduce drag and thus improve performance.

Appendix B

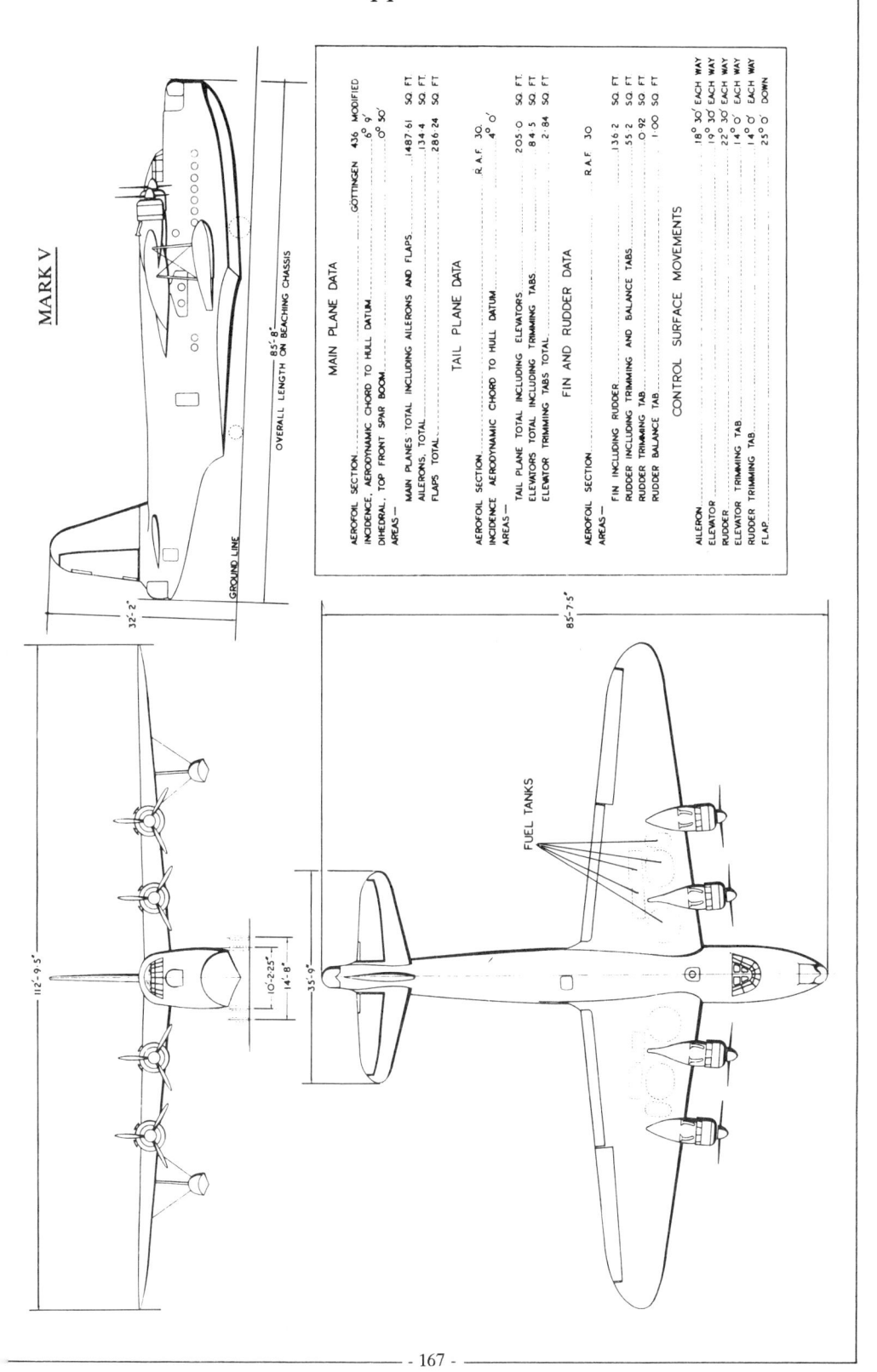

MARK V

32'-2"
OVERALL LENGTH 85'-8" ON BEACHING CHASSIS
GROUND LINE

112'-9.5"
10'-2.25" 14'-8"
35'-9"

85'-7.5"

FUEL TANKS

MAIN PLANE DATA

AEROFOIL SECTION	GOTTINGEN 436 MODIFIED
INCIDENCE, AERODYNAMIC CHORD TO HULL DATUM	6° 9'
DIHEDRAL, TOP FRONT SPAR BOOM	0° 30'
AREAS:—	
MAIN PLANES TOTAL INCLUDING AILERONS AND FLAPS	1487.61 SQ FT
AILERONS, TOTAL	134.4 SQ FT
FLAPS TOTAL	286.24 SQ FT

TAIL PLANE DATA

AEROFOIL SECTION	R.A.F. 30
INCIDENCE AERODYNAMIC CHORD TO HULL DATUM	4° 0'
AREAS:—	
TAIL PLANE TOTAL INCLUDING ELEVATORS	205.0 SQ FT
ELEVATORS TOTAL INCLUDING TRIMMING TABS	84.5 SQ FT
ELEVATOR TRIMMING TABS TOTAL	2.84 SQ FT

FIN AND RUDDER DATA

AEROFOIL SECTION	R.A.F. 30
AREAS:—	
FIN INCLUDING RUDDER	136.2 SQ FT
RUDDER INCLUDING TRIMMING AND BALANCE TABS	55.2 SQ FT
RUDDER TRIMMING TAB	0.92 SQ FT
RUDDER BALANCE TAB	1.00 SQ FT

CONTROL SURFACE MOVEMENTS

AILERON	18° 30' EACH WAY
ELEVATOR	19° 30' EACH WAY
RUDDER	22° 30' EACH WAY
ELEVATOR TRIMMING TAB	14° 0' EACH WAY
RUDDER TRIMMING TAB	14° 0' EACH WAY
FLAP	25° 0' DOWN

Appendix C

HULL EQUIPMENT

MARK V

STARBOARD

PORT

- D CLOTHING HEATING LEAD STOWAGE
- E CAMERA LEAD STOWAGE
- A FIRE EXTINGUISHER
- B INTERCOMMUNICATION SOCKET
- C ARMOUR PLATE

DE-ICING SYSTEMS SEE SECTS. 8 & 11

AUTOMATIC PILOT SYSTEM SEE SECT. 7, CHAP 4

ELECTRICAL & RADIO INSTALLATIONS SEE SECTS. 6 & 10

TURRET HYDRAULIC SYSTEMS SEE SECT. 9

- 168 -

Appendix C

Controls and Equipment at Crew Stations

KEY

1. Nose turret (F.N.5) 2 Browning .303 in. guns
2. Bomb-firing switch and lead—stowage
3. Pilot-operated bow guns—.303 in. Browning guns (2 port, 2 starboard)
4. Ammunition box
5. Boathook
6. Slip-line
7. Bomb sight stowage bracket
8. Bomb sight adaptor
9. Spent cartridge holder
10. Bomb sight computor
11. Signal and illuminating cartridges
12. Signal pistol
13. Drift-sight recorder mounting
14. Adjustable lamp
15. Mk. I air thermometer
16. Mk. IIIF computor mounting
17. A.P.U. fuel supply cock
18. Manual release for type J dinghy
19. Navigator's instrument panel
20. Astrograph mounting—under base of radio set
21. Plan range finder—stowage
22. D.F. aerial control
23. Oil coolers louvres controls
24. Engine starting panel
25. Navigational computors—stowage
26. Cowl gill operating gear
27. A.P.U. tank refuelling hand pump and cock
28. Aerofoil de-icing controls
29. Carburettor de-icing control panel
30. Engine turning handles
31. Engine and propeller servicing safety belt—stowage
32. First-aid outfits
33. Flap emergency winding handle—stowage
34. Flap gearbox
35. Bomb carriage emergency traversing handle—stowage
36. Bomb carriage traversing gearbox
37. Observation dome back rest—stowage
38. Mid-upper turret (F.N.7, Mk. V) 2 Browning .303 in. guns (emergency exit when turret is not fitted)
39. Beam gun—Browning .5 in. stowed position
40. Beam-gunner's hatch
41. Rear entrance door
42. Dinghy mooring hand-grip
43. Projectile type kite—stowage
44. Emergency rations—stowage
45. Emergency packs, types 5 and 7
46. D.R. compass master unit
47. H.T.V. sea markers or flame floats
48. Aluminium sea markers
49. W/T aerial winch
50. Tail-gunner's escape hatch
51. Tail turret (F.N.4) 4 Browning .303 in. guns
52. F.24 camera stowage bracket
53. Type "D" dinghy
54. Hull leak stoppers—stowage
55. Beam-gunner's fire step
56. Bunk—crews
57. Galley guns, 2 Vickers K guns—stowage (early aircraft only)
58. Bilge hand pump nozzles—stowage
59. Bilge-water hose
60. Hand bilging discharge connection
61. Bilge-water pump.
62. Bomb door operating mechanism
63. Bomb door.
64. Twin-unit filter-power bilging system
65. Power bilging connection
66. Cooking stove—paraffin.
67. Fresh-water tanks—two, 5 gall. each.
68. Drogue container
69. Drogue hatch (used for galley guns when fitted)
70. Drogue pennant and trip-lines
71. Cooking utensil locker
72. Paraffin tank for cooker
73. Rack for plates
74. Spare ammunition—galley guns.
75. Spare filaments—galley gun sights
76. Observer's platform—for use at engineer's hatch
77. Bunk—wardroom
78. Lavatory and wash basin
79. Bomb sight scuttle stowage
80. Spare drogue stowage
81. Water tank for wash basin
82. Nose turret and fairing retracting gear handle
83. Mooring pennant—stowage
84. Air-bomber's folding seat.
85. Height-and-airspeed computor stowage
86. Bow mooring hatch
87. Wedge plate stowage—camera push-switch control
88. Wedge plate stowage—camera control unit
89. Wedge plate stowage—camera motor
90. Bomb door operating lever
91. Windscreen wipers
92. Wedge plate stowage—camera control unit
93. Height-and-airspeed computors
94. 1st pilot's bomb-firing switch and lead—stowage
95. Spare glasses for signalling lamp
96. Signalling lamp
97. Marine type sextant—stowage
98. Astro compass mounting tray—stowage
99. Signal-pistol firing sleeve.
100. Emergency key—engineer's hatch
101. Engineer's hatch
102. Aerial lead—stowage
103. Sextant—stowage
104. Inspection lamp—stowage
105. D.F. loop aerial plug and coil—stowage
106. Trailing aerial winch
107. Crash axe
108. Fuel and oil funnels
109. Sea markers (ten)—stowage
110. Smoke or flame floats (ten)
111. Reconnaissance flares (six) (see also item 120)
112. Oars for dinghy
113. F.24 camera mounting—stowed position
114. Flare release lead—stowage
115. Wedge plate stowage—No. 4 lead—stowage
116. Camera cover and Camera motor
117. Camera heating muff lead—stowage
118. Camera and flare chute hatch.
119. Flare chute
120. Reconnaissance flares (four) (see also item 111)
121. Tool locker
122. Foot bellows for type D dinghy
123. Bomb winch hand-hoisting chain—stowage
124. Ice chest and food cupboard
125. Trailing aerial fairlead tube
126. Trailing aerial watertight cap
127. Trailing aerial fairlead—stowed position
128. Bow guns—stowage
129. Mooring ladder
130. Front entrance door
131. Fog bell
132. Anchor winch.
133. Camera leads—stowage
134. Anchor (special order only)
135. Retractable mooring bollard—stowed position.
136. Mooring bridle—stowed position

Appendix D

GLOSSARY OF TERMS AND ABBREVIATIONS USED

ABEAM – abreast or to the side of a boat or ship, at right angles to its heading
ABORT – to cancel a manoeuvre, eg a take-off
ACRC – Aircrew Reception Centre
ADJUTANT – an administrative officer in the services
AFC – Air Force Cross
AHQ – Air Headquarters
AILERON – a narrow hinged control surface on the outer trailing edge of the wing enabling its aerodynamic shape to be changed simply by turning the wheel or tilting the joystick sideways. Port and starboard ailerons operate in opposite mode so that when the aircraft is banked, lift increases on one wing while it decreases on the other
AIRFRAME – the framework of an aircraft (fuselage, wings, etc), mainly made in Duralumin(*qv*)
AIRSCREW – the technical name for a propeller. The blades are set at an angle or pitch so that when the prop is turning, it behaves like a screw relative to the air mass around it
AIRSPEED – the speed of an aircraft relative to the surrounding air. This will only be the same as the groundspeed if there is no wind
AIRSTREAM – the flow of air past the aircraft as it is propelled forward
ALDIS LAMP – a powerful hand-held signalling lamp with a hinged mirror connected to a trigger, the operation of which enables messages to be sent in Morse Code to ships, shore, aircraft, etc
ALTITUDE –   1 the height above mean sea level;
                2 the angle of a heavenly body above the natural horizon
ANNAPOLIS OF THE AIR – the popular name given by the US Navy to their flying training establishment at Pensacola, Florida. Annapolis is the capital city of Maryland and the site of the US Naval Academy
AOC – Air Officer Commanding
APRON – the tarmac or concrete hard standing on which land-based aircraft are parked
APU – auxiliary power unit. A small petrol engine located on the Sunderland in the leading edge of the mainplane between hull and starboard inner engine. The gearbox could be engaged to drive the refuelling pump, bilge pump and 2 air compressors
ASDIC – type of hydrophone used by ships to detect submarines (derived from Anti-Submarine Detection Investigation Committee)
ASP – anti-submarine patrol
ASR – air-sea rescue. The process of recovering survivors from disasters at sea either by means of ASR launches, ships or aircraft. In suitable conditions, flying boats could land on the water and effect the rescue. Otherwise, they would alert seagoing ships and sometimes home them on to the survivors
A/S SWEEP – an anti-submarine patrol in which a particular method of covering a given area thoroughly was used. See CLA
ASTRO-HATCH – a hatch, incorporating transparent perspex dome, in the top of a Sunderland's hull above the navigator's position. Replaced the engineer's hatch in flight, enabling the navigator to obtain bearings or fixes (on sun and/or stars) using the sextant. Also a convenient lookout point, eg for coordinating firepower in an aerial attack
ASV – air-to-surface vessel. Radar equipment used to locate ships, aircraft, etc by bouncing radio signals off them and measuring the time it took for the signals to return to the aircraft. Early equipment had a linear trace along a vertical diameter of a circular cathode ray tube and blips (or spikes) on either side of the trace indicated responses from targets. Later versions used a PPI (*qv*)

APPENDIX D (contd)

AUTOMATIC PILOT – or autopilot. A gyrostabilized system, affectionately known as George, used to maintain aircraft in steady flight with minimum help from the pilot
AVM – Air Vice Marshal. Senior RAF rank equivalent to Major General in the Army
BACK – (of the wind) to change in a counter-clockwise direction. *See* Veer
BANK – to incline or tilt an aircraft laterally. *See* Aileron
BAROMETRIC ALTIMETER – a height measuring instrument making use of the fact that barometric pressure is inversely proportional to height above sea level. Necessary to adjust the instrument for changes in sea level pressure. *See* Radio altimeter
BEACHING EQUIPMENT – Sunderland flying boats were not amphibious, so special equipment was needed to enable them to be towed up the slipway for servicing. It consisted of two legs (on wheels) which were bolted to the hull under the wings and a small trolley which was fitted to the tail end of the keel
BEAD – the forward sight of a gun. To draw a bead on a target was to line up the sights on it
BEARING – the direction of an object from an aircraft measured as an angle relative to north
BEAT UP – fly low in a simulated attack (RAF slang)
BEAUFORT SCALE – the international scale of wind velocity:

Force 0:	less than 1 knot	– calm
" 1:	1 – 3 knots	– light air
" 2:	4 – 7 "	– light breeze
" 3:	8 – 12 "	– gentle
" 4:	13 – 18 "	– moderate
" 5:	19 – 24 "	– fresh
" 6:	25 – 31 "	– strong
" 7:	32 – 38 "	– moderate gale
" 8:	39 – 46 "	– fresh
" 9:	47 – 54 "	– strong
" 10:	55 – 63 "	– whole
" 11:	64 – 75 "	– storm
" 12:	over 75 "	– hurricane

BELLY LANDING – said of a landplane when it landed with its undercarriage (wheel assembly) up
BEND – to drive (someone) round the bend was RAF slang, now absorbed into the language, meaning to drive someone out of his mind
BFB – British Flight Battalion. Name given to the unit made up of Royal Air Force and Fleet Air Arm cadets at Pensacola
BILGE – the space between lower deck and keel of a flying boat. If any water entered the bilges and was not pumped out before take-off, the added weight and/or its uneven distribution could cause problems
BIND – an all-embracing RAF slang term (both noun and verb) which could refer to nuisance, tedium, boredom, grumbling, etc
BLACK OUT – to lose vision temporarily due to blood draining from the head as a result of increased gravitational force when the aircraft's direction changes suddenly
BLIND FLYING – flying solely by observing, and responding to, the behaviour of the instruments. The pilot did not have the benefit of relating the aircraft's attitude to anything outside it. Also known as flying on instruments or instrument flying
BLIP – a definable response (from a target) on a radar screen
BLISTERS – in Catalinas, the bulbous waist gun positions. In the Mk V Sunderland, it referred to the ASV scanner (or directional aerial) housings located under the wingtips
BOAC – British Overseas Airways Corporation (Civil airline)
BOAT GUARD – crew member(s) detailed to keep watch in a flying boat at anchor or moorings, particularly in adverse weather conditions

APPENDIX D (contd)

BOLD – a decoy device used by the Germans to simulate the presence of a U-boat. A canister, containing a chemical which gave off hydrogen gas when in contact with water, was ejected into the sea, causing a cloud of bubbles to rise to the surface

BOOST – engine power applied by the operation of the throttle lever

BRIDLE – a wire hawser attached to eyes on the front of the keel and used to moor the flying boat to one of the pendants or strops on the buoy

BRIEF – to provide the crew with instructions and necessary information on the objective of the sortie, the weather, communications codes, etc before a flight. The briefing normally took place in the Operations Room. *See also* Debrief

BULKHEAD – upright partitions (like the walls of a room) dividing compartments of a flying boat

CALLISTHENICS – the art and practice of bodily exercises calculated to produce strength and grace. More commonly known among the British cadets at Pensacola as physical jerks

CAT – Catalina, the Consolidated PBY-5B. Amphibious version was the Canso (PBY-5A)

CATWALK – a sloping wooden ramp on wheels giving access to a beached flying boat

CHARGE SHEET – the official form 252 on which a charge (for an offence) was recorded

CHARPOY – a lightweight Indian bedstead. Commonly shortened to charp

CHOCK – wedge shaped block placed on the ground in front of and sometimes behind a landplane's wheels to prevent the aircraft moving

CIRCUITS AND BUMPS – the complete process of taking off, making a circuit and landing an aircraft for practice or testing

CLA – creeping line ahead. A method of searching an area thoroughly for submarines, ships, etc. Fully described on page 65

CLAMP – a device used when an aircraft is on the ground or water to prevent control surfaces from moving, for example in a high wind

CLOT – a derogatory RAF slang term meaning a blockhead, stupid person, fool

CO – Commanding Officer

COASTAL COMMAND – the arm of the RAF responsible for cooperation with the Royal Navy, reconnaissance of enemy harbours and shipping and for attacking the targets found. Subsidiary activities included ASR, passenger and freight carrying and meteorological flights

COCKPIT CHECK – a systematic procedure carried out by a pilot before take-off. Included checking that the engines and control surfaces were working satisfactorily and that the front turret and all hatches were closed

COME UNSTUCK – to leave the water on take-off. Expression probably came into use because in certain marine conditions the hull of a flying boat adhered to the water stubbornly, requiring special techniques to free it

COMPANIONWAY – nautical expression for ladder or steps from one deck to another

CONTROL COLUMN – the column, supporting the pilot's wheel, which transmits movements to the elevator and ailerons

CONTROL SURFACES – those movable surfaces on the aerofoils (wing, tailplane, fin) of an aircraft which determine its attitude in the air. They consist of ailerons, elevator, rudder and flaps, together with their trimming tabs

COURSE – synonymous with heading. The compass direction in which the aircraft is pointed. To this has to be added the deviation, a correction depending on the effect of magnetic material near the compass, to obtain the magnetic heading. Since magnetic north is not the same as true north, a further adjustment known as variation has to be made to arrive at the true course. (Note that the course is not the same as the track, or the direction in which the aircraft is actually moving over the ground, except when there is no wind)

COWLING – the housing around an aircraft engine. The rear hinged parts of it, called the gills, could be opened to provide additional cooling when necessary

APPENDIX D (contd)

CUMULONIMBUS – tall, dense cloud, often with anvil shape at the top, usually associated with thunderstorms
CUMULOUS – billowy white cloud associated mainly with fine weather in summer
CYPHER (or cipher) – to manipulate the words, letters and figures of plain language or coded messages to make them unintelligible to an enemy
DALTON COMPUTER – a navigational instrument with circular dial and movable blind on which vector diagrams of courses, tracks and winds were drawn and calculations made. See plate 15
DC – Depth charge (qv)
DEAD RECKONING – system of navigation in which the aircraft's position is mainly determined by measuring drifts and calculating wind direction and speed. See page 61
DEBRIEF – to obtain from the crew all the relevant information about a sortie when the aircraft has landed. As with briefing, the process normally takes place in the Operations Room
DEPTH CHARGE – the main weapon used by flying boats against submarines. Of cylindrical shape with a concave nose, it weighed 250lb and was filled with torpex. Eight DCs were carried by Sunderlands in bomb racks
DETACHMENT BASE – in order to be able to cover large areas of sea, eg in the search for enemy submarines, flying boat squadrons had small subsidiary bases with certain minimum facilities (eg mooring buoys, refuelling arrangements). At these detachment bases, crews often had to live on board their aircraft
DFC – Distinguished Flying Cross
D/F RADIO – direction finding radio. Using rotatable aerials, these radio receivers could provide bearings of transmitting stations by orientating the aerials for maximum or minimum signal strength, etc
DICE ON – RAF slang expression implying pressing on and risking one's life. More generally, carrying on heedless of any risk or hardship
DIRECTIONAL AERIAL – See D/F radio
DISTRESS FREQUENCY – an international radio frequency used by aircrew in distress. In addition to the aircraft's normal long-range radio equipment, there were facilities for transmitting a distress call on the IFF equipment (qv) and in the aircraft dinghy
DITCH – to make a forced landing at sea (RAF slang)
DOPE – cellulose paint applied to fabric parts of an aircraft to keep them taut, airtight and weatherproof
DORSAL TURRET – the mid-upper turret
DOWNWIND LEG – that part of an aircraft's landing circuit which is parallel to and the reciprocal of the approach heading
DR – Dead reckoning (qv)
DRIFT – the angle between an aircraft's heading or course and its track or path over the ground. Its magnitude depends upon the wind direction and speed
DRIFT RECORDER – instrument for measuring Drift (qv above). The ground or water over which the aircraft was flying was observed through a rotatable grid which had parallel lines across it. When the grid was adjusted so that objects appeared to travel along the lines, the drift could be read off the calibrated ring
DRILL – 1 procedure;
2 military exercise or training
DRINK – the water/sea (RAF slang)
DROGUE – an open ended canvas cone used to create drag in the water to limit the speed of a flying boat's approach to a buoy
DUFF GEN – inaccurate information (RAF slang)
DURAL(UMIN) – light, hard aluminium alloy containing copper, manganese and magnesium, used as the main fabric of the aircraft
DYAK – member of a head-hunting aboriginal tribe in Borneo

APPENDIX D (contd)

ECHELON – a single line flying formation in which each aircraft is on the port quarter (port echelon) or starboard quarter (starboard echelon) of the aircraft ahead of it

ELEVATOR – the control surface, hinged to the trailing edge of the tailplane, whose position determines the attitude of the aircraft in the vertical plane

ERK – aircraftman (RAF slang)

ETA – estimated time of arrival

EXACTOR – the hydraulic system which transmitted the throttle lever movement to the appropriate engine throttle valve. Exactors were also used for the mixture controls

FAIRLEAD – a long rigid tube which carried the trailing aerial through the bottom of the boat when in flight

FAN – airscrew or propeller (RAF slang)

FEATHER – 1 to adjust the pitch of a propeller to the extent that it ceased to rotate in the slipstream;
    2 the wake of a periscope in the water

FFI – Free from infection. Medical examination for venereal diseases

FIN – the vertical tail assembly on which the rudder is hinged

FIX – a position determined by more than one bearing on astronomical bodies, radio stations or known landmarks

FIZZER – a Charge sheet (RAF slang)(*qv*)

FLAK BATTERY – a concentration of anti-aircraft guns normally mounted on the deck of a U-boat aft of the conning tower

FLANNEL – to flatter or soft-soap (forces slang). To flannel one's way through was to bluff one's way out of a situation

FLAP – 1 hinged control surface on the inner trailing edge of the wing, used to increase lift for take-off and to lower landing speed;
    2 to get in a flap is to get agitated/fussed (RAF slang)

FLARE-PATH – series of lights marking the boundary of a flying boat's alighting area at night. Normally consisted of three flares equally spaced in a straight line. The pilot always had them on his port side when taking off or landing

FLIGHT DECK – the upper deck of the aircraft, normally occupied by the pilots, navigator, wireless operator, radar operator and engineer

FLIGHT PLAN – a written statement of route and procedures to be adopted for a flight

FLIGHT SIMULATOR – or Link Trainer. A machine which incorporated a fully equipped cockpit and responded to the controls as in an aircraft. It helped to reduce the cost of Instrument flying training (*qv*)

F/LT – Flight Lieutenant, the RAF commissioned rank equivalent to an Army Captain

FLOTSAM – floating debris which had to be cleared from the alighting area by a launch before a flying boat could take off or land

FLUKE – a flat, pointed (often arrow-shaped) projection at the ends of the arms of an anchor

FLYING BOAT – this term applies solely to an aircraft in which the fuselage is designed as a hull to rest on the water. Where floats only are in contact with the water, the aircraft is referred to as a seaplane

FLYING HOURS – this was an inaccurate term when applied to flying boats. The recorded flying hours were actually measured from the time of slipping moorings to the time of mooring up again after a flight

F/O – Flying Officer, the RAF commissioned rank equivalent to an Army Lieutenant

FORCE 0 to 12 – *See* Beaufort Scale

F/SGT – Flight Sergeant, the next senior NCO rank above Sergeant in the RAF

GATE – a hinged flap located at the top of the travel of the throttle levers. When lifted, it enabled the throttles to be advanced to their furthest possible settings, so developing maximum engine power. Normally only used in an emergency

G/CAPT – Group Captain, RAF senior commissioned rank equivalent to Army Colonel

GEN – information (RAF slang)

APPENDIX D (contd)

GEORGE – Automatic pilot (RAF slang) (*qv*)
GLIDE – to lose height without using power, that is with the engines just ticking over (or stopped)
GOSPORT – the headset in a rudimentary intercom system used in open cockpit training aircraft. The instructor could speak through a rubber tube to the trainee who could only respond with signs
GROUNDSPEED – the speed of an aircraft relative to the ground. *See* Airspeed
GUN – throttle (*qv*)
H2S – a centimetric radar system, used by Bomber Command, from which the advanced ASV used in Sunderlands was developed. Display was on a PPI (*qv*)
HATCH – common nautical term, referring specifically in a Sunderland to a door or to an opening in the upper deck
HEADING – Course (*qv*)
HOLDING UNIT – a personnel unit in which airmen were accommodated until their postings to operational or training units were arranged
HOME – to direct, particularly on to a target
HORIZON, INSTRUMENT HORIZON OR ARTIFICIAL HORIZON – the natural horizon was simulated on the pilot's panel by an instrument using a gyroscope. This was mounted in housings (gimbals) so that orientation was independent of the plane's attitude
HOUSEWIFE – pronounced 'huzzif'. A canvas case containing sewing and darning equipment, issued to all airmen to enable them to carry out running repairs to their uniforms
IFF – Identification Friend or Foe. A radio transmitter installed in RAF aircraft enabling Allied forces to distinguish them from the enemy. In an emergency involving ditching, the set could be switched to a distress frequency. There were also facilities for detonating the equipment if there was a risk of it falling into enemy hands
IMMELMAN TURN – an aerobatic manoeuvre in which the pilot completed half a loop and then assumed straight and level flight by executing a half roll. The aircraft ended up flying in the opposite direction to its original course, but at a higher altitude. From the originator, Leutnant Max Immelman, a first World War German ace
INSTRUMENT FLYING – *See* Blind flying
IRONS – knife, fork and spoon (RAF slang)
ITW – Initial Training Wing. The unit at which aircrew cadets learned the theory of flying etc and developed their physical fitness by means of exercise, sport and military drill
JETTISON – the process of discharging fuel from an aircraft in order to reduce its landing weight
JOYSTICK – *See* Control column
KAPITĀNLEUTNANT – the German Navy rank of senior lieutenant
KITE – aircraft (RAF slang)
KNOT – a speed of one nautical mile per hour. Originally measured by means of knots tied in the log line of a ship
LEADING EDGE – the front edge of an aerofoil (wing, tailplane or fin)
LEE SIDE – the downwind (or sheltered) side
LEND-LEASE (or Lease-Lend) – an agreement signed in 1941 between the USA and Britain whereby the former loaned military equipment and supplies to the latter and her allies
LEUTNANT – the German Navy equivalent of Royal Navy Sublieutenant
LIB – Consolidated Liberator aircraft
LIMEY (or lime-juicer) – American nickname for an Englishman. Derived from the practice started in 1795 of giving lime juice to sailors in the Navy to prevent scurvy
LINE AHEAD – naval formation in which all the vessels are one behind the other
LINK TRAINER – flight simulator (*qv*)
LOOP AERIAL – a directional aerial in the shape of a loop used with D/F radio (*qv*)

APPENDIX D (contd)

LOOP SWING – the procedure of measuring errors in loop aerial bearings due to reflections of signals from various parts of the aircraft

LIEUTENANT – Army officer rank equivalent to Flying Officer or Naval officer rank equivalent to Flight Lieutenant

MAE WEST – a life jacket for use in emergency at sea. After the film star of that name

MAGNETIC COMPASS – instrument indicating magnetic north (after applying deviation) and an aircraft Course (*qv*) relative to it

MAGNETO – a modified form of dynamo with permanent magnets used to generate the ignition spark in engine cylinders

MAINPLANE – the main wing of an aircraft

MAIN SPAR – the airframe member supporting the mainplane. The strongest part of the aircraft

MAYDAY – international distress signal given by aircraft when ditched or about to ditch

MEDICO – doctor and sometimes other medical staff (services slang)

MERCATOR CHART – map drawn as if the world were a cylinder, lines of longitude and latitude being at right angles to each other. Greatly simplified dead reckoning navigation. After Gerard Kremer (Latin name Mercator), 16th century Flemish geographer

METOX – A French-built radio receiver used by U-boats to pick up the radiations from Coastal Command's metric ASV equipment, thus giving warning of an aircraft's approach. When centimetric ASV radar was introduced, Metox was not capable of detecting it.

MIXTURE CONTROL – lever in cockpit controlling petrol/air ratio in engine

ML – motor launch. Usually applied to a Royal Navy vessel of this type

MO – Medical Officer

MV – used in this book to denote merchant vessel

NAUTICAL MILE – one sixtieth of a degree of longitude = 6080 feet. (*cf* statute mile = 5280 feet)

NCO – noncommissioned officer (Warrant Officer, Flight Sergeant or Sergeant)

NIP – a Japanese (from Nippon = Japan) (slang)

NISSEN HUT – a currugated iron military shelter of semicircular cross section. After Lt Col Peter Nissen, its pre-war inventor

NOISE – extraneous signals on radar and radio equipment. Often wanted signals were lost in the mush or noise due to unwanted reflections from, for example, the waves

OBERLEUTNANT – the German Navy equivalent of Lieutenant

OC – Officer Commanding

OM – Old Man. Affectionate family nickname for the author's father-in-law

OPERATING TEMPERATURE – in the interests of engine life and reliability, the cylinder head temperature which had to be reached before engines were opened up

OPERATIONAL – engaged on, or used for, war activities

OTU – Operational Training Unit in the RAF

OVERSHOOT – 1 to approach a landing area at too great a height, making it necessary to return to the circuit and try again;
2 to drop one's bombs (or DCs) ahead of the target

PACK – a concentration of U-boats, increasing the chance of success in sinking vessels in convoy. The term Wolf Pack was coined by the Germans in the First World War

PD – Pembroke Dock, a leading flying boat base in South West Wales

PDC – Personnel Distribution Centre

PE – Port Étienne, a small settlement on the West African coast, on the border between Spanish Sahara and Mauritania

PEI – Prince Edward Island, located in the mouth of the St Lawrence River in eastern Canada

PISTOL – device fitted to a depth charge to enable the depth at which it would detonate to be preset

PITCH CONTROL – the cockpit lever which controlled the pitch or angle at which the propeller blades were set. Fine pitch created more thrust than coarse pitch

APPENDIX D (contd)

PLUMB LINE – a line terminating in a lead weight for taking soundings (measuring depth of water)
P/O – Pilot Officer, the most junior commissioned rank in the RAF, equivalent to an Army 2nd lieutenant
POST – to transfer a serviceman to another unit
POSTIE – Scottish term for postman or postwoman
POW – prisoner of war
POWERED APPROACH – an engine assisted landing approach. *See page* 82
PPI – Planned Position Indicator. A circular cathode ray tube giving a trace through 360 degrees, thus providing a map of the area over which the aircraft was flying
PRC – Personnel Reception Centre
PX – Post Exchange. American term for the camp shop
QUADRANTAL ERROR – distortions in the readings given by a loop aerial due to signals being reflected from different parts of the airframe and arriving at the aerial with time delays
RAAF – Royal Australian Air Force
RADAR – from RAdio Detection And Ranging. A system for ascertaining direction and range of a target by sending out radio waves of short wavelength and interpreting the reflections
RADIAL ENGINE – an engine in which the cylinders are arranged like the spokes of a wheel instead of in line
RADIO ALTIMETER – an instrument for measuring an aircraft's altitude using radio signals in a similar manner to radar (*qv*). The indicated height is that above the terrain directly below the aircraft, not necessarily above sea level, as in the barometric altimeter (*qv*)
RADIO BEARING – the direction of a radio station from an aircraft as measured by D/F equipment using a loop aerial (*qv*)
RANGE – 1 (of an aircraft) the maximum distance an aircraft can travel on a given load of fuel. Sometimes used loosely to mean the number of hours it can stay in the air. Note that when calculating range, the diminishing fuel consumption due to reducing load has to be taken into account
   2 (of a target) the straight-line distance of the target from the aircraft
RECCE – slang for Reconnaissance (*qv*)
RECONNAISSANCE – process of searching an area to ascertain, and sometimes photograph, the disposition of enemy forces, installations, etc
RELEASE GROUP – the group to which a serviceman was assigned in order to determine the time of his discharge from wartime service
REV-ALEE – American pronunciation of Reveille (*qv*)
REVEILLE – waking signal for service personnel. Usually pronounced re-vallee
REVS/MIN – (of an engine) revolutions per minute
RCAF – Royal Canadian Air Force
RIGGER – a flying boat crew member, usually an air gunner, responsible for the Airframe (*qv*). Functions included mooring and unmooring
ROLL – an aerobatic manoeuvre involving a corkscrew motion along the longitudinal axis of the aircraft, without appreciably changing height or direction
ROUND TURN – to bring up with a round turn is to check or bring to a stop abruptly
R/T – radio telephone. Short-range radio equipment enabling aircrew to communicate in speech with receivers in the air or on the ground
RUDDER – the hinged control surface on the trailing edge of the fin enabling the aircraft to change direction laterally
SCANNING – the process of carefully sweeping an area with the eyes or with a controlled radio beam as in radar (*qv*)
SEAC – South East Asia Command. These initials were also adopted by a service newspaper in the Far East

APPENDIX D (contd)

SECOND DICKY – second pilot or co-pilot (RAF slang)
SEMAPHORE – form of signalling using two handheld flags
SERVICEABILITY – the state of aircraft readiness for operations, measured as the percentage of available aircraft airworthy at a given time
SEXTANT – navigational instrument used to measure the altitude of heavenly bodies at a particular time. Tables were then consulted and calculations made to establish the bearing of the body from the aircraft
SGT – sergeant, a noncommissioned rank, next above corporal
SHACKLE – a U-shaped link with bolt (or pin) through the two ends, used for joining hawsers, chains, etc
SHORT SLIP – a short rope with loop at one end, used as a temporary means of securing a strop (pendant) or spreader to the bollard
SICK CALL – sick parade (in US forces)
SIDE SLIP – an aerial manoeuvre for losing height rapidly, in particular in order to land in a restricted space. A port slip required port wing down and starboard rudder, a starboard slip vice versa
S/LDR – Squadron Leader, the RAF commissioned rank equivalent to Army Major or Lieutenant-Commander in the Navy
SLIP – 1 a slipway or concrete ramp provided for flying boats to be hauled ashore by winch or tractor;
  2 side slip (qv)
SLIPSTREAM – airstream. The stream of air driven back by an aircraft propeller
SNORKEL – a device developed by the Germans during the European war which enabled a U-boat to spend longer periods under water. Sometimes called a snort, it was a breathing tube which was deployed when the boat was submerged
SORTIE – operational flight
SPAM – trade name for American processed ham supplied in tins (from SPiced hAM)
SPIN – an aeronautical manoeuvre involving a stall (qv) followed by a diving descent with continuous rotation of the aircraft
SPREADER – a floating hawser, attached to a mooring buoy, which could be picked up quickly by boathook for temporary mooring to be made
SPROG – a recruit. Used widely to suggest lack of experience (RAF slang)
SPRUNG RIVET – loosened rivet which weakened the structure of the hull, sometimes causing it to leak
SPUME – in an agitated sea, the white froth or foam on the surface. A useful indication from the air of the direction of the wind. The spume is seen as streaks running with it
SQUADRON – a unit in the RAF, usually of 12 aircraft with crews, groundstaff, etc
SQUALL – sudden violent gust of wind, rain, etc
STABILIZING FLOATS – floats, either suspended on struts from the wings or fixed to the hull, designed to prevent a flying boat from capsizing when the wing tilted to one side or the other
STACK OUT – to lie down to sleep (RAF slang)
STALL – condition when an aircraft's speed falls off such that there is insufficient lift and it ceases to respond to the controls. The nose drops and the aircraft dives, sometimes going into a Spin (qv)
ST.A/G – Straight Air Gunner. On flying boats, gunner duties were combined with Rigger duties (qv)
STAR SHOT – observation of a star with the aid of a sextant for navigational purposes
STEP – a break in the smooth under surface of the hull designed to reduce suction and facilitate planing. The last part of the aircraft to leave the water on take-off
STICK – 1 Joystick (qv);
  2 line of bombs across a target
STIRRUP PUMP – a hand pump, held on the deck by the operator's feet (hence stirrup), used to remove water from Bilges (qv)

APPENDIX D (contd)

STRADDLE – of depth charges or bombs used in an attack on a submarine, to drop them in a stick in such a way that they fall equally to port and starboard of the hull at a fine angle

STRAFE – to rake or spray with machine gun fire

STRATUS – horizontal layer of cloud

STRINGER – an auxiliary longitudinal member of an airframe. A primary longitudinal member is known as a longeron

STROBOSCOPIC EFFECT – applied to propellers seen in line with each other from the cockpit, the illusion that when they are revolving at the same speed they appear stationary

STROP – pendant, or cable suspended from a buoy, to which a flying boat was shackled

STRUT – a support or brace for a wing, float, etc

SUN SHOT – observation of the sun, with the aid of a sextant, for navigational purposes

SUPERCHARGER – device supplying engine with air or explosive mixture at higher than normal pressure to increase efficiency

SUPREMO – Supreme Commander. Overall commander of a theatre of wartime operations – in the narrative, South East Asia Command

SWEEP – 1 the process of clearing the flarepath of debris by means of a motor launch before a flying boat landed or took off;
2 the process of searching an area for U-boats

SWELL – heaving of the sea with long rolling waves which do not always break

SWO – Station Warrant Officer

TAILPLANE – the horizontal tail assembly, to which the elevator is hinged, which gives the aircraft fore and aft stability

TAXI – to move an aircraft along the ground or on the water under power

TENTHS – the standard of measurement of cloud cover. Thus ten tenths means that the whole of the sky is covered with cloud, ie overcast

THREE POINT LANDING – (of landplanes) landing with the two wheels of the main undercarriage and the tail or nose wheel touching down simultaneously

THROTTLE – 1 the valve which determines the quantity of fuel/air mixture delivered to the engine and so controls the power output;
2 the lever in the cockpit connected via the hydraulic system to 1

TOP BRASS – senior service officers, so-called because of the profusion of gold braid worn on their hats and uniforms

TRACE – the path of the luminescent spot on a cathode ray tube (in a radar system) which is seen as a line on the screen

TRACK – path an aircraft follows over the ground

TRADE WINDS – winds blowing towards the equator from about the thirtieth latitude north and south. They are deflected westward by the earth's rotational force, so that they blow from the north-east in the northern hemisphere and from the south-east in the southern hemisphere

TRAILING AERIAL – long wire aerial which was run out through the bottom of a Sunderland's hull to improve long-range radio communication

TRAILING EDGE – the rear edge of an aerofoil (wing, tailplane or fin)

TRIM – make adjustments to the setting of a tab on a control surface to achieve balance in the aircraft's attitude. Necessary because of variations in weight distribution

TRIP – the process of emptying the drogues of water to take them inboard

TROTS – lines of mooring buoys

TURNING CIRCLE – the minimum width of a stretch of water in which a flying boat could be turned through 180 degrees

U-BOAT – German submarine, from the German Unterseeboot

UNDERSHOOT – 1 to approach a landing area at too low a height, necessitating the application of more power to check the rate of descent;
2 to drop one's bombs (or DCs) short of the target

USN – United States Navy

APPENDIX D (contd)

USNAS – United States Naval Air Station (Pensacola, Fla)
USNRAB – United States Naval Reserve Aviation Base (Grosse Île, Mich)
VEER – (of the wind) to change in a clockwise direction. *See* Back
VERY PISTOL – sometimes spelt Verey. A gun which fired cartridges giving coloured lights for identification purposes and when in distress. From the inventor, Lt S W Very
V (or Vic) – aircraft formation shaped like an arrowhead
VIP – Very Important Person. Used in this book mainly to denote senior service officer
WAAF – Women's Auxiliary Air Force. Now known as the Women's Royal Air Force (WRAF)
WAIST HATCHES – doors amidships which opened to reveal gun positions
WARDROOM – the main compartment (or room) on the lower deck of the Sunderland. While originally intended for officers only, as in ships, it was used for meals, resting and recreation by all members of the crew. Free movement between different compartments of the boat would otherwise have been difficult
W/CDR – Wing Commander, the RAF officer rank equivalent to an Army Lieutenant Colonel or a Navy Commander
WEATHERCOCKING – the tendency for a waterborne flying boat to swing into the wind if left to her own devices
WHALER – a double-ended clinker-built boat 20-30 feet long used by the Royal Navy for general duties, incl. pulling and sailing
WHEEL – that part of the control column operating the ailerons for banking an aircraft
WHITE RAJAH – white ruler of Sarawak. The third and last Rajah was Sir Charles Vyner Brooke, who retired in 1946
WINDWARD – towards the wind
WINGMEN – the aircraft (or their pilots) on either side of the leader in a V-formation
W/O – Warrant Officer. Top senior NCO rank
WRNS – Women's Royal Naval Service
YAW – to deviate from a straight course on the water due to a strong wind. Effect could be produced in the air by applying rudder without banking
YELLOW PERIL – affectionate nickname for N3N aircraft

Appendix E

BIBLIOGRAPHY

1) Air Publications and Pilot's Notes AP1566A & E

2) Sunderland design certificate, type record, flight test report, etc

3) Squadron operational records for 204, 240 & 209 squadrons RAF

4) *Aircraft of the Fighting Powers* by O G Thetford and E J Riding (editor D A Russell), The Harborough Publishing Co 1946

5) *The Last Viceroy* by Ray Murphy, Jarrold Publishers (London) Ltd 1948

6) *U-Boat 977 (8th edition)* by Heinz Schaeffer, Wm Kimber & Co Ltd 1955

7) *Aircraft of the RAF since 1918* by Owen Thetford, Putnam & Co Ltd 1957

8) *Flying Boat (The story of the Sunderland)* by Kenneth Poolman, Wm Kimber & Co Ltd 1962

9) *Shorts Aircraft since 1910* by C H Barnes, Putnam & Co Ltd 1967

10) *Squadron Histories RFC, RNAS and RAF since 1912 (2nd edition)* by Peter Lewis, Putnam & Co Ltd 1968

11) *Queen of the Headhunters* by Sylvia Brooke, wife of the last White Rajah of Sarawak, Sidgwick and Jackson 1970

12) *Famous Maritime Squadrons of the RAF (Vol 1)* by James J Halley, Hylton Lacy Publishers Ltd 1973

13) *Sunderland at War* by Chaz Bowyer, Ian Allan Ltd 1976

14) *The Battle of the Atlantic* by Terry Hughes and John Castello, Collins 1977

15) *The Critical Convoy Battles of March 1943* by Jurgen Rohwer, Ian Allan Ltd 1977

16) *Aircraft Crash Log No 3* – Short Sunderland by Nicholas Roberts 1977

17) *An Illustrated History of Seaplanes and Flying Boats* by Maurice Allward, Moorland Publishing Co Ltd 1981

18) *Coastal Support and Special Squadrons of the RAF & their aircraft* by John D R Rawlings, Jane's Publishing Co Ltd 1982

19) *U333 – The Story of a U-Boat Ace* by Peter Cremer, Verlag Ullstein GmbH 1982, The Bodley Head 1984

20) *Men of Coastal Command 1939-45* by Chaz Bowyer, Wm Kimber & Co Ltd 1985

APPENDIX E (contd)

21) *Flying Boat Haven* by John Evans, Aviation and Maritime Research 1985

22) *The Right of the Line (The RAF in the European War 1939-1945)* by John Terraine, Hodder & Stoughton 1985

23) *The Forgotten Pilots – A story of the Air Transport Auxiliary* by Lettice Curtis, Nelson & Saunders Ltd 1985

24) *The Sunderland – Flying-Boat Queen (Vol 1)* by John Evans, Paterchurch Publications 1987

25) *Salute to the Sunderland* by Ken Robinson, series of articles in Aeroplane Monthly, Dec 1987 to May 1988 incl.

26) *The 'Boat* by Ken Robinson, article in FlyPast, Oct 1987

27) Air Force List

28) *Who's Who*

Index

Note: 1 Place names are those used during the period of the narrative
2 Ranks and titles relate to the last entry for the person

Advanced training, 26-28
Aircraft recognition, 97
Aircrew medical, 5
Aircrew Reception Centre (No 1 ACRC), London, 6,*plate* 1
Aircrew training, 11-34
Aldis lamp, 64,73,141
Allward, M, 154
Alness, 90,107-8
Andaman Is., 125,135,141-2
Anderson, (Ensign, USN), 18-19
Anglo-Polish Ballet Company, 149
Annapolis of the Air, 20-31
Ansbro, W B (Ensign, USN), 29-30
Anti-sub patrols (ASP), 2,56-60,62-70, 75-9,82-3,85-6,88,91-3,95
ASDIC, 55
Atomic bombs on Japan, 123,137
Augusta, 112,116,119
Auxiliary power unit, 123,141
Avonmouth, 11
Avro Anson, 32

Bahrein, 120,122
Bandon Bay, 126,137-8
Banton, D (F/Lt), 136,140,146
Barometric altimeter, 113-4
Bathurst (Half Die), Gambia, 53-88,92, 101
Bayley, C A (F/Lt), 91
Bay of Biscay, 49,60,96-7
BBC News, 134
Beaching the boat, 95
Beaumont, M (F/Lt), 139,144
Bedouin camp, 68
Belleek (NI), 105
Benghazi (Libya), 112
Bertram, (F/Lt), 148,150
Bilges, water in, 86-7,94-5,142
Bircham Barrel, 73,128,
Blackburn, T H (F/O), 131-2,134
Blockade runners, 77-8
Bold decoy, 69
Borneo, 147-8,150-1
Borrowman, W (F/Sgt), *plate* 29, *plate* 31
Bowman, N J (Sgt), 91
Bremen (Germany), 96

Bren gun carrier, 144
Brien, D (F/Sgt), 99,104-5,108 130-1,142,146,*plates* 34 & 39
Bristol Beaufighter, 128
British Flight Battalion, 20
Brooke, Sir Charles V, 147
Brown, R A (F/Lt), 100
Buckmaster, Hon Colin, (F/O), 105
Burton, H B (F/Sgt), 99,104,119-20, 131,146,*plates* 34 & 39

Callisthenics, 21
Cape Verde Is., 83
Captain's course, 98-106
Caspareuthus, R F (Capt BOAC), 115
Catalina, *see* Consolidated Catalina
C-Class (Empire) boat, 115
Charge, disciplinary, 8,33,36
Clabaugh (Ensign,USN), 13-16
Clarkia, HMS, 72
Class B release, 146
Class C release, 144
Cleaning the boat, 87,147-8
Colvin, (Capt BOAC), 115
Consolidated Catalina PBY-5B, 30, 41,92,102,105,115,122-5,139, *plate* 6,*plate* 23
Consolidated Liberator, 58,72-4, 127-9,133, *plates* 41-42, *plate* 46
Consolidated P2Y, 28-30,*plate* 5
Convoy escort, 55-66,68,77,82-3,88 *plate* 27,*plate* 33
Coulson, (F/Lt), 123
Cowle, J (F/Lt), 124
Creeping-line-ahead (CLA) search, 65-6,77,93,127-9
Cremer, P (Kapitänleutnant), 60,69, 73,153
Crew, first flight with, 29
Cross, D A (Sgt), 33
Crowther, J (F/Sgt), 123,134
Curtis, Lettice (ATA pilot), 2

Dakar (Senegal), 72,86
Dalton Computer, 45
Danzig, 96

-183-

INDEX (contd)

Dar-es-Salaam, 115
Depth charges, 77-8
Deferred service, 5
Deneen, (Lt USN), 21
Detachment bases, 53,67,78-9,
 88,122-3,125-7,136-8,144
Detroit hospitality, 13
D/F, 55,62
Dickson, K F (F/O), 38-70
Different skills, 2
Discipline, 25
Donaghy, J (F/Lt), 123-4
Donegal Bay, 102,105
Dönitz, K (Grossadmiral),56,59,154
Douglas Dakota, 125-6
Drill & exercise, 7,8,19,21
Dunn, R E (F/O), 82
Dyak, 147-9

Empress of Australia, SS, 151
Enigma coding machine, 58
Escort of single ships, 67
Evison, C E W, (W/Cdr), 55,70,88,
 plate 26

Fairlead, 142
Fall of France 1940, 57
Fayia (Egypt), 120
Feilding, H (F/Lt), 99
Ferry Training Unit (302 FTU), Oban &
 St Angelo, 109-11,117-8
Finney, J G, (F/O), 75
First flight, 13
First solo flight, 19
Fisherman's Lake, 91,93
Flare-path, 103-4,141-2,144
Flak batteries, 60
Flat calm conditions, 93-5,113,
 plate 32
Flying bedstead, 28,*plate* 5
Flying boat training, 28-30
Flying checks, 24
Flying Training Schools, 11
Focke-Wolf Condor, 58
Formation flying, 27-28
Foulds, R J (F/Lt), 91
Frame, A (S/Ldr), 88,91
Free French Air Force, 86-7
Freetown (Jui), 88-93,95

Gavin Robinson, C B (W/Cdr),
 122,145,*plate* 47
G-Class boat, 115

General Reconnaissance School
 (31 GRS),PEI, 32-4
George, the autopilot, 50,90,114,
 150
Gibraltar, 51,111,118-9
Gordon, D M (G/Capt), 107
Gosport, 14
Graham, R (AVM), 93
Grant, D (F/O), 96-7
Gulf of Martaban, 127-9,133

Habbaniya (Iraq), 120-1
Haigh, J (F/Sgt), 141-4
Halifax (Nova Scotia), 11
Hallisey, W D (F/O), 103-4
Hamburg (Germany), 96
Harrogate (7 PRC), 34-7,152
Hawkins, H J L (W/Cdr), 81,88
Hay, J C M (W/Cdr), 6-7
Heliopolis (Egypt), 115
Hibberd, T J (F/Lt), 68,71,91-2
Highland Brigade, SS, 11-12
Hoare, L C (S/Ldr), 122
Hogan, J P M (F/Sgt), 85,
 plates 30-1
Hong Kong (Kai Tak), 149
Horner, H V (F/Lt), 70-1
Hospital, US Naval, 17,23
Hulton, E, 95,157
Hulse, H (W/O), *plates* 30-1
Hurricane 1987, 157

Indo-China, 125
Initial Training Wing (9 ITW), 6-10
Instrument Flying, 26
Ismailia (Egypt), 120
Iwakuni (Japan), 149

Jettisoning fuel, 85,138
Johnston, F N (F/Lt), 81,83,90-1,
 108,*plates* 30-1
Johore (Malaya), 142,144-5
Johore Strait, 137,145

Kallang (Singapore), 148-9
Kandy (Ceylon), 148
Karachi, Korangi Creek (India),
 122-3,139,142
Kasfareit (Egypt), 112,119-20,*plate*
 37
Kenyan plateau, 113-4
Khartoum (Sudan), 112
Kilimanjaro, Mt (Kenya), 113,115

INDEX (contd)

Killadeas (NI), 98,102-6
Kisumu (Kenya), 112
Koggala (Ceylon), 122-3,125,137-9, 142-4,*plates* 41-2
Kra Isthmus (Siam), 136-7
Kuching (Sarawak), 147-8

Labuan (Borneo), 150-1
Lamb, D H (P/O), 131
Lend-Lease, 11
Leigh Light, 59
Liberia (W Africa), 91,93
Liberator, *see* Consolidated Liberator
Link Trainer, 35
Living on board, 67-9,126,156
Lockheed Hudson, 92
Lord's Cricket Ground, 6
Lough Erne (NI), 98,105
Lowestoft, HMS, 97

Madras, Redhills Lake (India), 122-5, 127,137-40,142-4
Maintenance, 1,70,86,92,95,141,155, *plate* 29
Malacca Strait, 137
Malaria, 144
Malaya, 125,135,137,142
Mansfield, W (W/O), 99,102,118,*plate* 34
Marine crews, 1,80,82,*plate* 11
Marshall, L H (F/Sgt), 73
Martin, T J (F/Sgt), 99,104-5,119-21, 124,126,135-7,146,*plates* 34 & 39
Mayberry, C C (F/Lt), 69,81
Mayday, 76
McGowan, J (P/O), 131
Mechanical problems, 2,39,70-1,75-6, 83,85-6,90,92,95,100,103-4,155
Mergui (Burma), 135
Met flights, 124
Metox receiver, 59
Mitsubishi Zero, 136
Moffatt, P (F/Lt), 109-10,120
Moffitt, A G (F/Lt), 99,102,108,114, 116,119,121,127-8,130-3,139,*plates* 34 & 39
Mombasa (Kenya), 115
Moncton (31 PD), New Brunswick, 12,32, 152
Monro, H S P (F/Lt), 149
Montreal (Quebec), 12
Moore, T (Sgt), *plates* 30-1
Morgan, D F (Capt), 148

Morgan, R (F/Sgt), 139,145-6,148
Morocco, 80,88,91,119
Mountbatten, Lord Louis (Adm.), 135,137,147-9
Mountbatten, Lady Patricia (3rd Officer, WRNS), 148
Murray, R B (W/O), *plates* 30-1

N3N-3, 13-25,*plate* 2
Nancowry (Nicobar Is.), 135
Navigation (DR), 41,61-2,129, *plate* 15
Navigation training, 31
Nears, C A (W/O), 91,109,124
Needle, ball & airspeed, 18
Newbon, R (Sgt), 72
Nicobar Is., 135,137,141
Night attack strategy, 107,155
Night flying techniques, 81-2
North American Harvard (SNJ), 26, *plate* 3
North American Yale (NJ), 26, *plate* 4

Oban (Argyll), 109-11,118
Objectives of book, 1,3
Ogle Skan, W E (W/Cdr), 115, 149-50
Ootacamund (India), 139-40
Operational Training Unit (131c OTU), Killadeas (NI), 98-107
Operation Overlord, 96
Operation Zipper, 137
Osborn, F (F/Sgt), 99,111,127, *plate* 34
Owens family (Wyandotte, Detroit), 13

Pallett, D W (F/Lt), 92
Parades, 27
Paré, J C (F/Lt), 55,71-3,91
Paris, J W (Sgt), 131
Parry, J C (S/Ldr), 125
Pearl Harbor (Hawaii), 9,30,58
Pearson, D (F/O), 100
Pegu (Burma), 131
Pembroke Dock (Wales), 37-49
Penang Is. (Malaya), 125,135,138, 144-5,*plate* 38
Personnel Distribution Centre (PDC), Manchester, 11
Phuket Is. (Siam), 138
Pirie, G C (AVM), 139
Planned maintenance, 100-1

INDEX (contd)

Planned position indicator, 109
Poole (Dorset), 116
Port Blair (Andaman Is.), 135,141
Port Dickson (Malaya), 137
Port Étienne (Mauretania), 53,67,78-81, 87
Port Lyautey (Morocco), 119
Port Reitz (Kenya), 115
Port Swettenham (Malaya), 137
Powered approach, 81-2
Practice bombing/gunnery, 71,91
Pressure chamber, 21
Price, (Sgt), *plate* 29
Prien, G (Käpitanleutnant), 58
Primary flying training, 13-25

Queen Elizabeth, RMS, 34

Radar (metric ASV), 41,58-9,62-3,66,69, 77,107,153
Radar (centimetric ASV),59,109,114,155
Radio altimeter, 107,114
Radio equipment, 41,55,62,*plate* 16
Rangoon, Syriam (Burma), 125-7,133,135, 137-8,144,*plate* 40
Recreation, 21
Republic P47 Thunderbolt, 137-8
Rescue, Air-Sea (ASR), 3,125-134,137-8, *plate* 45
Robinson, Mrs Mary, 5,27,31,34-6,49,69, 79,88,98,106,110,116,149
Role of Sunderlands, 2
Ruston, A M (S/Ldr), 122-4,145,148-50
Ryan, D (W/O), 99,102,113,118,*plate* 34

Saigon (Indo-China), 127
Salbani (India), 127
Sarawak (Borneo), 147,150
Say, L (LAC), 8
Scanners, 109
Schaeffer, H (Leutnant), 59,153
Schamong, K (Oberleutnant), 73
SEAC newspaper, 134
Seamanship, 29,42,46,121,144,*plate* 22
Seletar (Singapore Is.),142,145,150
Shat-el-Arab river (Iraq), 121
Shawcross, G (F/Sgt), 131
Short, C J G (F/O), 33,124
Short Sunderland:
    Numbers built, 156,Appx A1
    Mk I, 41,71,Appx A1,*plate* 27
    Mk II, 48,Appx A1,*plate* 9
    Mk III, 39,100,109,116,Appx A1
        plates 7-8,*plate* 10,*plate* 36

Short Sunderland (contd):
    Mk IV, Appx A2
    Mk V, 92,108-10,112,116,140, 155-6,Appx A1,Appx A2, *plates* 33 & 35
    Post-war service, 156-7
Siam, 125
Silburn, L (F/Lt), 100
Simon, R M (Lt), 142,144
Singapore, 125,137-9,144-50
Sittang Estuary (Burma), 127,132
Smith, R G (F/Sgt), 99,104,111,128, 130,*plates* 34 & 39
Snorkel, 96
South East Asia Command (SEAC), 135
Special flying boat conditions, 1
Special Duty Flight, 122,125

Squadrons:
    10, 108
    95, 68,70
    204, 38,55-95,100-1,155,*plate* 26
    209, 110,115,125,145-51
    212, 122
    230, 125,145
    240, 122-145,*plate* 47
    259, 115
    355, 127
    461, 108
Staffiere, A G (F/Lt), 64,75,93-5, 101
Standards of comfort, 2
St Angelo (NI), 117
Stapleton, R (F/Sgt), 127,141, *plate* 45
Stevens, F W H (F/O), 91
Stone, D (F/Sgt), 72
Stranraer, 117-8
Sullom Voe (Shetland Is.), 105
Sumatra (Indonesia), 135
Sunderland:
    airscrews, 92,108,Appx A1, *see also* under A
    armaments, 62,77-8,108,125, Appx A1,*plates* 18-20
    crew stations, 40-2,44-5,Appx C
    dimensions, Appx A1
    engines, 39,92,108,Appx A1, Appx A2,*plate* 17
    first flight in, 42
    fuel capacity, 49,Appx A1
    introduction to, 38
    manufacture, Appx A1

INDEX (contd)

Sunderland (contd):
    radar, Appx A1; *see also* under R
    speed, 140,Appx A1
    weight, 47,110,Appx A1
Supermarine Spitfire, 126
Swaffer, H (F/Sgt), *plates* 30-1

Teamwork, 2
Terraine, J, 11
Thongwa (Burma), 131
Todd, C (F/Sgt), 81
Torobzoff, G (F/Sgt), 99,104, *plates* 34 & 39
Toronto (Ontario), 12
Trade winds, 60,80
Trailing aerial, 135-6
Training, *see* Aircrew training
Trevor, D, 4
Trigg, L A (F/O), 73

U-boat, air attack conditions, 69-70, *plate* 25
U-boat pens in France, 57
U-boats:
    Landwirt Group, 96
    Milch Cow, 58
    Type XXI, 96,155-6
    750-ton, 69
    U110, 58
    U333, 60,69,73
    U468, 72-3

U-boats (contd):
    U977, 59
Unaccompanied vessels, 34,67,76-8, 81
US enters war 1941, 9,58
USNAS Pensacola, Fla, 20-31
USNRAB, Grosse Île, Mich, 12-20

Very pistol/cartridges, 63-4,73, 128,130
Volunteering for the RAF, 4
Vultee Valiant (SNV), 27,*plate* 4

Watkinson, C H (W/O), 72-3,80-1
Watson, K J F (P/O), 131
Wavell, Lord (Field Marshal), 141
Weather conditions, 62,83-4,86, 92-3,102,113-4,149
Western Approaches Command, 57
White Rajah, 147-8
Wildlife, 143,152
Winch, J P (P/O), 131,134
Wings, award of pilot's, 31
Woods, C V (F/Sgt), 84,*plates* 30-1

Yellow Peril, 13,21,*plate* 2
Yendell, M (W/O), 82,91
Young, A (F/Sgt), 85,*plates* 30-1
Young, P N (F/O), 118-21,127-8, 130-1,133,135,142,144-6,*plate* 39

Zero, *see* Mitsubishi